"The sharp, hardboiled prose you would expect from a detective novelist... Smith shares vivid details, hard-earned insights, and stories of courage and terror, told with crisp, raw dialogue, a feeling for the drama of potentially violent confrontations, and an undercurrent of despair, despite many heartfelt tributes to cops he trusted and the mentor whose murder he had to look into." - BookLife Review

"Danny R. Smith has told his story with open and raw emotion that few would be willing to share openly and with such brutal honesty. His story leaves the reader with a better understanding of the hardships that a career in law enforcement can take on one's life, and hopefully leaves society with a better appreciation of those who chose to protect us." – Andrea Self

"*Nothing Left to Prove* is a gritty, gut-wrenchingly honest and compelling inside look at the life of a law enforcement officer. This author pulls no punches as he lays bare the violence and horrific atrocities that took place during his career." – Heather Wamboldt

"I was at times, shocked, appalled and repulsed by what one human being could do to another human being. I was also amazed, appreciative and extremely respectful of those who serve so resolutely to protect others." – Michele Carey

"This is an outstanding, exciting, and superbly readable account from a man who lived it all. Poignant, gut-wrenching and, at times, amusing, this is definitely an unputdownable narrative." – Michele Kapugi

"A riveting law enforcement memoir." – Bud Johnson

NOTHING LEFT TO PROVE

A LAW ENFORCEMENT MEMOIR

DANNY R. SMITH

ISBN-13: 978-1-7349794-5-9 (Paperback edition)

ISBN-13: 978-1-7349794-6-6 (Hardcover edition)

Cover by Jon Schuler

www.schulercreativelab.com

❀ Created with Vellum

For my partners, with whom I witnessed the best and worst of humanity, endured the brightest and darkest days, and survived the exhilarating and terrifying moments. Thank you for the ride.

FOREWORD

Every cop has stories to tell. All cops are forever altered–scarred and hardened by their experiences. They carry with them the memories of sights, sounds, and smells that are embedded in their psyches and can never be erased. Those memories will emerge throughout their lives, often randomly and always disturbingly. Cops find various ways to cope with these demons. Many find relief in dark humor. But many of the mechanisms are self-destructive: drugs, alcohol, isolation, and, too often, suicide. Not surprisingly, more Law Enforcement Officers die at their own hands than are murdered by criminals.

Some write books. Fiction based on experiences, or perhaps memoirs—all of it a form of catharsis. Many of these writings fall short, however. Having a story to tell and the ability to tell it are not always aligned.

Danny R. Smith is a notable exception. Smith has written several novels, loosely based on his experiences as a Los Angeles deputy sheriff working some of the toughest and most demanding assignments. He was successful in each of his roles from patrol deputy, training officer, and station detective, to headquarters detective at both Major Crimes and Homicide Bureaus. His novels—spellbinding, fast paced, and easy to follow—touch on the events that taught, molded, and hardened him.

Nothing Left to Prove is his memoir. A compelling narrative that takes the reader from his early days to his retirement, and illustrates his unique experiences and how they shaped his life. You'll share the repulsion of having to deal with a mangled body of a child thrown from a cliff while meticulously gathering evidence and conducting interviews to eventually hold accountable the savage responsible–his obligation to the dead. It tells of having to put one's grief on a shelf to conduct business, and you'll see firsthand the heavy burden which he will forever carry.

Nothing Left to Prove is a beautifully crafted tapestry that also reveals the pure joy, fun, and brotherhood shared in the law enforcement community. Cops will nod their heads. Civilians will gain deep insight into the visible and hidden aspects of the job that shapes the men and women who proudly and bravely serve.

Dennis Slocumb, Legislative Director
International Union of Police Associations

PART I

BEGINNING OF THE END

1

WEST LOS ANGELES

DECEMBER 2003

T he end came the day I rushed to investigate a human head hanging in a tree. It would be my 143rd death investigation as a homicide detective with the Los Angeles County Sheriff's Department, and normally, just another day at the bureau. Dead kids. Dead cops. Human fucking heads. At some point, everyone breaks.

A nurse had taken my vitals, asked a few questions, and jotted some notes in my chart. When she left me alone in the room, I fixed my gaze on the drab wall across from where I sat and pondered my destiny. In my heart I already knew, and the doctor would confirm it moments later.

Doc entered the room with my chart in his hand and a somber expression I hadn't seen on him before. He rolled a stool close to my chair and lowered himself onto it, and then he asked me to describe what had happened earlier that day. He wanted details, not the highlights which I had already relayed to his nurse. If that brief summary had bothered him—which it obviously had—wait until he heard the particulars.

I began by telling him about that morning in the office, how I had been greeted with stacks of reports and subpoenas, a revised on-call schedule that now showed my partner and me first up for murders—again—and half a dozen phone messages along with scores of emails to answer. It was the normal burden of working Homicide in the County of Los Angeles, a job that turned healthy young cops into worn-out men and women with broken hearts and tormented minds. Before I finished my first cup of coffee, we had an assignment: a human head had been found hanging in a tree. I gathered my gear and got a refill of coffee to go. With it I washed down the first pain pill of the day, something that could normally wait until lunch.

Doc waited, his stoic gaze revealing nothing about his thoughts. But I knew.

I continued: Then, while doing seventy on the Long Beach Freeway and talking on the phone with my partner, discussing this forlorn head, I glanced over my shoulder to change lanes when it happened again—my neck froze. Each of the previous four or five times it had happened had been during times of tremendous stress, and it was always preceded by a throbbing headache and tightening muscles. This time, the intense spasm surprised me, and it left me stuck looking behind me while traveling in the other direction at a high rate of speed.

Doc took a breath and let it out slowly, the sound amplified in the relative silence that now hung between us.

I broke his gaze and looked around the room, suddenly aware of the antiseptic smell of cleansers. My mind flashed to the coroner's office, images of cadavers on stainless steel gurneys populating its colorless hallways, a dreadful place that I hoped never to visit again. Like a runner who can see the finish line, there was relief in knowing it was almost over, and in my mind I certainly knew that to be the case. No more autopsies. No more bloody scenes. No more dead kids and murdered cops and women hacked and slashed and strangled by hands they had trusted.

The muffled sounds of a busy office permeated the walls, stirring me from my contemplation: ringing phones, chattering staff, hasty footsteps moving purposefully as doors were opened and closed up and down the hallway outside, medical staff tending to the needs of others. I could feel Doc's gaze still upon me, perhaps waiting for me to come back to him. But was I ready to hear his words? I wasn't sure. After a moment, I took another breath and looked him in his eyes.

"You're finished," he said. It was unequivocal and not negotiable.

For a moment I sat silent, digesting the reality of my career ending. For cops, it's so much more than leaving a job. It's leaving behind a family. It's the loss of loved ones. It's losing your identity and stepping into the abyss, where you can only hope that you'll someday find your footing, realize that you'd done enough and that it was okay to hang up your gun and badge. But getting there—to that point of knowing it was okay to walk away—would be a long journey for me.

As I sat and absorbed the harsh words—*You're finished*—a dark fog rolled over me and began smothering me. I saw myself standing at the bottom of a gorge, looking up at the first light of day, stranded and alone with no hope of climbing to safety. Lost and cold. Hopeless. And I wept uncontrollably. Like an inconsolable child, but also like a broken man. The latter, I would eventually realize, I was.

2

THE LOS ANGELES RIOTS

APRIL 1992

Black soot floated down from the heavens, covering buildings, streets, and cars throughout South Los Angeles. With darkness came desolation: the streets, alleys, and parking lots vacated in response to a curfew. All that remained were violators of the law—those striking with violence and destroying property in the name of justice—and those who were there to stop them. The peacekeepers. I was one of them.

It was Wednesday, April 29, 1992, five weeks from the day I would marry my one and only bride, and ten weeks shy of my turning thirty. I was nine years into my 21-year law enforcement career with the Los Angeles County Sheriff's Department, and six months into my assignment as a detective at Firestone station in South Los Angeles. Just weeks before, we had buried a colleague, Nelson Yamamoto, a young Firestone deputy gunned down in the line of duty.

The verdicts in the case of four LAPD officers involved in the Rodney King incident were announced as I drove home from work that Wednesday afternoon. I arrived home in time to see Los Angeles mayor Tom Bradley's press conference wherein he denounced the verdicts, using what many considered inflammatory language. His words stoked anger among some elements of the black community, many of whom were upset that the cops had been acquitted by a mostly white Simi Valley jury, and some who would use the occasion to riot and loot and to act out with violence upon their fellow man.

My fiancée and I went down the road and had dinner at a little Mexican joint, successfully pulling ourselves away from the news for a while. I had a feeling I would be called back to work that night, but until then there was nothing I could do other than to wait for the phone to ring. Shortly after dinner, that call came.

I spent the next half hour collecting weapons, food and water, and assembling these things along with extra underclothes in what is now referred to by preppers as a bug-out bag. My wife-to-be helped load rifle magazines with ammunition, and then I drove her to my childhood home—a place far from South Los Angeles. There, she wouldn't be alone, and I wouldn't have to worry about her safety. The man who had raised me and shaped me would protect the family while I put myself in harm's way. Dad had seen his share of action long before as a paratrooper in the Korean War; now it was my time to serve.

From the Santa Clarita valley I descended into the City of Angels on empty freeways in my old GMC pickup, something I didn't normally use to commute, but a vehicle I would be able to use as a ramming device if needed. Gang members were known to set roadblocks using furniture and cars in order to capture their prey. Cops who worked in areas like Watts knew never to stop to clear a roadway; rather, to go around, over, or through said barricade, and to have a weapon in hand, prepared to fire.

The extra weapons I had brought to the station remained with me on patrol for the next several weeks. Like many others at Firestone, I was qualified to carry an AR-15 rifle, but the station armory had a limited supply of these weapons and the .223 caliber ammunition they required. We had learned from our predecessors who had experienced events such as the Watts riots of 1965, the East Los Angeles riots of 1970, the SLA (Symbionese Liberation Army) shootout of 1974, and scores of civil unrest incidents, that it was imperative to carry extra weapons and ammunition when working in volatile and violent communities.

My first encounter occurred before I exited the freeway. A carload of Hispanic youths pulled alongside me, carefully appraising me. These weren't hardcore gang members, just boys not old enough to legally buy liquor who were caught up in the flood of emotion that had quickly swept through the poorer communities of Los Angeles, while everyone else sat glued to their televisions behind locked doors.

"Why do you have to go down there?" my sister had asked. *Down there.* To the parts of the city most citizens dared not journey—South Central Los Angeles. The beginnings of gentrification were yet a decade away, the prettying up of this area and making it sound nice by renaming it "South Los Angeles." I was headed to South Central; it was hardcore and there was nothing pretty about it. She said, "They should just let them kill each other and burn down their own communities."

The images of a bloody and beaten Reginald Denny writhing on the pavement in the intersection of Florence and Normandy had horrified her. A group of black men—later to be called "The L.A. Four"—had savagely beaten the unsuspecting truck driver after seizing his rig and pulling him from it. The four men—there were others, but primarily these four—viciously assaulted Denny. They punched him, they kicked him; one man beat him with a claw hammer, while yet another bounced a brick off his head. They robbed him, rifling through his pockets as he lay unconscious, this working man who knew not the evil of his fellow citizens until that very moment. It was a time before YouTube when few knew what we knew, that an element of our society embraced violence beyond most people's level of comprehension.

The conversation with my sister had taken place not twenty minutes before the carload of hooligans pulled alongside me. She had called, emotional and scared, uncharacteristically indifferent to the plight of her fellow humans while fearing for the safety of her baby brother, the smart-alecky little redhead who had grown into a man and who now drove into the abyss with a shotgun on his lap. She was but one of millions who had been unable to turn away from the images on TV: the bloody trucker, groups of thugs looting, shooting, burning their communities to the ground. And it had terrified her.

I answered her question about why I had to go. There were a lot of good people in that community too, decent people who lived in fear behind security screen doors and windows, and who counted on us to be there for them at times like this. We were their only hope. My sister already knew this, of course, but it had been lost on her in the moment.

And it was true; there were many kind and caring citizens in South Central Los Angeles, a place where liquor stores and churches were prominent, but which lacked grocery stores and strip malls and parks that were free of thugs. Most of the good people had lived there all of their lives and were unable or unwilling to leave. It was their home, battered though it might have been.

I watched in my sideview mirror as the carload of young men, which had backed off for a moment, now came roaring up beside me again. I feared they had prepared a weapon and were now ready to try me. But I wouldn't give them the chance. As they arrived, I leveled the business end of a short-barreled shotgun at them, prepared to light it off. They must have been outgunned, or perhaps surprised to see me prepared for battle. Either way, they slammed on the brakes and then faded away. I continued my journey toward the battlefield.

Normally, an encounter like that would require an off-duty incident report. But by the time I reached the station, that incident seemed insignificant, so I never bothered to mention it in any formal report. As I continued toward my reporting district, I hit the Harbor Freeway and snaked through downtown, and then south into a blanket of thick smoke. My standard route to work would have me exit onto Florence Avenue and drive through the intersection of Florence and Normandy, Ground Zero. Not only did I avoid that intersection, but many times I was forced to abruptly change directions to avoid roaming groups of angry mobs. It was nearly ten when I slid into the station parking lot, safe at the plate, as if I had stolen home for the winning run. And for the first time in my career, I found our station to be fortified, locked down, guarded by heavily armed deputies who were posted at the doors and driveways and on the roof. In the following days, military personnel took over these positions. A pair of camouflaged Marines sat concealed in the bushes just feet from the front door, armed with automatic weapons. A scout/sniper team had been stationed on the roof. No, I didn't need to report pointing my shotgun at a carload of punks.

Throughout that week there were many "incidents," both on- and off-duty, that occurred across the southland and would never be reported. It was as if we had gone to war and everything had changed. Civility had vanished, and martial law was the result. There were exchanges of gunfire that, when no injury had resulted, sometimes went unreported. No harm, no foul. At times it seemed surreal.

Inside the station, deputies moved with purpose and urgency. Radios crackled and sirens wailed as radio cars and other emergency personnel regularly came and went. Helicopters streaked through the skies, appearing and disappearing through patches of smoke. Gunshots rang out in the night, regularly accented by bursts of automatic gunfire. It was a war zone.

Within days there were federal troops stationed at all major intersections as we rode four-deep in black and white patrol cars, clad in riot gear. When we weren't racing from call to call, we prowled the streets, blacked out at night, looking for looters. Twelve-hour shifts and no days off turned into 16-hour shifts and short periods of rest in the station bunkhouse.

The presence of the military helped us take control of our jurisdiction; they were primarily used to hold the areas we had secured. Previously, we would sweep a block and arrest looters, who would then be replaced by new looters once we moved on. With the military in place, we secured our area one block at a time while soldiers and Marines held the ground behind us. The National Guard had been the first military assistance to arrive. Most of these troops had never seen combat; they were bankers and plumbers and regular citizens who drilled once a month and a couple of weeks each year. Some of them were visibly frightened being in Watts with their unloaded weapons.

A call for assistance came over the radio. The National Guard was "taking rocks and bottles" at Santa Fe and Florence Avenues. We raced over, but as we did, I said, "Aren't those the guys in tanks?" meaning, why would they have to call the cops for help.

One of the guys in our car, ex-military, said, "Humvees aren't tanks, dumbass." Still, I argued, they had cool shit and they should've been using it.

But they hadn't. When we arrived, they pointed out the problem location, a shithole apartment from which gangsters would pop outside and throw something at them before retreating. We weren't the types to retreat, so we came up with a plan. One particularly big, fast, and tough deputy sheriff snuck around the apartments and positioned himself just ten feet from the door, hidden behind a car. The next time a gangster popped out, he was mugged before he could launch another missile in our direction. He and a few others inside went to jail, and *that* problem was solved.

I walked into the station wearing a bandolier filled with shotgun shells across my chest, a shotgun in my hand. A lieutenant—one with whom I never saw eye-to-eye, and not only because he had barely passed the height requirement when hired—snapped at me to remove the bandolier from my uniform. "Why?" I asked, sincerely, but also in my ever-challenging-authority way.

"Because it looks too aggressive," he said.

I didn't hesitate in my response: "Maybe you haven't noticed, Lieutenant, but we've got tanks out there driving up and down Compton Avenue."

His nostrils flared, and he restated his order. I removed the bandolier until I departed the station, at which time I promptly replaced it and added a second one for spite. I hadn't even bothered to argue that a curfew was in effect and that no citizen was to be on the streets lest they be subject to arrest. The furious lieutenant wouldn't have cared; he had butter bars on his collar and a stick up his ass.

There were many exciting moments during the riots: foot chases, shots fired, fights. One night, my partner and I were patrolling along Firestone Boulevard when we spotted an unmarked sheriff's unit abandoned in the street. It was a far nicer car than those driven by our detectives, but clearly a sheriff's vehicle, nonetheless. We sped to the location and skidded to a stop, bailing out of the car with our attention directed to the burned and looted liquor store in front of which the unmanned car sat. Moments later, one of the two assistant sheriffs for the County of Los Angeles strode out of the smoldering ruins with a handcuffed prisoner. The third-most senior-ranking man of a 10,000 sworn officer department, the Los Angeles County Sheriff's Department, a former Firestone deputy himself, had observed a crime and made the arrest. He was accompanied by his driver, but it was only the two of them. They hadn't called for backup and it hadn't been staged for any cameras. I have never been prouder of any department executive.

One of the best lieutenants we worked for at the time was Sid Heal. And that was really saying something because, other than the lieutenant who had worried about appearances during a riot, and one or two others over the years, we at Firestone always seemed to be blessed with great lieutenants and sergeants. Sid had served with the Marine Corps and had seen combat in Vietnam, and again in Desert Storm, having remained as a reserve for more than twenty years while serving the county of Los Angeles as a deputy sheriff. With the sheriff's department, he had been a member of our SWAT team, and later returned to SWAT as a captain. Sid stopped me as I strolled through the station hallway during a brief respite from the action outside and said, "Smith, who are you working with?" I could tell that he and the two army intelligence officers who stood with him had been engaged in a strategy session.

"Okamoto," I replied. Geody Okamoto was a good friend and a great cop, and he also happened to have been one of my codefendants during a federal lawsuit not long before. This night we had been teamed up and tasked with handling a special detail in which Okamoto was known to specialize, appropriating supplies from various outside sources.

Lieutenant Heal smiled. "Good. You and Geody take these guys down to the projects and get me a report on the gang activity in the Downs."

We had all heard that the Bloods and Crips had gathered in the Jordan Downs housing project, and that a truce had been made as they united against The Man. At the time, most of us in law enforcement would never have believed it possible. However, we always knew that if the thousands of gang members in Los Angeles County were ever to unite and become organized, they would be a force of considerable power and violence. But the odds were always against that happening, we knew. Until that night.

The Jordan Downs housing project is located in the southeast corner of Firestone's jurisdiction near 97th and Alameda Streets, in Watts. There were industrial buildings along Alameda, and we found one with a high outside catwalk that overlooked the projects. From our elevated position, we watched in amazement as hundreds of Bloods and Crips partied and shot guns in the air and not at each other. It was more than a bit disconcerting, to say the least. Our position was only a hundred yards or so from the masses, and we knew that if they spotted us, they would shoot at us. My partner and I were armed with AR-15s. The soldiers were carrying some type of automatic rifles, though I don't recall now what they were. Lieutenant Heal showed up not long after we were in position. He had come out to get a report and see the action firsthand, because he wasn't a sitting-in-the-office type of leader. We neither heard nor saw him until he whispered a warning that he was coming up behind us. The five of us watched for a while longer before carefully exfiltrating with the confirmation that there was indeed a truce—however temporary—in place between the largest and most violent black gangs in America.

For the remainder of that first night, my partner and I mostly continued gathering intelligence and reporting to Lieutenant Heal. Our department had sent scores of undercover cops into the various communities and churches to gather additional information on the uprising and its instigators and participants. We met with several of these operatives and learned that a few politicians had been observed stoking the flames of hatred and unrest. A particularly vocal Democrat congresswoman was among the instigators of violence. I shall refrain from naming her, but most who read this will know her. She has a history of corruption, connections to the radical Nation of Islam leader, Louis Farrakhan, and she has been an outspoken supporter of murderous dictator Fidel Castro. It is said that she stood among the gun-toting gangsters that night in the Jordan Downs housing project, though I did not personally see her there.

After a couple of nights, we had mostly regained control of our jurisdiction with the assistance of deputies from other stations, the National Guard, and federal troops. On about the third night, it was decided we would be staged in a parking lot near our station, and from there we would be given assignments. A sergeant and two radio cars, each containing four deputies, would respond together to any situation. None of us liked the arrangement. We felt we should still be out prowling the streets, hunting for looters, arsonists, and killers.

And the arrangement did come to a screeching halt when a broadcast came over the radio announcing that firefighters were being shot at in the vicinity of Firestone Boulevard and Maie Avenue.

I led the charge, primarily because my vehicle was closest to the exit, and partially because I had more seniority than almost all of the other deputies there that night. Also because I didn't hesitate. None of us did. We sailed out of the lot, car after car, a parade of lights and sirens and armed men ready for battle. The shooting had stopped by the time we arrived, and the firefighters had little information about the origin of the attack. We searched the area but never figured out who had shot at them.

The lieutenant, John Martin, would later say I nearly ran over him on my way to the call. He had come from the station and was crossing the street to where we were staged, hoping to keep a handle on the recently instituted policy of coordinated responses. I had worked for John for a long time by then, and we had a good rapport. Privately, he said he had expected nothing less from a group of Firestone deputies. He also said if I did it again, he'd choke me out. John Martin easily could have, so I told him yes sir and that was the end of that.

After about a week of not seeing much of me, and with no end to the unrest in sight, my bride-to-be started to fret over the wedding plans. In the best of circumstances, planning one is stressful; imagine having a wedding date a few weeks out when the would-be groom and almost everyone on his guest list were engaged in a fight against civil unrest. Should we postpone our wedding? Cancel it? When was the madness going to stop? As April turned to May and the date drew nearer, these were our concerns. Hers more so than mine, but still. The decision was made not to cancel nor postpone the wedding; we were holding out hope that order would be restored by June 6 (D-day).

Eventually, I returned to my regular duties working day shift as a detective. We were still working twelve-hour shifts with no days off, and we needed those extra hours to get caught up; we had quite a mess now that the smoke had cleared. Firestone personnel, and those who had been sent to assist us, had arrested hundreds (if not thousands) of people in the first days of the rioting. Looters, vandals, arsonists, and an assortment of other lawbreakers had been rounded up and stacked like cordwood in booking vans and hauled off to the pokey. Once we had—for the most part—gained control of the situation, the judicial system returned to normal operations. All of those arrests had to be filed with the court, so we detectives were busier over the next couple of weeks than we had been during the riots, and not nearly as entertained.

Soon thereafter, we were all back to working semi-normal hours. Days off and vacations had been restored, and the wedding was on!

PART II

PATH TO LAW ENFORCEMENT

3

A DUMB WHITE BOY FROM NEWHALL

JANUARY 1987

"**Y**ou read their expressions. It's the way they look at you, or sometimes the way they don't. But a dumb white boy from Newhall probably won't know what he's looking at. Now if we were hunting lizards or snakes," he started, then glanced over from behind the wheel and grinned.

The words were an answer to a question I had asked of a tough and savvy street cop named Sal Velazquez: "How did you know they had dope?" Sal, who had grown up in a barrio himself, hadn't the learning curve that I and others with backgrounds like mine had had when we hit the streets. Sal knew the streets, and he knew the players. He had instincts you didn't get growing up in Newhall or Torrance.

This conversation took place when I was a trainee at Firestone station, and Sal and I were patrolling on a street just outside of the Jordan Downs housing project in Watts. It was during the eighties when the use of crack cocaine had spread insidiously throughout the nation like a cancer, and the ghettos of South Los Angeles were Ground Zero. Gang members were killing each other daily, in deadly competition for their shares of the market. The question I had of Sal had come a short time after he had slammed our dented and scratched black and white Chevy Malibu into park, bailed out, and pulled a man from the driver's seat of a parked car. I jumped out and rushed to the other side of this parked car to detain the passenger, while Sal, his big hand clamped around the man's throat, commanded of the man, "Spit it out! Spit it out!"

The two men in the car had been preparing to smoke rock cocaine (crack) when we happened upon them, but I had been oblivious to it. The driver had eaten the evidence before Sal could get to him. Possession was a felony; being under the influence was only a misdemeanor. We detained both men and searched their car, finding a crack pipe and some liquor, but no additional cocaine. By then I had learned that misdemeanors were often overlooked in this high-crime district, so I wasn't surprised when Sal kicked them loose, telling them to get their asses out of the area or they'd go to jail next time. We drove off, and a few minutes later I had asked the question. I had no idea what he had seen that made him jam *those* two. There were guys just like them everywhere —on the sidewalks, in parking lots, sitting in cars, riding bikes. Most of these men and women were openly drinking alcohol in public and carrying on in ways that would draw the attention of cops in Newhall and communities like it. But this was a different world than the one I knew. This was Watts, and I had a lot to learn about it.

4

NEWHALL, CALIFORNIA

CHILDHOOD

Throughout the sixties and seventies, Newhall was still small-town USA, mostly white, and relatively free of serious crime. As a boy, I could ride bikes or play football and baseball on the streets with my friends, or I could go to the nearby elementary school to play basketball with little concern for my safety. Other than the occasional schoolyard fistfight, no part of my childhood had prepared me for a career in law enforcement, at least not one in Watts, a place where violence and death were rampant, constant, and abiding.

I grew up on Atwood Boulevard, which was a dirt road during my early childhood. As a young boy, I played in the street with my sturdy metal Tonka trucks until the construction crews arrived to pave it and bring us into the modern world. It wasn't long after that everything north of nearby Lyons Avenue, which had remained as agricultural land through the sixties, began giving way to a sprawling housing development called Valencia. Much later, the entire region would be incorporated as the City of Santa Clarita and become home to nearly a quarter-million residents. The days of six-year-olds playing with Tonka trucks on Atwood Boulevard are but a distant memory, as are the sprawling fields of carrots and potatoes and hay for livestock.

But even with the growth that Valencia brought to the Santa Clarita

Valley, my high school class was relatively small and unburdened by crime and gangs and clashing cultures, all of which were reported and rumored to have been commonplace in the San Fernando Valley, not far south of us. It wasn't that we had no diversity; there was a large Hispanic population, as one might imagine from the region's history of agriculture, and there were black families also in our valley, though few. But race was never counted as a contributor to any problems we may have had—at least none of which I was aware. One of my high school friends was a black kid named Shane. He drove a lowrider and had a reputation as a tough guy, but I never saw him in a fight. In fact, he was one of the most popular kids at school, as were the few other black students.

At that time, Santa Clarita was unincorporated Los Angeles County, and it was policed by both deputies from the Newhall sheriff's station and traffic officers from the California Highway Patrol. I maintained the same healthy respect and fear of them as I had for my father. If I didn't screw up, there was nothing to worry about. But on those occasions when I would cross some boundary, I would soon feel the repercussions from the cops, my dad, and even the school officials. I grew up at a time when the school dean would administer swats with a paddle for those of us who had difficulty following the rules. In junior high, I had been the recipient of several spankings, though I don't recall how many. All I remember is that I had earned enough to sign the dean's paddle, and I did.

Though I loved baseball and football, I didn't have the opportunity to participate in organized sports as a child. Hart High has seen its share of championship teams, and it has been traditionally well-represented in professional sports by more than a few students who have gone on to have successful careers in the NFL and MLB. I played football during my freshman and sophomore years, but since I didn't have the experience of my teammates, I never came close to obtaining a starting role. Not having a shot at being put in to play in any game, I gave up sports so that I could work. If I wanted to drive, I had to earn enough money to pay for a car and put gas in it. My folks couldn't and wouldn't provide those things to me or my siblings. When I was sixteen, my dad co-signed a loan for $1,200 and I was able to buy my first car, a 1968 Mercury Cougar. By working part-time, I could make the $68 per month payments and usually keep gas in the tank. My parents paid for my insurance until I was eighteen.

My work experience was varied, and it began long before high school. At about age twelve, I held a paper route, a job I would keep for a couple of years. At fifteen, I bused tables and washed dishes at Happy Steak, a local steakhouse that was similar to a Sizzler. I also worked for a general contractor part-time during the school years and full-time during the summers, building patio covers, room additions, and other projects. I even helped on exactly one roofing job, and it was a great education—I knew I didn't want to be a roofer after that. My junior year I worked at a gas station, at K-Mart, at a shooting range, and I even held a janitorial job at a dry cleaner. My senior year I worked at a machine shop in nearby Pacoima, a city known to be mostly Hispanic and, in parts, a rough place to be. Thus began my cultural education. I was one of only a couple of white employees, and one of only two who weren't related to the owner. But I was unskilled, so I worked jobs that required sitting or standing in one place the majority of my shift, processing machine parts. One part, one task. Drill a hole, cut a bar, et cetera. The same thing all day long. Forty-nine hours per week in the summertime—we only worked nine hours on Fridays—and twenty or so hours during the school year, depending on if we had work on a Saturday or not. While most of the students from my school either worked at nearby Magic Mountain—a theme park—or didn't work at all and were able to enjoy high school and sports and the like, I had sampled a wide breadth of occupations and had been able to eliminate each of them from my future plans.

However, I still had no interest in law enforcement, and cops were still not my friends. Not that I was an outlaw but I was a hotrodder, a street racer, a guy who liked to hang out on cruise nights in various locations: Lyons Avenue in Newhall and Van Nuys Boulevard down in the San Fernando Valley, to name a couple. As such, I would often be subjected to the "harassment" of cops.

My other interest in those days was music. Like my father, I was a drummer, and I played in an assortment of garage rock bands and even in our church's music group. And as a musician in the seventies, I had taken on the look of a rock-n-roll band's drummer, with a head full of reckless red hair and a gold stud in my left ear. It amazes me to this day that my parents allowed either one. It amazes me more that I just admitted to the hair and earring in my memoir.

The church I attended was Grace Baptist. When our family joined circa 1970, the church consisted of one small building located on a dirt road in Placerita Canyon. We, the family of James L. and Beverly Joan Smith, were the 96th through 100th members of the small community church. We helped build a larger church and multipurpose room—financially and physically—and over the years I watched as the church grew to be one of the biggest in the valley. It was eventually relocated to a much larger site on a hill in the midst of the sprawling, populous, and prosperous City of Santa Clarita, and a megachurch was erected. But by then I was long gone, living—and surviving—in the big city south of the sleepy community from where I had come.

5

GRADUATING HIGH SCHOOL

JUNE 1980

After graduating from William. S. Hart High School in Newhall in 1980, I did what many of my fellow Hart High Indians at that time did: I promptly signed up at the local community college, College of the Canyons—or, as some of us called it, College of the *Crayons*. My first instinct had been to join the military, so I took the test and spoke with recruiters. But my father talked me out of joining. He had been a paratrooper and had fought in Korea. Two of his brothers had also served: Robert John Smith, also a paratrooper, was killed in action in Korea. The other, Lt. Col. Bascom P. Smith, served as a pilot in the Air Force during WWII, Korea, and Vietnam. He and his crew were shot down during WWII, but he survived. Our family had served honorably and had sacrificed plenty, and like most parents of my father's generation, he only wanted a better life for me than what he had lived. "Get an education, boy, and make something of yourself."

But an education was not working well for someone who hated school. I had barely graduated from high school, but only because of lack of interest and poor attendance. Attending classes at the community college turned out to be no different for me, it just wasn't my thing. I had taken some criminal justice classes only because it beat math, and a journalism class because I had some strange notion about wanting to write. Later, when I joined the sheriff's department, I would breeze through the academy both academically and physically, and I would be one of fewer than a dozen cadets from a class of 135 to be chosen for the honor guard. But it would take finding something that interested me before I magically wouldn't be as dumb as my school records may have suggested.

But the sheriff's department was yet a few years away, and at that time, not even in my sights. My first inkling that law enforcement was in my future came when I landed a job working security. My drum teacher, Dave Compton, had worked as a security guard at Bendix Corporation in Sylmar, just a short drive south from where I lived. They were hiring, he told me, and it was a great job for college students as there was time to study and do homework during one's shift. Also, it paid $4.50 per hour! I jumped on it.

6

BENDIX SECURITY

SYLMAR 1980

My interview at Bendix was conducted by one of the two chiefs of security, George Betsworth. He and the other chief, Ron Borgstrom, had both retired from the Los Angeles Police Department. At the end of the interview, Betsworth called Borgstrom in front of me and told him that I seemed okay but needed a haircut. He hung up and sent me to North Hollywood, where they would do the paperwork and fit me for a uniform. From there I found a barber shop.

It was while working at Bendix over the next year or so that I decided I wanted to be a cop. I loved everything about the two former cops for whom I worked: the way they walked, the way they talked, the way they studied people and were mindful of their surroundings at all times. I enjoyed listening to them reminisce about their law enforcement careers, and I loved hearing their "war stories." They represented the epitome of real men, and I wanted to be just like them.

Both encouraged me to join the sheriff's department rather than Hollywood's favorite police department, the LAPD. Its best days were behind it, they told me, and later, a background investigator for the LAPD would echo what my two mentors had said. I had applied to LAPD as a backup to the sheriff's department, and when I called to retract my application because the sheriff's department had offered me a job, the investigator said, "Congratulations, young man, you've chosen the better department."

At that time the minimum age to be a sworn deputy sheriff was twenty-one. You could apply six months prior to your twenty-first birthday, as it would take that long to complete the application process. That left me a couple years before I could even apply, and a couple years at that time felt like an eternity to me.

It was then that I started to realize that military service would have been a great primer for law enforcement, and I regretted my decision to continue with school rather than enlisting. However, between my father discouraging me and Jimmy Carter having been our President when I graduated from high school, it hadn't been in the cards. Few were joining the service during those days as there was little incentive to do so, and the military had suffered great cuts during the previous years. And now it was too late. It wasn't really too late, but I felt like it was, since the prospect of being a cop was only a couple of years away, while going into the service then would have been a four-year commitment. This is when I made the second bad choice in not joining the military, the first being when I hadn't gone straight in from high school. I chose to forego the military so that I could be a cop in two short years. By then, I had set my mind on law enforcement, and I couldn't be deterred.

7

WESTEC SECURITY

1981

W ith a career in law enforcement on the horizon, I made it my business to move up the ladder of security work. I discovered that all across the southland there were private security companies whose services were contracted by residents of more prosperous communities, many of whom had elaborate alarm systems that would be installed, maintained, and monitored by these companies. Arguably the best company at the time was Westec Security, and I was hired by them once I obtained my state licenses. I was now an armed security patrol officer, a real live wannabe cop.

My colleagues and I took pride in our work, and we tried hard to remove some of the stigma that came with being a security guard. That was the goal of Westec as well, and it was said that they hired a higher quality of officer than some of the competition did. They took training seriously, especially when it came to firearms. One of the managers was a nationally ranked handgun competitor, and he saw to it that we were well trained and that we regularly qualified on the range. Later, as a cadet in the sheriff's academy, the skills I learned from those days would help me qualify as a Distinguished Expert with my sidearm.

Westec was an interesting place to work. We patrolled Bel Air, Beverly Hills, Brentwood, Santa Monica, West Los Angeles, and beyond.

Many of our clients were celebrities: movie stars, music moguls, executives, and other persons of substantial wealth and notoriety. I met Priscilla Presley (who was truly beautiful, sweet, and charming, even when awakened by her alarm at three in the morning), Don Meredith's wife (who was as funny as he himself had been), two of *Charlie's Angels* (one of whom was as crazy as the other was pretty), and a host of others. Such as the great Muhammad Ali.

Westec provided security for the gated community in which Mr. Ali lived. Our duties there included alarm response and patrol, and a sentry was stationed at the gate twenty-four hours a day. This was circa 1982, and Mr. Ali had not yet been officially diagnosed with Parkinson's syndrome.

One afternoon, the sentry at the guard shack radioed for assistance because a well-known former child actor—who as an adult had struggled to stay out of trouble with the law—had walked into the private community, dismissing the sentry's efforts to stop him.

The procedure for visitors was to check in at the guard station. Their visit would have to be cleared by the resident they wished to visit before permission to enter was given. Expected or welcome guests were on a list in the guard shack. But this uninvited guest walked in without stopping at the gate, and as he did, he told the guard where he could stuff it.

I arrived at the guard shack along with another patrol officer, and we contacted the sentry, Mike, a short, robust Englishman with a great sense of humor who was easily excited. He told us what had happened and identified the suspect to us by name. We were familiar with the intruder from previous encounters and from his childhood celebrity.

I asked, "Where'd he go?"

"Where the hell do you think he went?" was the reply. "He went to Ali's house!"

There were few problems in this community. Unfortunately, when there were, it seemed they would stem from the unwanted, perhaps uninvited, guests of The Champ.

We drove in and parked on the street near Mr. Ali's home.

A neighbor—who also was famous and black—stood watching from his property. He must have witnessed the incident, and he was none too happy about the intrusion. He called out to us, "Arrest that nigger!" referring to the former child actor.

I knocked on Mr. Ali's door and was shocked when he answered it himself. I had expected a servant to do so. What I hadn't expected was to have the giant of a man himself, the great Muhammad Ali, open the door and stand in front of me, no more than an arm's length away.

I had seen the legend on other occasions, but I had never actually met him. There had been times when I was parked at the guard shack and Mr. Ali passed through, driving his Bentley. Each time he had smiled and waved, leaving me with the impression that he was a decent, friendly man. Other guards who had met with him had nothing but nice things to say about him. Some celebrities were not so nice to the hired help, which was all we were.

When Mr. Ali answered the door, he greeted us with a warm and friendly smile. I took the lead over my partner, who was a decade older and who had worked at the company for at least eight years.

"Where is he?" I asked, forgoing the pleasantries and getting right to it.

"Who?"

"You know who, Mr. Ali. He walked past our security officer at the gate and came straight to your home."

"Nobody's here."

At that moment, the intruder in question walked through the house in plain view from the open door. I pointed past Mr. Ali and said, "He's right there!"

He turned and glanced inside, then looked back at me and shrugged with a hint of embarrassment.

I said, "Mr. Ali, there are rules established by your association regarding guests entering the premises. You each have signed a contract that authorizes us to enforce laws on the private property within these walls on your behalf, and we do. In return, we expect our clients and their guests to abide by the rules, not make our jobs more difficult. Mr. (name withheld) cussed our sentry and walked through the gate without permission or prior approval. Your neighbors aren't happy with the situation either. Quite frankly, Mr. Ali, had I arrived before he made it into your home, I would have arrested him for trespassing."

He said, "I'm sorry, it won't happen again."

"Thank you."

There was nothing else to say. Though he had initially tried to cover for his guest, Mr. Ali offered a sincere apology and assured us it wouldn't happen again. That was good enough for me; I had no doubt he would handle it.

We shook hands, and my partner and I walked away.

Standing near our vehicles in front of the mansion, my partner said, "Jesus, dude, you just chewed Muhammad Ali's ass."

His remark caught me off guard. I didn't think I had chewed his ass. To me, I was only doing my job. I was careful to be respectful and reasonable, but I also had a duty to the clients—each of them.

In the two years I worked for Westec, I had many other encounters with big-name celebrities. I treated each of them as I would treat anyone, the glamorous star or her gardener. Some were pleasant, others were not. With no regard to their wealth or fame, I did my job without favor or prejudice.

Our experiences shape who we are and what we become. The encounter with Muhammad Ali is one such experience that helped shape me, reinforcing the adage that a person is a person, no matter how large or small. That I had not hesitated to address him in a professional manner stayed with me. It had been instinctual, not planned or considered, and it told me something about myself as I later considered it.

Albert Einstein said: "I speak to everyone in the same way, whether he is the garbage man or the president of the university."

I would be remiss if I didn't emphasize how decently Mr. Ali treated me, whereas many in his position may not have been so kind. He was polite and gracious, and exhibited class in choosing to deal with the guest outside of our presence. I wish I could have heard their subsequent conversation. [1]

ONE NIGHT I WAS PATROLLING THE UPSCALE LOS ANGELES SUBURB KNOWN as Brentwood when a colleague, John Babbitt, asked me to meet him for a cup of coffee on Santa Monica Boulevard. I would later attend the sheriff's academy, work the jail, and transfer to and work at Firestone station with Johnny, but on this night, we were a couple of kids with adequate training for responding to alarms and not much more. While en route to the coffee spot, my attention was drawn to an audible alarm at a liquor store. It was about 3:00 a.m. and the streets were mostly empty. I stopped in the middle of the intersection and looked in both directions. Nothing stirred around the liquor store, and at a glance, it appeared to be secured. But across the street was an all-night restaurant, and a young black male was walking away from it—away from me, in fact. He looked back over his shoulder as he moved away, and he had a look of surprise or fear on his face, an expression that made it clear he hoped to avoid me.

I pulled alongside him and called out for him to stop. As I was exiting my car, he attempted to conceal a large metal object beneath his coat. My lack of training and experience likely played a part in my guessing that it was a crowbar he was trying to hide, as my only thought at the time was that he may have tried to break into the liquor store. After all, a burglar alarm had been sounded. But as I stepped toward him, he removed the item from beneath the coat, and I saw that it was a sawed-off shotgun. I drew my gun and was quickly on target, ready to shoot. Thankfully, the young man in my sights made it immediately clear that he was putting the gun down. I ordered him to step away from where he had placed the shotgun, and then instructed him to lie prone on the sidewalk. I then handcuffed him and excitedly called for backup.

The shotgun was a double-barreled 12 gauge, and both barrels were loaded and ready for action. As I unloaded it, my adrenaline pumped, and I realized just how deadly the situation had been.

In instances when security officers apprehend a criminal, the agency of jurisdiction is called to "take" the arrest. LAPD was summoned, and they responded quickly. They would arrest and book him, and their detectives would present the case to the district attorney, who would review the case and determine what if any, charges would be filed. I later learned that as a result of this arrest, detectives had been able to clear a number of armed robberies that had occurred in the area. The suspect had been described as a black male, 16-21 years of age, who, while armed with a sawed-off double-barreled shotgun, had robbed several restaurants late at night.

I look back on that night and recall it vividly, and I realize that had this young felon been a hardened criminal by then, the encounter could have ended very badly.

THE NEXT DEADLY ENCOUNTER I EXPERIENCED WHILE WORKING AT WESTEC happened a few months later.

A rapist had been regularly striking in the Hancock Park district of Los Angeles, a wealthy area south of Hollywood where the mayor's home is located. Westec maintained a large clientele in this area and there were two units that patrolled it on the graveyard shift. I had been assigned that beat for a few months when the rapist had begun his crime spree. He would break into homes in the middle of the night and rob the residents, and on the few occasions when a woman was found inside alone, he raped her. One particular case was that of an elderly woman who had been beaten, raped, sodomized, and robbed. One of the items stolen from her was a .38 caliber revolver.

For several weeks, my colleagues and I had a heightened sense of awareness for prowlers, suspicious vehicles, and activity. In the wee hours when nobody other than cops, guards, and paperboys would be seen moving about, we would black out (turn our vehicle's lights off) and patrol the streets, hugging the curb lines to the extent we could. One night, owing to this diligent search for the rapist, I arrested a car burglar. On another night, I caught a pair of car thieves in the act of hot-wiring a client's vehicle. And then late one night, or maybe more accurately, early one morning, a silent alarm came into our dispatch. I responded to the corresponding residence along with the other unit in the area. This particular call had been a panic button activation, and those were rare. Though most alarms are false activations, meaning the alarm was set off accidentally or by some glitch in the system, each was taken very seriously, as we knew any of them could be the next victim of a brutal rape, or even a murder.

We arrived stealthily, each of us coming in blacked out and parking our patrol cars out of view of the home. Together, we approached the home on foot, proceeding down a long, dark driveway until we were along the south side of the residence. We found an open kitchen window with muddy footprints on the wall and a corresponding large footprint in the damp flower bed beneath it. All were fresh, and we were confident that an intrusion had been made. My partner asked our dispatcher to try calling the homeowner to see if there was a response. We also requested an estimated time of arrival for LAPD.

One of the reasons that private patrol is so popular in the City of Los Angeles is that LAPD is very typically slow in their responses to routine calls for service. This has always been the case and will likely never change, but I can't explain why it is that way. Where I would later work as a deputy sheriff, in the Firestone District, our average response times for priority calls was one to two minutes. Routine calls would be expected to have no more than a five-minute response. LAPD could, at times, take more than an hour to respond to a non-emergency call such as an alarm, absent any evidence of a life-threatening situation in progress. This night was no exception; LAPD had an extended ETA.

The homeowner had answered the call made by our dispatch and told the operator that an intruder was in her home. The dispatcher asked if they could get out safely, advising her that two officers were waiting outside. A woman and her husband appeared moments later, each nearly hysterical.

"There's a black man inside," the woman said. "He's upstairs."

"Where?"

The woman told us that she had awakened to see the intruder walk through her bedroom and into the walk-in closet. She said, "It's where I keep my jewelry." She said she had pretended to be sleeping when he first passed through, and that he was still in the closet when she and her husband snuck out and came downstairs. One of us asked if anyone else was in the home. Her answer stunned me. "Yes, both of our children are upstairs, asleep in their bedrooms."

My partner and I exchanged glances. We had to go in; there was no time to wait. Our field supervisor had arrived, a lieutenant with Westec who was also a reserve police officer for South Pasadena. He had more experience than we did, so he formulated the plan and led the charge. My partner was told to stay outside and watch the front and side of the home from the southeast corner. The lieutenant and I would go into the home with the intention of securing the children. We were not going to take any time to clear the downstairs first; if he escaped out the back, so be it.

Once inside the darkened interior, we heard the heavy footsteps of a man traveling across the floor above us. The intruder was on the move.

The lieutenant suggested that we let him think that there were many of us on scene. It was brilliant, really. The bad guy likely knew we were there by then, so trying to sneak around would have been of no use. We began speaking to each other loudly, coordinating with other officers who didn't exist, calling out to Joe or Tom to watch the back, stay downstairs, et cetera. We talked about the home being surrounded outside, and that SWAT was on the way. The truth of it was, we weren't even sure that LAPD was on the way!

We worked our way upstairs, the beams of our flashlights leading the way. The first bedroom to the right was a playroom. A glance inside, and we moved past it. Our greatest concern was to get the children safely out of the home. The next two rooms belonged to the children. I covered the playroom and the master bedroom from the hallway, keeping in mind that the suspect could be anywhere, while the lieutenant picked up one sleeping child at a time and rushed them downstairs and out to safety. As he did, I kept talking to the fictitious officers who were upstairs with me —my pretend backup.

After both children were safely removed from the house, we did what we never should have done; we continued the search for the bad man. As the years have passed and I have had thousands of hours of training and experience in law enforcement, I look back and again thank the good Lord for his grace toward the ignorant. Once the family had reached safety, we should have backed out and let the real professionals come and do their jobs. They might not be the fastest to a call, but LAPD is a top-notch police agency and many of their officers are among the best in the country. Their training, like the sheriff's department, is world-renowned and second to none, and they would have been better equipped to safely search the home and arrest the intruder. But we didn't wait for them; we continued our search for an exceedingly dangerous man, two guards with guns.

The first room we searched was the playroom that we had passed by with only a glance inside while looking for the children. We worked our way into it, carefully approaching the closet at the far side of the room. I stayed closer to the door, trying to watch the hallway beyond this room so that we wouldn't be surprised by the suspect coming from behind us. The lieutenant pulled the closet door open, and as he shone his light inside the dark compartment, it spilled upon a large man who stood eerily still in the corner, waiting.

The lieutenant screamed, "Let me see your hands!"

We both had our firearms pointed at him. I remember my gun was shaking slightly, and I thought about all of those hours of shooting at the range. I focused on controlling my breathing, and I was able to calm myself. My lieutenant ordered the intruder out of the closet and into a prone position on the ground among the scattered building blocks, balls, and dolls. He covered the suspect as I holstered my weapon and hand-cuffed him. Gripping the arm of this man in order to move him was akin to trying to palm a basketball. He was a giant of a man, and I was thankful that he hadn't resisted arrest.

We found a gun on a shelf in the closet among the children's toys. The family confirmed that they didn't own any weapons, so we knew the intruder had stashed it there once he made the decision not to try shooting it out with us. After all, he knew from our contrived conversations that we were many. It turned out that the gun we recovered was that which had been stolen from the woman who was raped and sodomized a week or so before this night.

A DOZEN YEARS AFTER THE MANSON FAMILY TURNED THE BENEDICT Canyon home at 10050 Cielo Drive into a house of horrors—the manic cultists slaughtering actress Sharon Tate, her unborn fetus, and four others who were either guests or lived on the property, and leaving behind their unsettling messages that shocked the nation—the summer winds still whispered sounds of terror through the shadowy canyon road on the outskirts of Beverly Hills.

The top of this infamous canyon offered breathtaking views of West Los Angeles from a plateau that was popular among kids and young adults who drove there to indulge themselves with alcohol and drugs and carnal pleasures with lovers, friends, and sometimes strangers. With the darkness of times past still weighty and real, the locale—in spite of its appeal—was still ripe for misadventures and tragedies.

In the early morning hours of just such an ominous summer night, the dispatch center of Westec Security in Santa Monica was suddenly abuzz with activity: the board of phone lines lit up as panic alarms sounded, and the operators hastily gathered as much information as they could while fear struck residents of Benedict Canyon once again. A man, most said—frantic and covered in blood—ran house to house pounding on doors and ringing bells while screaming for help.

It came over the radio as a check-the-area call with a notation that an unknown person covered in blood was crying for help. And of course, it would be my call. Though I hadn't realized it at the time, I was destined to dwell in the most extraordinary, bizarre, and dangerous situations. Whether it be a chance encounter with a boy wielding a sawed-off shotgun and roaming the streets of West L.A., an armed rapist discovered hiding in a playroom closet, or any of the dozens of deadly encounters I would face in the years to come, these were the cards I'd been dealt.

There was no backup coming. LAPD had been notified, but they could never be counted on to respond quickly to the calls of a security service. I was on my own as I drove slowly through the region where the calls had originated, scanning the road and homes and yards for a deranged man or perhaps a desperate one. Was he a victim, or a killer? If the former, where might the real danger lurk? The history of this locale had not escaped even me as I trolled with my hand resting on the butt of my holstered weapon, eyes wide open and pulse racing. After all, I was still just a kid, maybe twenty at the time, and with limited training and experience. Truthfully, my life had just begun, though back then I had no idea. The preponderance of my existence had yet to be realized, the adventures and disasters, wins and losses, anecdotes of love and loathing still unwrapped packages. Without even knowing it, I relied on fate.

Beams of light washed over a man as I turned slowly around a blind corner and found him staring into my headlights like a deer on the road. His clothing was torn and covered in blood, his arms and face patches of road rash. I stopped. He froze. I had the instinct to scan my surroundings before exiting my car, searching for danger lurking in the shadows. Seeing no other threats beyond this crazed man covered in blood in the middle of the road, walking distance from Cielo Drive, I exited my car and directed him to the front of it where I had him remain while I heard his tale.

He had been hitchhiking through West Hollywood on Sunset Boulevard when a bearded man driving an older sedan stopped and offered him a ride. The man had beer and marijuana, and he offered our midnight rambler both. They decided to head to the plateau where they could party undeterred while enjoying the lovely Los Angeles summer night, and that is what they did.

However, it was on the way back down the canyon, the man driving carelessly as the summer wind rushed through their open windows, when this stranger suddenly said, "Hey man, open your door, I have to throw some trash out."

Not too bright to begin with, an assumption we could all make from his actions to this point, my bloody prowler did just that—he opened his door—and his elder, wiser friend shoved him from the speeding vehicle onto the road in Benedict Canyon.

This is a story I told my daughters when they were only children, in part to reinforce the stranger danger warning, and in part because my twisted sense of humor had always found it amusing. From then on it became a family joke to say, when any passenger happened to irritate the driver, "Open the door, I have to throw some trash out."

My elder daughter insisted that I include this story in my memoir, saying it otherwise wouldn't be worth publishing at all. If we had been riding together when she told me this, I would have, of course, asked her to open her door...

UNFORTUNATELY, THIS PROPENSITY TO HAVE BRUSHES WITH DEATH continued throughout my law enforcement career and beyond. As a deputy sheriff, I had many deadly encounters, as you will read in the following pages. Since retiring, I've narrowly escaped a number of other harrowing accidents involving livestock, heavy equipment, and even a very close encounter with a mountain lion. But by the grace of God, here I am, telling my story.

---

1. Though quotations were used to tell the story of my encounter with Mr. Ali, the incident occurred nearly forty years ago and there is no record of it with which to check for accuracy. The quotes are only used to establish dialogue in the manner of storytelling, not to indicate factual dialogue. The black neighbor did use the N-word when he called out to us to arrest the intruder. That I'll never forget.

8

PROCESSING WITH THE SHERIFF'S DEPARTMENT

1983

While working at Westec, several of my colleagues and I began applying for jobs in law enforcement. Some guys applied with every department that was accepting applications; others were more selective, applying to only a few. By that time, with the advice of my Bendix supervisors and several others along the way, I had decided that it would be the Los Angeles County Sheriff's Department for me. The day I turned twenty and a half, I submitted my application. LASD was recruiting at a record pace during that time, and the process had slowed because of it. Typically, it would take six months to complete the process and be hired, but due to the volume of candidates, it was taking longer. I waited three months before applying to the Los Angeles Police Department as a backup plan, the idea being that if for some reason the sheriff's department didn't hire me, maybe LAPD would.

LAPD was a fine department filled with great cops. Some of their specialized units were second to none, such as their SWAT team, their Metro unit, and their Air Support unit. However, by the time I was applying, their department had gone through tremendous scrutiny. They were constantly under some sort of judicial review and the overall morale of the line troops was low. At least, that was what had been reported to me, and it is what I had seen as an outsider. It was indisputable that politics had corroded their agency, and the mayor, at that time, was seen as an adversary to the police. As a city agency, the LAPD would always be held accountable to the police commission and mayor.

The sheriff, on the other hand, being an elected (rather than appointed) official, and being the chief law enforcement officer of the county, was far more powerful than any chief of police. Although LAPD is a very large agency, they are but one of more than forty municipal police departments within the County of Los Angeles. The sheriff can (and has) taken over the policing of municipalities for any number of reasons, though corruption would be (and has been) the most likely of scenarios. The point is, as stated, that the sheriff is the chief law enforcement officer of his county. Period.

I applied to the sheriff's department and soon thereafter had successfully completed the written examination and physical fitness test. I was then promptly scheduled for the oral interview, which I passed with ease after making a great first impression.

The interview had been scheduled for 1:15 p.m. at the Hall of Justice in downtown Los Angeles. At the time I drove a 1969 Volkswagen Bug. When you are young (and "a dumb white boy from Newhall") and haven't spent much time in downtown L.A., the freeway system, the one-way streets, and the traffic on both, can be daunting. So I left early and arrived before the interview boards had recessed for lunch at noon. There were three rooms going at once, each having a team of two sergeants conducting interviews. The hallway outside of the interview rooms was filled with young, nervous, clean-cut men, (I don't recall that any women were there that day) wearing suits and ties and sporting recent haircuts. I sat among them and waited in one of the many old wooden chairs.

When one candidate was ushered from an interview room, one of the two interviewers would see him off and then call out the name of their next victim. As the noon hour approached, I found myself alone in the hallway. Finally, one of the sergeants who had eyeballed me each time he came out, exited the room with his partner and said goodbye to their final interviewee of the morning. Then the sergeant looked at me and asked what time my interview had been scheduled for. "Thirteen-fifteen hours, sir."

He glanced at his watch, looked at his partner, and then frowned at me. "Why are you so early? We're breaking for lunch."

"Sir, I drive a 1969 Volkswagen Bug. I gave myself enough time that if I had car troubles on my way in, I could abandon my vehicle on the Hollywood Freeway and jog the rest of the way here without being late."

He smiled. "Okay, well, we'll be back in an hour."

The same two returned an hour later with the other interviewers and acknowledged me silently. I sat as I had before they left, at attention in a hardwood chair. They went into their respective rooms and soon the chairs around me filled with a fresh batch of applicants—scared kids who looked to me for direction, since I had been at this much longer than they had. Have a seat and wait, was my instruction—they'll call you in when they're ready. I had it down by then, having watched the process for hours. A short time later, I was summoned by the sergeant who had spoken to me earlier. Once I was seated inside the room, he told his partner, "This is the kid who's been here all morning."

I found the interview to be easy, and the sergeants seemed pleased with my answers. I scored in the high nineties, which meant that my file would be moved along to the next steps in the process: medical examination, background investigation, and possibly polygraph and psychological examinations.

Once I cleared the medical, I had only the background investigation remaining. At the conclusion of this is when they would decide whether or not psychological and polygraph examinations would be administered. The decision as to who would be subjected to those things would be made by the background investigator, based on his/her findings. I hoped to avoid all of it. My background was relatively unblemished, or so I thought, and if all went according to Hoyle, the rest of the remaining steps would be no problem.

But the process came to a halt. Months had passed and I hadn't heard anything about even having had a background investigator assigned to me, and none of my references had been contacted. I began to worry. In the meantime, LAPD seemed to be moving much more quickly than the sheriff's department. I had passed all of their examinations and tests as well, and I had already heard from my background investigator. They had nearly completed the process and I expected to hear something about a hire date from them very soon. It had now been six months since I had applied to the sheriff's department, three months since I dropped an application with the boys in blue, yet it seemed the city was going to beat the county in spite of the head start I had given LASD.

So I donned a suit and tie and pointed my VW south from Newhall, the windows down in the heat of summer. I was headed back to the Hall of Justice.

Looking up at the beautiful architecture of the structure located at 211 West Temple Street, Los Angeles, I had a vague feeling that I had been there as a child, one of those déjà vu moments. I would later learn that when I was young, my parents had driven me there a couple of times. My mother would stay with me and my sisters while my father visited his brother, the only one who hadn't served his country, and who always seemed to have hard luck and make bad choices. No, my uncle was not a member of the sheriff's department; he was a guest of the sheriff at the Hall of Justice Jail (HOJJ) which occupied the top five floors of the historic fourteen-floor building. I would later learn that my dad had worried about his brother's criminal background affecting my chances of being hired, though by then the brother was deceased. My dad had hoped that having a convicted felon for an uncle wouldn't hold me back. Fortunately, the background investigations were neither that thorough nor that discriminating.

I went inside and up to Personnel where I asked to speak with a supervisor in the hiring department. A man in shirt sleeves and a tie, a gun on his hip and a badge pinned to his belt, appeared and stated he was a lieutenant. I asked if there was any news about my background, or if anything had been decided about my employment. I told him that LAPD was close to hiring me, but that I preferred to be a deputy sheriff, and that is why I had applied there three months before applying with LAPD. He seemed legitimately concerned, or at least empathetic to my situation, so he asked me to wait while he checked into the status of my process. Soon thereafter he returned and apologetically informed me that my file had been sitting in a stack of many others, untouched. He assured me it would be assigned to an investigator that day.

Not long after, I was offered a job. The call came from the recruiter's office on a Monday afternoon. The timing was great; I had just awakened after a few hours of sleep that followed a long night of working my security detail in Hancock Park, which, by then, was shy one rapist. I answered the phone that sat on a table in my bedroom. The man on the other end identified himself and offered me a job as a deputy sheriff trainee, and he asked if I could come in Wednesday to be sworn. I quickly made a difficult but principled decision and asked if I could extend my hire date two weeks so that I could give proper notice to my current employer. It was so scheduled, and on October 12, 1983, I returned to the Hall of Justice once more, raised my right hand, and swore an oath to protect and serve the citizens of Los Angeles County. The next twenty-one years and two months would bring great pride, joy, sorrow, and heartbreak.

And I'd do it all over again.

PART III

THE PATH TO HOMICIDE

9

SHERIFF'S ACADEMY CLASS #220

NOVEMBER 1983

A formation of 135 cadets wearing green shorts and white t-shirts with last names printed across the front and back in bold green letters, gun belts fastened around our waists, ran through the streets of East Los Angeles carrying batons in our hands, the weapons moving forward and backward as we pumped our arms and legs in unison.

One of the several drill instructors would lead us in a jody, bellowing out one line at a time to be echoed by the class with enthusiasm, lest the time marching or distance run be doubled.

Eighteen weeks of living hell
Just to work the county jail
But I won't cry and I won't moan
Soon I'll be out in Firestone

Jodies are military-style cadences used to keep a large group marching or jogging in time. Between the jodies, one of the drill instructors would keep us in time with the simple cadence: *Left, left, left, right left.* Traffic would be diverted as we commanded the use of two lanes of traffic and did not stop at red lights. We were the sheriff. *The mighty, mighty sheriff...*

Here we go again

(Here we go again)
Same old run again
(Same old run again)
Up and down Eastern Avenue
(Up and down Eastern Avenue)
Twelve more weeks and we'll be through
(Twelve more weeks and we'll be through)
Here we go
(Here we go)
Up the hill
(Up the hill)
Down the hill
(Down the hill)
Around the hill
(Around the hill)
What the hill
(What the hill)
Bring it on down now
(One, two, three, four...)

Though physical training was only a small part of our daily routine at the eighteen-week Sheriff's Academy, it was certainly one of the hardest parts for many cadets. I had prepared for it since I first decided to pursue a career in law enforcement, and for the most part, the PT was a welcome part of the day. As for the academics, I would no longer maintain the D average I had carried in high school; in fact, I graduated in the top ten percent of my academy class. I loved the subject matter and I enjoyed most of the lectures. It was extremely interesting to hear the experiences of veteran officers and deputies as they lectured on officer survival and tactics. Even subjects such as court procedures and case law could be interesting when the instructor mixed in personal stories that related to the topics at hand. I would sit and imagine what it would someday be like to work the streets, to bring bad guys into the jail wearing stainless steel handcuffs, to raise my right hand and swear to tell the truth, and send bad men (and women) to prison.

The academy, at that time, was located in East Los Angeles on Sheriff's Road, and was referred to by most as "The Hill." It moved to Whittier a couple of months after my class started. The class behind ours started on The Hill but graduated from the new academy. The new location, a former high school campus, was thought to usher in a new breed of deputy, the result of a less stressful approach to training by the academy staff. The truth was, no LASD academy has ever been easy or without a rigorous and stressful program in place. At any rate, our class was the last to graduate from The Hill for several decades until the academy was moved back to East L.A. in 2014.

The Hill featured a series of classrooms, a large flat, paved area called The Grinder where formations were held, a weapons training (and qualifications) range, and a track and field, not unlike that of every high school in America, though probably the only one where runners wore guns on their belts and carried batons while engaged in physical training. There was also a gymnasium, but unlike high school, we didn't move our PT indoors due to inclement weather. Ever.

The academics took place inside the classrooms where rows of desks were occupied by uniformed cadets who sat at attention. There was no slouching or kicking back in class. Weekly tests were given for spelling, radio codes, penal codes, and vehicle codes. There were also weekly notebook inspections. Each cadet would maintain notes of all lectures, and those notes would have to be maintained in a specific, orderly manner within a notebook that would be a part of your academic scoring. Everything was written in pencil, because back in that day and throughout my patrol career, that was how we wrote reports: by printing them onto report forms using all upper-case letters that were—at least during the academy—expected to be as neat as if each letter had been typed.

There were morning formations wherein inspections would be peppered with planned fits of disgust and rage from the drill instructors who couldn't believe they had found a bare thread on the uniform of Cadet Jones. "Are you trying to hang yourself, Cadet Jones?" one would bark. The other instructors would watch carefully to see if any cadet glanced in the direction of Cadet Jones and the sharply dressed drill instructor who stood spitting his comical rant in the cadet's face. Such a wayward glance by another cadet would lead to that cadet being screamed at by another DI. "What are you laughing at, Cadet Smith? Do you think it's funny that Cadet Jones is trying to hang himself and get the rest of us killed while doing so? Drop and give me twenty (pushups)!"

Morning formation might be followed by time spent marching, and then it would be inside for lectures. They would usually save PT for after lunch. Digestion was not a concern of theirs, nor was the rising afternoon temperature. It was mind over matter, they would often say: *We don't mind, and you don't matter.*

After a month or so, some of the more enjoyable parts of academy training would begin: firearms training, self-defense instruction, role playing, emergency vehicle operations, and eventually patrol rides. The firearms training, of course, took place at the range. Self-defense instruction was held on the infield of the track. Role playing took place at various locations throughout the academy grounds and beyond, including a couple of days and nights at Universal Studios, where training came to life just as movies do with the ambience of city streets, towns, and buildings.

Much time was spent marching and running in formation. This was where the class really came together, the cadets learning that we would succeed or fail as a unit. Once we were all in step, there was a feeling of pride and unstoppable strength like that of an army.

In order to graduate, there were many tests that had to be passed and requirements that had to be met. PT tests had a maximum score of 500, but the qualifying score was much lower (though I can't remember now what that was). Three tests would be given throughout the course of the academy, and every cadet had to pass each one or risk being dropped. (That was the threat, but the term "remedial training" was often used for those who didn't meet minimum requirements.) The PT tests comprised a certain number of pushups, pull-ups, sit-ups, and burpees, and each movement had its own set time limit. There was a mile and a half run (ten minutes was the mark for the maximum points) and a 220-yard dash, the latter of which was my greatest nemesis. I scored in the high 400s on the first three tests, never having a score lower than 470 and increasing with each test. It had been my speed (or lack thereof) on the 220 that held me back, but I set my mind, pushed myself, and with some motivation from my good friend, Johnny Babbitt, I passed the final PT test with a perfect score of 500. (John was/is a great runner, and for the final test, I used him as the proverbial rabbit that I'd chase. I had told him my plan, and he, while flying around the track with me a short distance behind him, yelled encouragement for me to run faster and push harder every step of the way.)

Firearm qualifications were similarly spaced throughout the academy, and of a possible 300 points, one only needed 210 to qualify. The course required 30 shots fired at a target set 25 yards downrange. If you placed all 30 shots into the ten-ring, you'd have the perfect score of 300. Each shot that landed outside of the ten-ring lowered that score proportionately. One shot in the nine-ring and three more in the eight-ring would lower a score to 293. To stay above 290 was no small feat, but to require only 210 was a ridiculously low standard, in my opinion.

Before graduating, one only had to qualify once at a certain rank in order to wear the shooting medal for that qualification. Scores between 290-300 were awarded the DX (Distinguished Expert) pin, and it was my goal to wear one on the day of graduation. I qualified as Expert on the first test and Distinguished Expert on all of the others. I believe (if my memory serves me correctly) that Expert was awarded for 270-289. The bulk of cadets wore those pins.

There was also combat firearms instruction which was far more intense with the use of shotguns, radio cars, and barricades, and required weapon changes and reloading while moving from one station to the next. Stress was a factor too, inserted into the exercises by the instructors who would yell at you while you were going through the course. It was top-notch training, perhaps the best to be found anywhere.

As mentioned, we had weekly spelling tests on the twenty words we would be assigned each week. Some of the more difficult words included: phencyclidine, psychological, and rehabilitation. I would later learn that the former would be used regularly in reports I would write as a patrol deputy in South Los Angeles, and that the latter was a farce. I always scored at least 90% on the weekly spelling tests, and I scored 100% on many of them.

The emergency vehicle operations training was a blast. There are deputies who do nothing but train department personnel in high-speed pursuit driving, how to recover from a loss of control, and how to drive backwards at a high rate of speed, safely. A "skid pan" is used to intentionally put the trainee's vehicle out of control. It is a large, flat, smooth surface which would be slicked with oil, and the cadets—one at a time— would be required to drive onto this surface at a moderate speed and then turn or brake, which would send the vehicle into an uncontrolled spin. We were taught how to recover from such an event and drive through these types of scenarios without panicking. We trained on the racetrack of the Pomona Fairgrounds using cars that were specially equipped and maintained for this purpose. I would later hone these skills as I would spend thousands (if not hundreds of thousands) of hours behind the wheel throughout my career. These acquired proficiencies would keep me safe in numerous high-speed pursuits on the streets, through parks, and even—once—along the sidewalks of Los Angeles.

PATROL RIDES WERE WHAT WE ALL HAD WAITED FOR. I WANTED A TASTE OF the action, as did most of my colleagues. With twenty-some sheriff's stations at the time, the scheduling of cadet rides throughout the county must have been an arduous one. By the time we began participating in station patrol rides we had lost a fair number of cadets who had quit or been fired, but there were still more than a hundred of us. Each week the drill instructors would distribute patrol ride schedules, and most of us anticipated the lists with the excitement of children at Christmastime. I wanted to be sent to Firestone, but I received a steady diet of stations that didn't thrill me: Malibu, where the deputy I rode with spent his shift collecting errant golf balls around the perimeter of a golf course; Temple station, where the deputy to whom I had been assigned worked hard to find criminals, though they were scant in the mostly middle-class community wherein we were working; East Los Angeles, where the activity was high and the cops were topnotch, but it still wasn't Firestone. I wanted to go ride at the mystical, legendary station that we sang jodies about while marching or running through the streets of East L.A., and that seemed to be mentioned by at least every other instructor during their lectures.

Each week the drill instructors would call the cadets from their platoons, one by one, to their desks at the back of the room and ask how their patrol rides were going, and go over the cadet's evaluations that were completed by each deputy with whom they had ridden. When my DI asked how I liked the rides I had had, I was daringly truthful in my response: "Sir, the rides have been fine, but I was really hoping to go to Firestone."

He said he would see what he could do. Later that day he summoned me again and informed me that I was going to Firestone in the coming weekend for two shifts. He smiled and said, "I'm pretty sure you'll see some action there." Did I ever.

The atmosphere at Firestone was intense. There was so much going on, it was difficult for a cadet to decipher. I mostly tried to stay out of the way, but that seemed impossible. It started with where I had parked. A deputy yelled at me, telling me I hadn't earned the privilege to park in their parking lot, and I needed to move my car to the street. In Watts! I was yelled at for which door I walked through, for the manner in which I approached the desk to ask where I was expected to report, for where I sat in the briefing room...

I learned later that part of the extra hazing had been due to the actions of a fellow cadet who had ridden there the week before. He had forgotten his gun in a gun locker after booking a suspect, and he had returned to the field unarmed. This obviously meant that all cadets were trying to get all Firestone personnel killed.

On my first shift there, I was teamed with a veteran deputy, Danny Cruz. He took me aside and dressed me down for the actions of my predecessor, having been the deputy who had been partnered with the cadet who had forgotten his gun. Deputy Cruz closely inspected my firearm to make sure it was loaded, went over his expectations of me, and told me what actions to take in a number of possible scenarios such as fights, foot pursuits, and shootings. Then he told me to forget all that shit I had learned at the academy, that these were the streets where real blood was spilled. Pay attention and maybe I'd stay alive for eight hours.

Less than an hour had passed before we made a felony stop and arrested half a dozen gang members with numerous weapons, likely intercepting them on their way to commit a drive-by shooting. *Action!*

Later, after a substantial amount of paperwork and time expended in the station booking the suspects and evidence, we were back in the field where it seemed we raced from one hot call to another, many of which would call for our firearms to be drawn and pointed toward dangerous individuals. Several of these calls resulted in more people going to jail. *More action.* The next night I was back at Firestone, and it was a repeat of the previous one as far as my being busy and seeing action. However, I apparently had garnered some respect for my performance the night before and was only subjected to vicious hazing while in the station. The hazing was a tradition, one that I would endure again a few years later when I would return to Firestone station as a patrol trainee. But it would be worth it, I knew, because after experiencing just two shifts there as an academy cadet, there was no doubt in my mind that this was where I belonged. Firestone was where I wanted to be a street cop.

I won't cry and I won't moan
Soon I'll be out in Firestone

A deputy once said that being a cop in South Los Angeles was the most fun an adult could have with his clothes on. I would have to agree with that assessment. Since leaving the department, I look back at the days spent at Firestone station fondly. They were some of the best days of my life, all but just a few of them, anyway. Those other few were among the very worst days I ever had.

As my time at the academy neared its end, and as I became more accustomed to the processes, the games, and the torment, all of it seemed easier. Graduation was in sight and very much attainable. The twelve- to fourteen-hour days had subsided to more manageable ten hour days, not including the commute and the homework and studies we each took home. But with familiarity comes a level of comfort and even relaxation. Seeing the light at the end of the tunnel, my good friend Johnny Babbitt and I began taking a few chances. We weren't the only ones.

Chambers was a shoeshine parlor in South Los Angeles. Located on the east side of Central, north of Firestone Boulevard, it was within the boundaries of Firestone station's jurisdiction. Inside there were raised platforms on top of which a customer would sink into a comfortable chair and read the paper or a magazine while a shine man turned their leather into glass and soul music played in the background. If you added some images conjured from movies and videos that show the fellowship of a black barbershop or a soul food café, you can see in your mind the interior of Chambers shine parlor. However, you won't likely place in your mind any white people inside enjoying the company of the employees, patrons, and loiterers, nor will you see the junkies, gang bangers, and thieves prowling through the alleys and adjacent streets. For two skinny white boys with motivated haircuts to go to Chambers in order to get award-winning shines rubbed, buffed, and polished—with a little spit—onto our academy shoes, would be an act of insanity. Absurdity. Ridiculousness. It couldn't be done without tremendous risk to personal safety.

So, to Chambers we went, but not without packing our pieces. We were only a few weeks from being able to legally carry concealed weapons anyway, and we were in fact fully qualified—not to mention Distinguished Experts—in our firearms training. Also, Johnny B. argued, the drill instructors were always emphasizing that we needed to take initiative in matters. Well?

The first time we walked into Chambers (yes, there were several visits before we would graduate from the academy, and scores of others during our tenures working Firestone Station), all eyes were on us as if we were wearing the robes of Klansmen or the outfits of clowns—though that might be redundant. Nonetheless, it was fairly clear to all that we were "not from around there." My dumb ass from Newhall, California, raised on a dirt road, and Johnny B., from Torrance, California, an even skinnier kid who appeared—at the time—to be about fifteen years old. Board shorts and flip-flops would have better suited him, but there he stood, on the threshold of Chambers in Watts, alongside his friend and academy classmate, the both of us dressed as off-duty cops: blue jeans resting on cowboy boots, white t-shirts beneath untucked flannel button-ups to cover our .38 specials. We didn't fit in.

"Come on in, officers," said one of the shine men, a grin stretched across his face. The others laughed and jeered, and we smiled ear to ear and swaggered across the floor and climbed onto two vacant chairs that sat side by side with their backs to a wall where we would be facing the front door and windows. *Taking initiative.*

We each greeted the collective assembly warmly and smiled widely as we looked around the room, making eye contact with all in attendance. I only noted one or two who didn't seem friendly. The others were gracious and inviting. It was my first encounter with some of the wonderful people who live—rather, survive—in South Los Angeles, but who are seldom thought of when one thinks of the ghettos.

The best part was that Johnny and I had the best shines on The Grinder come Monday morning. Fellow cadets asked our secrets, and Johnny B. would smile knowingly as I would explain in great detail the tricks of a good spit-shine that I had learned from my father, a paratrooper of the 82nd Airborne. All were impressed. Only nods would be received from the instructors, and maybe the occasional, skeptical glance.

WAYSIDE HONOR RANCHO, LATER NAMED THE PETER J. PITCHESS Detention Facility, is one of several jail facilities spread throughout the county. Located in the Santa Clarita Valley, the 2,620-acre property features several academy training firing ranges and an equine center. At one time, some of its land was cultivated and the produce was used to feed the inmates. The farmers were "trustees," low-level criminals who spent their days working in various supervised positions.

There is a time during the academy when all cadets are sent to Wayside for several days of intense firearms instruction, the previously mentioned combat shooting courses, and also a night shoot. Many cadets would try to stay in the area rather than commute from their homes in the southern areas of the county, or the counties south or east of Los Angeles. When the Wayside schedule was revealed to us, I invited my closest academy friends who lived far away to stay with me at my parents' home during those few days of training. I told all to bring sleeping bags, as there was plenty of space on the floors. Several accepted my offer, and my childhood home was filled with adventurous, shorthaired young men who would spend the next several decades seeing and being involved in unspeakable sufferings, and who would remain my brothers as no other friends ever had. Early the next morning, my dad stepped over and around the smattering of campers to head to work, and my mom started cooking breakfast for all. Yes, I really did have that great a home life and childhood.

Once the shooting had been completed that first day, we were called to formation, at which time the drill instructors cautioned us to not go out and get into trouble, knowing that many cadets would be staying locally rather than commuting each day. "This is sheriff's jurisdiction. We better not get any calls from Santa Clarita station telling us that our cadets were running amok."

Shortly after we were dismissed, those staying at my house gathered in a circle. The self-appointed spokesperson for the group, Tommy Jimenez, said, "So, Danny, where exactly should we run amok?" I suggested a nightclub that seemed to be popular with the young crowd in town, and that is exactly where we landed several hours later, showered, shaved, and dressed like off-duty cops. We took a table near the dance floor and just waited for all the girls to show up. But rather than flocks of young ladies, we were stunned to see the entire academy staff stroll in and take a table across from us. Obviously, they noticed us.

We all looked at one another until finally someone asked what we should do. Johnny B. took a swig of his beer and said, "My motto is, if you get caught with your dick in your hand, you look like a fool trying to put it away. You might as well go ahead and wag it at 'em." Tommy concurred and then upped the ante, sending a round of drinks to the drill instructors who sat nearby, glaring.

The consensus was that we would need to get our instructors drunk. If any ladies ever happened in, we'd sacrifice them as well. We were in deep shit and we knew it. We sent one round after the other, and gladly paid our tab. One of the instructors ended up drunk and belligerent after trying to woo an attractive waitress to no avail. At some point, the waitress, whom we continually sent with trays of liquor to our leaders, told us that the one with the particularly large, black mustache had been cut off. We laughed. But only then, and not the next day. And it was not he who called us out early the next morning during formation. In fact, he—and his prominent 'stache—were nowhere to be seen.

"Okay, where are the winos?" one of the instructors barked. I knew, and about half a dozen others knew, exactly who he was talking about. But none of us stepped forward. "Come on, you winos, you know who you are. Step up now or face worse consequences."

This was it, I knew, my last day in the academy and back to Westec as a disgraced, fired sheriff's cadet. But what about the drunken DI, I pondered. Why were we in trouble and the one who had made a spectacle of himself and had been cut off was beyond reproach? It didn't seem fair, but I knew I had to step forward. My partners in crime had come to the same conclusion, and after exchanging a few knowing glances, we all stepped forward. We took a serious ass-chewing, were assigned to write lengthy papers on alcoholism, and were henceforth collectively called The Winos. But we would prevail, each and every one of us so-called derelicts.

ON MARCH 30, 1984, THOSE OF US WHO HAD SURVIVED THE *EIGHTEEN weeks of living hell, just to work the county jail,* donned our sharpest uniforms and put on our shiniest shoes—mine and Johnny Babbitt's leading the pack. We survivors marched sharply and stood as statues when called to attention at the Los Angeles County Sheriff's Academy Class #220 graduation, held at the La Mirada Theatre for the Performing Arts. The 1,251-seat venue filled quickly with family members and friends of the hundred or so graduating sheriff's deputies. After a short ceremony, we stood up from our seats, one row at a time—as practiced—and marched down the aisles and up the steps to the stage where Sheriff Sherman Block—the last great sheriff—shook each of our hands as he provided us with our certificates and offered his sincerest congratulations.

I remember feeling as if this was my greatest accomplishment in life. Up to that point, it certainly had been so. A few years later, I would be even prouder to complete the six-month training regimen at Firestone station. I hadn't cared about graduating from high school and had no pride in doing so. I hadn't graduated from college, so I didn't have that to compare to it. My good friend, Frank LaFlamme, has said that he considered becoming a Firestone deputy one of his greatest achievements in life. This from a man who also earned a Bachelor of Science degree from the University of Southern California, an achievement he claims doesn't even rank among his top five.

10

MEN'S CENTRAL JAIL

1984 - 1986

T he sheriff is responsible for the care and custody of all arrestees in his county. There are 20,000 inmates in the Los Angeles County jail system at any given time, more than in any other system in the country. The next closest, Rikers Island, New York, houses about 13,000, while Harris County jail in Houston, Texas, and Cook County jail in Chicago, Illinois, each report inmate populations of about 10,000—half of the inmate population in L.A. County. Unlike in prison facilities, many of these inmates are moved daily for release, court, or to be shipped to prison. Given the daunting task of running such an operation, a large percentage of deputy personnel is assigned to custody division. Like most cops, I had signed on to work the streets, and I never would have volunteered to work the jail. That is why a deputy sheriff's first assignment is—with very few exceptions—Custody Division. Johnny and I were both assigned to Men's Central Jail, otherwise known as MCJ—or, simply "CJ."

MCJ was home to some of the nation's most notorious criminals: Charles Manson, Richard (the Night Stalker) Ramirez, O.J. Simpson, and the Menendez brothers—two spoiled Beverly Hills brats who shotgunned their parents to death. Lesser known but far more dangerous were the various killers who represented the most vicious prison and street gangs of Southern California and beyond. There were nearly daily assaults, weekly fights involving deputies, and several murders a year within the facility. During my two-and-a-half-year stint, there were three major riots, two involving the Crips, and one involving the Bloods, both notorious black street gangs. During the early eighties, the two gangs had been segregated from the rest of the jail population for the safety of staff and other inmates alike. Having them locked up together was convenient in some ways, dangerous in others. After the last riot, which had occurred in a chow hall, the two modules housing these gangs would be essentially placed on permanent lockdown status. The gang members would receive all of their meals inside their cells, and their movement within the jail was limited to only that which was absolutely necessary.

One murder that occurred while I was there happened in Module 4800, the Crip module. An inmate was found dead in his cell among the six or eight inmates locked inside with him—there was no escape for the suspects. This murder had taken place before they were banned from going to the chow hall. After lunch, several inmates—who were assigned to other cells—had gathered in the dead man's cell where they would remain until ushered to dinner. This was not uncommon as there were no midday counts, so as long as a wandering inmate returned to his assigned cell after going to dinner, his having been in an unassigned cell during the afternoon would likely go undetected. Many times, gang members would do this to hang out with their closest homeboys. Other times, it was to discuss business. Sometimes, that business included discipline. I would later learn that the inmate who was killed that day was said to be a snitch, and therefore his "homies" murdered him.

We would later learn that the way they had killed him was by someone suggesting a pushup contest. One of the shot-callers went first, whipping out fifty or so. The soon-to-be victim was second to go, and he was challenged to top the number of pushups that his predecessor had completed. He gave it his all, and when he rolled over, exhausted from his efforts, the other inmates began stomping him. Too tired to put up much of a fight, he was quickly stomped to death. A short while later, the inmates summoned the assistance of staff to report a medical problem. With shoe prints all over his clothing and blood spilling out of his mouth and nose, it didn't take long to figure out what had happened. The list of suspects was short and definitive. Though I don't know firsthand, I would guess each of them was subsequently charged with murder.

For much of my tenure at MCJ, I was assigned to the floor known as 9000. It was the first stop for new inmates entering the jail after being processed through the Inmate Reception Center. They were unclassified, known as "fish," and housed by the hundreds in one of five large dormitories filled with bunk beds. This was the most dangerous place in the jail for inmates, and one of the most active for deputies. It was there where people who had been arrested for drunk driving or drugs were housed alongside men who had killed multiple people and others who had robbed and beaten hundreds.

Drugs and other contraband were plentiful on 9000, as the fish were fresh off the street. Some entrepreneurial criminals would swallow or hide in their rectums stashes of drugs to bring into the jails where they could sell them for ten times what they might go for on the street. At the time inmates were allowed to have cash on their persons if they arrived at the jail with it or if someone outside brought it to them. Robberies occurred every hour, though most went unreported. White boys were lucky if they could keep their shoes; rarely did any of them retain whatever cash or cigarettes they might have had. Eventually the cash would be removed from the jail, but that did not remove the crime, because criminals are a resourceful lot. Soon after cash left the jail system, the transactions were taken to the street. Both sides of a financial transaction would have someone "outside" handle the exchange of cash. Even protection would be sold. A vulnerable inmate would be compelled to have family pay a contact on the outside to secure his well-being inside. It was extortion, and I'm sure it still goes on today.

During the time I worked on 9000, I made numerous drug arrests and began building my expertise in the field of narcotics while honing my report writing skills. Johnny Babbitt worked on the same floor, because, after all, we had entered the sheriff's department on the buddy system, or so we would joke. (The military used to have such a system which they used to encourage enlistment.)

One night we had come into some information that an inmate had smuggled PCP (Phencyclidine) into the jail. PCP comes in a liquid form and is oftentimes stored in small glass vials. When we brought the inmate from his dorm into the hallway in order to safely search him, he resisted, and was taken to the ground and subdued by several of us. During the process, a vial containing PCP broke and the contents spilled. Four of us deputies came into contact with the liquid during the incident, and we were subsequently taken to White Memorial Hospital for evaluation. Each of us—to varying degrees—exhibited symptoms of PCP intoxication, and we all remained at the hospital for the remainder of our shift so that our vitals could be closely monitored until all had returned to normal. [1]

GEORGE ARTHUR WAS A LEGEND IN OUR DEPARTMENT, HAVING SURVIVED A harrowing, near-death encounter wherein he and his partner, Mike Waters, had, two days before Christmas in 1976, encountered a trio of black militants who were out to kill some cops. Arthur and Waters were working a gang car out of Firestone station when they came across the men in a dark parking lot behind a bank building. A vicious fight and shooting occurred, and when it was over, two suspects lay dead. Waters was critically wounded by gunfire, and Arthur was critically wounded with major head trauma.

Much like Firestone station, the floor known as 9000 at MCJ was a busy, action-packed place to work, and as with any such assignment, there were instances of violence that far exceeded those in other places. This would include instances wherein force would be used by deputies to intervene in fights and vicious assaults. There were four of us deputies, though, who were thought to be involved in too many uses of force. The fact that we also were finding and removing extraordinary amounts of drugs, weapons, and other contraband, didn't matter. A decision was made to split us up. We were each transferred from 9000 and sent to separate floors within the vast jail. On June 1, 1985, we arrived early for our 2:00 p.m. shift and promptly went into the jail's barber shop, where the four of us who had been transferred shaved our heads as a symbol of unity. Sergeant Arthur, sympathetic to our plight, called us into his office after learning what we had done.

In the first-floor sergeant's office, George Arthur told us that each of us was the type of deputy who would excel at stations like Firestone, a place where he had proudly served himself. He said there were always cliques of deputies at the various stations and facilities, some of whom played softball, or golfed, or were part of a bowling league. There were, he said, those who were hard-charging cops who lived and breathed to do police work. Although they might enjoy the aforementioned activities, it was not what defined them. And these were the types of cops that always had each other's backs during times of trouble. He loved that we had demonstrated our unity through the haircuts, though, he admitted, the rebellious act had exacerbated some of his peers. George used a Polaroid camera and snapped four pictures of us posing in front of a giant sheriff's badge painted on the wall. He gave us each a copy, along with his well wishes for grand careers. That night, George was murdered. He was shot and killed as he left work by someone who had lain in wait in the back of his van.

The case of George Arthur's murder remained unsolved for more than a decade, and I would later become involved in the investigation as a homicide detective. But that's a story for another part of this book.

IN 1984, THE SUMMER OLYMPICS CAME TO LOS ANGELES. SINCE THE killing of eleven hostages and one police officer by terrorists at the 1972 games in Munich, security was the number one priority for all law enforcement: city, county, state, and federal. The sheriff's department was responsible, in part, for safely escorting athletes from their hotels to the various venues. SWAT team members and other personnel were involved on the ground level, and our aero bureau closely monitored all movement from above. The airships were stocked with additional personnel for more eyes to survey the landscape along the routes, and most of those positions were filled by deputies working overtime. I signed up and received a spot in one of the birds. Truthfully, they wouldn't have had to pay me. But they did, and we watched all of the activity along the routes where buses of athletes were escorted by heavily armed and expertly trained sheriff's deputies.

It wasn't the last time I'd be up in the bird. Later, as a detective at Century station, my partner, Pat Tapia, and I were flown from Lynwood to Lancaster while investigating a high profile case. It was right after the 1994 Northridge earthquake, during which freeways collapsed and travel between the north and south ends of Los Angeles County was nearly impossible. Later, as a homicide detective, I was transported to various locations by helicopter on several other occasions. I've always found it enjoyable and exciting to be up in the bird, but I've always been exceptionally fond of being back on the ground.

THE PROCESS FOR BEING TRANSFERRED FROM CUSTODY TO PATROL COULD BE a nerve-wracking one. First, you had to list six stations you hoped to be transferred to—it was your Wish List. The stations that seemed to take the most bodies were also the busiest stations in the county, as the turnover of personnel was higher than at some of the more civil places one might choose to work, say, for instance Marina del Rey or Malibu. For some reason, the waiting lists to go to those stations were always long ones. (I say that sarcastically.) Firestone was a smaller station than some of the other high-activity stations such as Lennox and Lynwood, and the turnover rate was lower for that reason, and also because people who went there loved it and stayed. So if one put in for all of the fast-paced stations, he/she would most likely go somewhere other than Firestone.

Johnny B. came up with a strategy that would ensure that we both went to Firestone. We would list Firestone as our first choice, and select for the other five choices stations that were nearly impossible to be transferred to, stations like Malibu. The trouble was, it hadn't been as simple as one would think. At first, there was a bit of guesswork. We listed Firestone along with Santa Clarita, Malibu, Marina del Rey, et cetera. But when the first list came out, a few of our "Never Go To" stations weren't so impossible to get to, and we moved up too quickly on some of those lists. So we crunched the numbers and adjusted our alternate choices as necessary, making sure that none ranked highly enough to get us assigned to any of those less active stations.

Our strategy worked, though it cost us each an extra three months or so working at the jail. But it was well worth the wait to see that in December of 1986, Johnny and I were being transferred from Custody Division, Men's Central Jail, to Patrol Division West, Firestone station.

---

1. Phencyclidine, also known as angel dust, is a mind-altering drug that induces hallucinations and produces a feeling of detachment from oneself and one's surroundings. It is known to cause super-human strength and immunity to pain with some users.

11

FIRESTONE STATION PATROL

DECEMBER 1986

T he unincorporated county area of Watts is policed by the Los Angeles County Sheriff's Department. From 1924 to 1994, deputies assigned to the area worked out of Firestone station, the first patrol station in the history of the department. I had the privilege to be assigned there from 1986 until they closed the doors in 1994.

Training at Firestone was different from training at most of the other twenty-seven sheriff's stations throughout the county. The environment was stressful as hazing was encouraged, if not mandated. Though by this time in our careers we had been deputies for several years, we were once again considered rookies, boots, pond scum lower than the station inmate trustees. Trainees were not allowed to wear mustaches. You would address every deputy at the station as sir, no matter if you had worked together at the jail six months prior and were friends. You spoke only when spoken to, and you avoided eye contact with all other personnel while traversing the station. You knocked and asked for permission to enter the sergeant's office or to approach the front desk personnel. You prepared the car before briefing so that you were ready to depart at a moment's notice—which happened often—having your equipment, your training officer's equipment, and the shotgun inspected, loaded, and in place ahead of time. You would clean out any debris left from the prior shift, and you would take the car to the station gas pumps and fill the tank, regardless of how full it might have been. If the car was dirty, you would get the trustees to quickly wash it. And after briefing, but prior to departing the station (going 10-8, or "in-service"), you would check with the desk to see if they had anything for you, meaning if they were holding any calls earmarked for a trainee. "Contempt" was a common answer to that question.

Prior to actually starting at a newly assigned patrol station, every deputy is sent to patrol school. It is a three-week advanced training class designed to refresh what you had forgotten since graduating from the academy so that when you began with your station training officer, he could tell you to forget all that shit they taught you in patrol school. My first assignment as a Firestone deputy would take place just at the end of that three-week course and prior to reporting to the station. It was the Rose Parade in Pasadena.

The Rose Parade, at that time, attracted several hundred thousand attendees, many of whom would arrive the night before to stake their claim to a section of sidewalk from where they would view the parade the following day. Of course, we're talking about New Year's Eve, and the paradegoers are no less enthusiastic about celebrating it than anyone else. To maintain order, the rules about alcohol and the like are strictly enforced. We were assigned the "pre-parade" shift, which began at about 3:00 p.m. New Year's Eve, and finished up at about 7:00 a.m. the next day. It had been a busy night with numerous arrests, a few minor scuffles with those whose common sense had been drowned by Budweiser, and at times, a lot of fun with the many party-minded citizens who were there to enjoy the experience. It had also been freezing cold, and during the last few hours of the shift, as spectators huddled in sleeping bags to stay warm, we were to stand our ground, enforcing the codes and laws. That involved little movement, and by the time we were finished, I could barely walk. I've taken approximately six baths in my entire life, but when I got home that morning, I needed a hot one to thaw out and to soothe my aches and pains. I soaked for an hour before crashing for the rest of the day.

As a trainee, I had been drafted to the Rose Parade assignment. Many deputies would volunteer to work it each year, just for the overtime. But most Firestone deputies didn't because Firestone was a fun place to be on New Year's Eve, arguably much more so than Pasadena.

Though I had vowed to never again work the Rose Parade, I eventually took an overtime assignment working the World Cup when it came to Pasadena, and that was an entirely different experience. It was warm, and as such, it was a pleasant experience with a great deal of wonderful scenery—shorts-clad ladies as far as the eye could see. I was one of several deputies assigned to clear and hold an intersection when President George H. Bush's motorcade sped past, escorting him to the event. Though I had no idea in which vehicle the President rode, it was a powerful moment, one that sent chills up my spine as the President of the United States passed within feet of where I stood at attention.

THE PATROL TRAINING PROGRAM AT FIRESTONE ALLOWED FOR EACH TRAINEE to have three training officers during six months of training: the first would have you for three months, the second two months, and then the third would have you for your final month, which was considered the evaluation period. My training officers were: Mike Griffin, Steve Wilkinson, and Tony Baudino, respectively.

Mike had been at Firestone for about four years by then, which was equivalent to working ten years at many other stations. He had arrested hundreds of felons, had been involved in dozens of pursuits and a couple of shootings, and he had earned a reputation among his peers and supervisors alike as a solid deputy with great report-writing skills, which he passed on to me. He was also thorough with his investigations, a skill for which he would be rewarded with a promotion to Detective shortly after he finished training me. The other thing Mike was known for was his keen sense of humor. The man was funny, which made the job even more enjoyable while I endured the grueling training regimen.

Like most training officers, any levity with a trainee was absent in the presence of other deputies. Around others, Mike would growl and grump and speak to me as if I were the biggest dummy to wear a badge and potentially an enemy of the state. It was a Firestone tradition, and I embraced it.

We had only been together for a couple of weeks the afternoon I handled my first murder as a patrol deputy. Adell Leon Mixon, Jr. was shot in the head and dumped out of a car at 95th Street east of Laurel Street. It was a whodunnit, two blocks from the Jordan Downs housing project in an industrial area where there were no witnesses. He appeared to have been seated in a car prior to being shot and dumped onto the street as if he were trash. It was a case that would likely never be solved as there were no witnesses and virtually no workable information. Of course, if it could be solved, our homicide bureau would be the ones to solve it, and you never wanted to count the bulldogs out. But since I never received a subpoena to testify in court, I'd have to assume that the identity of Mixon's killer has remained a mystery. Over the years, I would marvel at just how many people got away with murder in Los Angeles.

The second murder I would handle came not long after, the brutal stabbing and slashing of Virginia Gonzalez. It occurred during broad daylight in front of numerous witnesses in the 1300 block of East Florence Avenue.

The call had come out as a "245 (assault with a deadly weapon) just occurred, stabbing victim." Griff grabbed the mic and quickly acknowledged the call with an excitement I hadn't previously seen from him. He flipped the lights and sirens on and shouted over the wind that rushed through our windows, "I hope you're ready for another murder." I later would ask him about his prediction, and he explained that people were shot all the time and survived, but when they were stabbed, they very often died. He was right. We arrived to find Virginia lying on the sidewalk, her white medical clinic uniform painted a solid red. Her neck was sliced from one side to the other so deeply it appeared as if her head was barely attached to her body. Years later, when Nicole Brown Simpson was murdered, I knew exactly what that scene had looked like; I had stood in a very similar one. Witnesses told us that it was Virginia's estranged boyfriend who had slashed the woman to death in front of a crowd. If he couldn't have her, nobody would.

The process of handling a murder as a patrol deputy is much simpler than one might imagine, with far less paperwork than many other crime reports. At a murder, the handling deputies secure the scene, maintain a log of all who enter, and notify Homicide. The first hour or so flies by, and then you hold the scene while homicide detectives conduct their investigation. With Virginia's case, I remember getting the call within a half hour after our shift had started, yet we weren't cleared until several hours beyond our normal ending time that night. So rather than handling four or five report calls and writing another two or three arrest reports in the shift, I had one report to write and the entire shift to do so.

When I arrived at the station the next afternoon, Mike met me as I came through the back door next to the booking cage. He pointed out a Hispanic man who had just been booked and who appeared as the everyday illegal in the area: he was dressed as a cowboy, had gold and silver teeth when he smiled—yes, he smiled—and he had a slight beer belly and was not of impressive stature. "There's our killer," Griffin said. He had been arrested shortly before we arrived for work that next day with the intention of continuing our search for him. "That man right there is the one who carved up Virginia Gonzalez and left her dead on the sidewalk yesterday. Take a good long look at him."

I did, and he met my gaze and held it, unflinching.

Griff said, "You wouldn't think that dude's a killer if you met him on the street, would you?"

I shook my head.

"That's why this place is so dangerous," he said, "and you best not ever forget it."

The killer nodded as if to agree—though I doubted he understood much of what was said—and smiled.

Virginia Gonzalez is a name I'll never forget. Adell Leon Mixon, Jr., another. Over the years to come, there would be dozens of names of victims burned into my mind, and scores more I would forget. Some of the victims stayed with me for any number of reasons: the manner of death, the level of violence, a loved one who wailed. While I can recall only some of the names, all of the images remain stored in my mind, and they are easily evoked at the slightest prompting.

Before Griffin and I parted company, we handled half a dozen murders and assisted on many others. A gangster had been killed in the front yard of his girlfriend's house when he was "caught slipping"— getting caught in a rival gang's neighborhood. An elderly man was beaten to death with a claw hammer by a younger female tenant of his home, a crackhead. There had been a shaken and battered baby, and a couple of gangsters killed in drive-by shootings. Mike looked at me while we stood at one of the scenes and asked, "How are you feeling, Smith?"

"Fine, sir. Why do you ask?"

"You've seen a lot of death in a short period of time. Just wondered how you're hanging."

I assured him I was okay.

The first of the murders I handled had come before I could reliably find my way back to the station. After three months, I knew the area like my own neighborhood, and I didn't worry about the type of call that might come our way. I had already been exposed to more crime and violence and harrowing moments than some cops would experience during their entire careers.

Mike and I tended to make a lot of gun arrests together. It may have been some sixth sense he had, and if it was, it rubbed off on me because I would go on to continue the tradition of taking more guns off the street than the average deputy. And that's measuring by Firestone's standards; I can't imagine how my stats might have stacked up against deputies from other stations. One night, Mike and I made five gun arrests during our eight-hour shift, a month we would boast a total of 35 such arrests.

The first time Mike allowed me to drive, we were traveling north on Compton Avenue when Griffin yelled, "Gun!" and told me to turn around. He directed me to the street we had just passed, and when we came around the corner, there was a man with a gun chasing another without one. We jumped out and, with weapons pointed at the gunman, yelled all of that magical police shit: "Stop! Freeze! Drop the gun!" The suspect chose the latter, and then he started to run. We quickly captured him and recovered the gun, which of course had been stolen, the serial number obliterated, and had likely been used in countless crimes of violence.

Another afternoon we responded to a call of shots fired and rolled into the back lot of an auto repair shop where a drunken Hispanic man was shooting his gun in the air. We repeated the magical phrases to no avail. Griffin, fluently bilingual, repeated the commands in Spanish. The man stared at us through bloodshot eyes while waving a pistol around, the one he was shooting into the air when we arrived. I was squeezing the trigger on my revolver. Mike was yelling at the top of his lungs, the Spanish rolling off his tongue as beautifully as a mariachi melody, as we found ourselves in a deadly standoff. I felt the pressure on my trigger, and I knew I might have to shoot this man. Some of my friends were still in college, others living at home, working at Magic Mountain or Taco Bell, and here I was, ready to take a man's life. If the muzzle came in our direction—intentionally or not—I would have to pull the trigger on him. You didn't wait until they let one fly in your direction before shooting; that wasn't how you won a gunfight—it wasn't how you went home every night. I kept the front sight of my revolver glued to his chest—*the ten-ring* —and I watched the gun in his hand with an intensity I had never before felt, but would feel many times again. Finally, after what seemed an eternity, the drunken idiot reached over and set his gun down on the 55-gallon drum that stood next to him, which I later found out was exactly what Griff had been telling him in Spanish to do.

We grabbed him and placed him in cuffs. The man smiled and asked, "*¿Hay problema?*"

Mike would later tell me I used great restraint in not shooting. He said that he, too, had come close to pulling the trigger throughout the incident. Nobody wanted to kill anyone if we didn't absolutely have to, and we both had sensed throughout the intense moments that the man meant us no harm; he was merely a drunken fool with a gun. There would be many more such instances in my career, and thankfully, all of them ended well. Mostly.

It was said that all good training officers would try their trainees at some point to see what they were made of. My testing happened one afternoon when Griffin and I were tasked with resolving a family issue. The disturbing party was partially mentally ill but mostly under the influence of drugs and not at all willing to listen to reason. "Hook him up," Mike called out to me as he left me one-on-one with the formidable young man and walked to the driver's side of the car. Griff watched as if he knew there would be a fight, and there was. The suspect, a tall black male, lean and sinewy, resisted arrest, and the two of us locked horns. Soon thereafter we went to the ground in a tangle of violence. I heard the car door shut as I was trying desperately to get control of this man and get him handcuffed while he was trying to keep me from doing so. It is far more difficult to handcuff someone who chooses not to be than anyone who has never tried might imagine. Soon, my training officer barked from the confines of our radio car, "Hurry up, Smith; we don't have all day." Thoughts about Griffin at that point rolled around in my head while I rolled around on the ground with Dipshit, who was more committed to his cause than I had anticipated him to be. More from the car: "Let's go, Smith." *The prick.*

Finally, I was able to get the disturbing party's hands cuffed behind his back. I tossed him into the backseat harder than necessary, taking my frustration out on him rather than on the driver waiting for us. As I climbed into the front seat, trying to catch my breath, Griffin smiled. "Good job, partner." I wanted to hit him. But of course, I didn't, nor would I ever. That relationship changed dramatically once I was off training. The relationship between a rookie cop and his training officer is like a father and son relationship in many ways, and as such, at Firestone, we referred to our training officers as our dads. Mike is one of my best friends to this day, nearly forty years later.

That little tussle, as it turned out, paled in comparison to another incident I would be involved in a very short time later.

A MAN WITH A KNIFE IS AS DANGEROUS AS ONE WITH A GUN, GIVEN RELATIVE proximity. Though still assigned to Griffin, I was scheduled to ride with another deputy for two shifts while Mike attended some type of training. The deputy I was put with happened to be a particularly tough ghetto cop, a large Hispanic man who had grown up in the barrios of East Los Angeles. His name was Sal Velasquez.

Sal was respected by all and feared by many, especially trainees. He claimed to hate "white boys," and all week leading up to our two shifts together, he reminded me of it often while warning me that I wouldn't last one shift with him. He suggested that I resign or call in sick. As tempting as it was, I showed up prepared for two long nights partnered with a man who swore I wouldn't survive in his car. To say I was nervous is an understatement.

Directly out of briefing the first day, we received a call of a rape in progress at Will Rogers Park, located in the south end of our jurisdiction. We rolled hard and were met there by the informant, a frantic woman who pointed us toward the women's public restroom. She told us that a man had followed a woman and her child into the bathroom, and she knew for sure they weren't there at the park together. Our sergeant, Jerry Taylor, had arrived, and the three of us stealthily entered the restroom together.

Inside, we saw several feet beneath the last stall, two of which appeared to be those of a man and which were facing the opposite direction as those of a woman. Jerry quietly climbed onto the toilet of the adjacent stall and peeked down into the stall in question. He pointed his gun toward the occupants and said, "Drop the knife! Drop the knife!"

The suspect opened the stall door with the knife still in his hand. Each of us was yelling for him to drop it while pointing our firearms at him. After what seemed like a long time but was probably only an instant, the man complied. He dropped the knife as he emerged from the stall and tried to run through me and Sal, who stood between him and the door. It would have taken one hell of a man to "run through" the deputy I worked with that night; there was no way he was going to run through him, me, and the sergeant who accompanied us, an accomplished martial artist himself. But the suspect fought viciously nonetheless—as if his freedom relied on it—and in doing so, we were compelled to use substantial physical force to overcome his resistance. As a result, the suspect had to be booked at the Los Angeles County Medical Center jail ward.

Truthfully, he was lucky we didn't kill him. We would have been fully justified in shooting the suspect up until the moment he finally dropped his knife, but we didn't. Contrary to a popular but false narrative being pushed by some vocal anti-police activists and politicians, 99.9% of cops do everything they can do to avoid using deadly force. This incident serves as just one of many examples of that.

Once the suspect was subdued, we took him out and placed him in the back seat of our car. The woman emerged from the restroom, hysterical, her young son at her side. She told us that she had taken the boy into the restroom with her, and shortly after she entered a stall, the stranger confronted her at knifepoint and forced her to remove her top and drop her pants. He placed the woman's top over her child's head so that he wouldn't watch, or maybe so he didn't have to look at the boy while defiling his mother. She told us the suspect had just begun raping her when we arrived.

By the time we finished booking the suspect at the medical ward downtown, a significant part of our shift had been expended. The remainder of that night and the shift we worked together the next day were enjoyable, far different than what I had been promised and what I had expected. I had proven myself to Sal, who decided that for a white boy, I was okay.

Sal would later be accepted into our department's elite SWAT team, where he excelled as a top-tier team member and where he remained for the duration of his career. He still professes to hate white boys, though he usually does so with a smile on his face.

At the end of three months, I was transferred to the early morning shift (EMs) and partnered with a new training officer, Steve Wilkinson. Steve was a good cop who excelled in tactics and officer safety. Where Griff had been a fast-paced, hook-'em-and-book-'em kind of guy, Steve was more methodical in his approach. He was attentive, detailed, and exacting—a cop who insisted on perfection in the application of police work.

Working early mornings, typically 10:00 pm to 6:00 am, has some unique dynamics. The start of the shift would often be the busiest. Right out of the gate, we often found ourselves chasing the radio, rolling from one hot call to the next—especially on warm nights. In contrast, the PM shift (2:00 - 10:00 pm), which I had been assigned to when I was partnered with Griffin, would often be steady in the first few hours and then really heat up later when the sun went down. With the early morning shift, almost always, there came a point when everything would die down, and the streets would empty. During this time, we would catch up on our reports from the earlier, busier time of the night, or we would train. Wilkie would set up scenarios for us to go over—over and over again—until I had whatever tactic we were practicing down pat.

Back in those days, our reports were written in pencil. The "bookman," the deputy riding shotgun—which is where a trainee would most often be found—would write his reports while riding in the car. He would learn to look up regularly and to always glance up at a turn to identify a street at any change of direction. A good training officer would catch any misstep in this process and make a trainee pay the price for it. If a trainee didn't look up, and the training officer knew he didn't know where they were, he would slam on the brakes mid-block and yell at the trainee: "I've been shot! Where are we?" Generally, one time is all it would take to make the trainee never again forget to look up. A standard rule was that if you missed the street, ask. You'd never be in trouble for asking your training officer to confirm what street you were on. Fortunately, my training officers never caught me unprepared, but there was a trainee or two I nailed in later years when I sat in the big seat.

When it did slow down, we would sometimes patrol the streets and alleys with our cruiser blacked out like a darkened gunship drifting through the moonless, misty night. One such night, at about two hours after the bars had closed—the time of night when cops and robbers alike prowled the City of Angels while her citizens peacefully slept—Wilkie suddenly hit the brakes violently. "Goddamn, look at that!"

I looked up and followed his gaze toward a darkened market, searching for open doors or broken windows, any evidence of a crime. He shoved his big finger past my face and aimed it toward the barred windows of a storefront. "In the liquor store, dangling from the ceiling."

He then switched on his spotlight and directed its beam to a pair of legs hanging from the drop ceiling inside. At first, it seemed surreal, but then the legs began pumping, walking against the air.

There had been a series of rooftop entry burglaries in the area. Smart street cops like Wilkie were patient, and they stalked with a hunter's instinct. The reward would sometimes come in the way of great arrests, the type that many cops would never have made. Sometimes you had to slow down and hunt if you wanted the big payoff.

We coordinated assisting units to set up a containment and watched as the burglar's legs disappeared back into the ceiling. The building was tall. Not a two-story, but as is the case with many commercial buildings, the top was probably twenty-five feet from the ground.

One of the things cops enjoy most is getting firemen out of bed. It's part of the healthy rivalry between us. With the use of their ladders, several of us deputies went onto the roof while the firemen waited below in their yellow pants with suspenders over wrinkled t-shirts.

It didn't take much to coax the burglar out of the ceiling once he realized he had nowhere to go. We may have threatened to unleash a dog as well, though I don't recall if one was there. I proudly slapped my handcuffs on him once he was in our grasp. It was a great arrest, and the crook didn't know I was just a rookie riding my partner's coattails. We walked him to the ledge where the ladder waited. A couple of deputies went down ahead of us and waited on the ground near the sleepy firemen, along with our lieutenant, who had come out to enjoy the show.

I looked at Wilkie for direction, now at a loss as to how we would safely lower our suspect from the roof. He said, "You're going to have to take the hooks off and let him climb down the ladder."

I'm afraid of heights, so I wasn't looking forward to climbing down myself. For me, it's worse than climbing up. I don't even put the Christmas lights up at our house; my wife and daughter do that. The last thing I wanted was to stand at the edge of a tall roof with an unrestrained, squirrelly prisoner. I didn't like this idea at all.

I told the arrestee to turn away so I could remove his cuffs. As he did, I lowered my voice so that my watch commander below wouldn't hear me. "You try anything stupid, I'll throw your ass off this building."

My partner stood to one side, grinning. Wilkie seemed to grin a lot. He seemed to grin the most whenever I found myself in undesirable or challenging situations.

After I had reluctantly removed the hooks, I stood ready to give the suspect a quick shove off the roof if necessary; I wasn't going to fight with him on the edge and take a chance of plunging to my death. He climbed onto the ladder and stopped, looked me in the eye, and said—loudly enough to be heard below—"You want to throw me off the roof?"

Before I could respond, he launched himself backward off the ladder.

With arms and legs spread wide, he sailed through the night sky and smacked onto the sidewalk below, flat on his back.

I gasped. That was the last thing I had expected him to do.

I looked over at Wilkie, who, for a moment, appeared to be shocked as well. But then he began to laugh. The man grinned and laughed at very odd times. But laughing or not, at least there was a witness who stood next to me and saw that I didn't throw our suspect off the roof. Wilkie would no doubt testify that this jackass hurled himself to the ground without my help. But I knew it could have appeared to those below—our watch commander, for one, and the firemen who only wanted their ladder back so that they could go back to bed—that he had been shoved or otherwise assisted in his fall.

"Holy shit!" I exclaimed, staring down at the flying burglar who was now sprawled on the sidewalk below and not moving.

The lieutenant frowned as he looked up from the pile of broken burglar at me and the laughing policeman by my side.

This was it. I was done as a cop, maybe headed to prison for murder.

When I stepped off the bottom rung of the ladder, I was glad of three things: I was once again on solid ground, the burglar was not dead, and the watch commander, Jim Mulvihill, who might not have ever believed the story had he not witnessed it himself—told me he saw that the burglar had jumped of his own accord.

Unlike my training officer, I didn't find it too funny at the time. But over the years, I have to admit, I've had a few laughs at the memory.

As was the case with Griffin, Wilkie and I saw more than our share of death and destruction together. One morning, shortly before six a.m., we were assigned to handle the call of a shooting victim on Compton Avenue at Slauson. We arrived to find a young woman dead on the sidewalk, her clothing soaked with blood that spilled out of her body and formed a crimson slick around her.

There were numerous witnesses as people were hurrying to their jobs at this time of the day. The victim, in fact, was about twenty feet from reaching the bus stop where she would catch her ride to the garment district of Los Angeles, a place where she worked long days for little pay. Now she lay on the sidewalk, her hair still wet from a morning shower, her blank stare fixed on the purple morning sky. Her lunch, previously contained in a plastic shopping bag, was scattered on the sidewalk. She had never seen death coming.

The suspects were three black males, last seen driving in a gray or silver sedan north toward the Pueblo housing project.

The Pueblos were home to the Pueblo Bishop Bloods, a notoriously violent street gang. Wilki and I and other Firestone units spent the next several shifts and days scouring the projects and the surrounding area in search of these killers. The suspects were eventually identified and arrested. The shooter was fourteen. He and two older boys had stayed out all night robbing people, and they were on their way home when they spotted the young woman walking alone in the predawn hour. The two older gangsters handed a shotgun to the fourteen-year-old and told him it was time for him to "make his bones" (prove himself worthy of gang membership). He exited the car, walked up behind the unsuspecting woman, and, with the barrel of the shotgun at her back, pulled the trigger. The pellets blasted through the woman, ripping through her heart and lungs. She was dead before she hit the ground.

I remember wondering what kind of savage could do such a thing. Later, when I appeared at juvenile court for the fourteen-year-old, the homicide detective told me about the boy's confession. I reflected on my life as a young teen: after school, I would get together with friends for a game of baseball on the street, or we would ride our bikes around the neighborhood. Once, a friend stole a kid's bike when I happened to be with him and another boy. I was certain we would all go to jail over it, and it nearly sickened me. And if my dad had found out about it, I would have wished the cops had found me first. I was happy when the father of the boy whose bike had been stolen drove up in a car, yanked the bike from beneath the thief, threw it in his trunk, and drove off without a word. Still, I worried for weeks about it. So how could these kids go out robbing and murdering people with nary a concern? Perhaps the answer lies somewhere in the fact that the kid was out all night to begin with. I would learn that all too often, many kids in South Los Angeles (and similar communities) aren't raised; they just grow up. And far too often, they don't.

As for the young killer, the juvenile justice system would treat him as if he were an otherwise innocent little boy who had made a mistake, not the vicious, murderous little bastard that he was. Just as the media portrays young men killed by police as pillars of society, showing pictures of them from when they were seven and playing sports, rather than any of their previous six booking photos depicting gang tattoos on their faces, they would lie about the intent and soul of this vicious killer, and mercy would always be part of the equation. I have no doubt that this monster went on to kill again, maybe numerous times. Most likely, he is now dead, long before his time, and I sincerely hope that he is.

THE FINAL PARTNERSHIP I WOULD HAVE WHILE STILL ON TRAINING WOULD BE with Tony Baudino, another great street cop who had the respect of all of his peers and supervisors alike. The sixth month of training was considered the evaluation period. A trainee was expected, at this point, to be able to function with very little guidance. After I had been with Tony for only a week, he informed me he was signing me off training early. We had been assigned to work on a gang task force and were being sent to Lennox Station. Part of their jurisdiction, the Vermont District, was out of control with gang violence and narcotics activity. This was, after all, the height of the cocaine epidemic that saw record numbers of assaults and murders throughout South Los Angeles. We spent the next several weeks working out of Firestone Station but driving each afternoon to Lennox, where we were teamed with three other pairs of partners from various stations in the region and a sergeant from Lennox. We received no calls, as our only objective was to take gang members to jail. As Mike Griffin would say, "What a great company we work for!"

And take them to jail we did. Every night we made numerous arrests, recovering guns and drugs and making solid cases against hardcore gangsters who would be sent to prison because of our hard work. We had fights, foot pursuits, vehicle pursuits, and on several occasions, we found ourselves beginning to squeeze our triggers while demanding compliance from armed suspects.

One night, we were involved in a high-speed pursuit across the southland that ended in the Nickerson Gardens housing project south of Firestone's area. Sheriff's units from Lynwood and Firestone responded to assist us, as the occupants were suspected of committing an armed robbery.

Once inside the projects, two of the occupants bailed out of the car when it briefly slowed, and deputies began chasing bad guys in all directions. We stayed with the driver and the vehicle as he turned off the road and began driving across the lawns. He crashed his car and immediately began running between the buildings. I drove as far as I could before we had to stop and chase him on foot. When I hit the brakes, my car slid uncontrolled across the grass until it abruptly came to rest against a clothesline pole. We left the car and chased the suspect. When we rounded the corner of a building, deputies in the airship overhead called out to us over their loudspeaker that the suspect was behind us while focusing their spotlight on the side of the brick building adorned with a ribbon of shrubbery. The suspect was taken into custody without incident, relatively speaking. The others were all captured by our assisting units.

Later that night, while cleaning our fish, so to speak, one of the Lennox deputies who had been with us during the arrest of the driver complained that he had lost his watch during the scuffle. Tony said we should go back and get it. The deputy declined, stating nothing good could come from going back into the Nickersons after the commotion we had stirred. It was not uncommon to be shot at while driving a radio car through the projects, and that night the gangsters were riled up.

On our way back to Firestone station in the early morning hours, Tony said, "Head to the Nickersons." He always had a smile on his face, and this night was no exception. I smiled too, and off to the projects we went, blacked out and under the cover of darkness. The next day, Tony handed the Lennox deputy his watch, which we had recovered from deep in the projects, where, just a few hours before, a melee had occurred. The Lennox deputy smiled and said something along the lines of having a newfound respect for Firestone deputies.

SEVERAL MONTHS AFTER JOHNNY BABBITT AND I WERE OFF TRAINING, WE were partnered together on the day shift, and neither of us could have been any happier with the arrangement. Don't get me wrong, we would rather have been working a P.M. shift, but we were happy to be partners in a place we had longed to one day work together.

On a warm L.A. morning, the first day of October 1987, at 7:42 a.m., our world was literally rocked. The most powerful earthquake to hit Los Angeles since 1971 had struck, registering 5.9 on the Richter scale. It would be dubbed the Whittier Narrows earthquake and leave in its wake eight people dead and another two hundred injured. The quake was felt as far south as San Diego, and north to San Luis Obispo.

Johnny and I had stood eating breakfast on the hood of our radio car in the parking lot of Spartan Burgers. There were no better breakfast burritos in a ten-mile radius, and normally this would be a great way to start the day. Though not the most scenic destination in Los Angeles, Spartan Burgers did offer a great view of the Tiki Motel, located directly across the street. And while Spartan Burgers was famous for one thing only—great burritos—the Tiki Motel was famous for two: The Arnold Schwarzenegger movie *Terminator*, and heroin addicts. But the movie stars, directors, and cameramen had moved on, and all that remained were the hordes of hypes (heroin addicts) and jumbo cockroaches.[1]

Both having been raised in Southern California, Johnny and I were familiar with earthquakes. As the ground shook, our eyes met. Each of us immediately recognized the gravity of the situation. When the initial jolt subsided and only shaking still remained, Johnny's eyes grew large, and his gaze drifted beyond me with great interest. Remarkably, the violent jolt and its continued shaking had stirred addicts and roaches alike, and each began scurrying from the darkest crevices of the Tiki Motel to Johnny's delight. Men and women with pinpointed pupils and scars from intravenous drug use were suddenly amassed in public, the sight of which had captivated him. Johnny set his burrito on the hood of our car, the dining table to ghetto cops of that era, and started across the street. I reluctantly followed, asking, "What the hell are you doing, Johnny?"

He looked at me as if I were dense. "Look at all the hypes! I'm going 10-15."

"You're arresting hypes during an earthquake?"

Firestone deputies abhorred day shift. At most stations, you had to earn seniority to avoid working nights. At Firestone, the opposite was true. Deputies who chose to work Firestone did so for the action. We used to say that you weren't a real cop unless half of your shift fell during the hours of darkness. For day shift deputies, the end of their shifts found the gangsters, dope-dealers, and killers just waking up and starting to move about. Hypes, on the other hand, needed their breakfasts, meaning they needed to score heroin first thing in the morning to "get well." (When heroin addicts come down from a high, they become sick with symptoms resembling the flu. Only more heroin will make them feel better.) After they got well, and once the euphoric high dissipated, they'd be out stealing to support their habits. As such, most daytime burglaries are committed by these junkies. Arrest a hype, you've taken a burglar off the street. Dayshift deputies found hypes to be the best source of entertainment, and Johnny wasn't going to let this opportunity slip past him. To hell with the earthquake.

Just then a car abruptly turned into the lot and stopped next to us. It was a nurse who worked downtown, someone I had known socially. Frightened—nearly frantic—she asked what had happened, what we knew about the shaker, and whether or not we thought she'd be able to commute all the way to downtown. It was enough of a distraction to keep my partner from loading the back of our car with Under the Influence arrests—for the moment. As we finished assuring Sandy it was safe to continue her travels, our radio began crackling with emergency traffic. Fires, medical emergencies, and general panic had struck our jurisdiction. Johnny looked like a kicked dog as we silently retreated to our radio car, foregoing his cleanup of the famed Tiki Motel.

We spent the next several hours responding to one emergency call after another. Everyone did. On one such call, we found an apartment building engulfed in flames. There were people running out, but others running in. They were going back into a burning building, but for what? That was the question, one for which we hadn't the luxury to guess.

They may have been trying to save material possessions, but they also might have been going back for children or pets.

Johnny and I didn't hesitate. We ran into the smoke-filled building several times to push, pull, and prod these residents to safety. It turned out there were no children left behind, and most had only been trying to recover their belongings. It didn't make sense to me at the time, but then again, I hadn't come to this country with few belongings and lacking the means with which to replace them.

Eventually, the fire department arrived and took over their fire-fighting duties (yawn). We drove over their hoses and headed to the next emergency.

The field sergeant had heard of our heroic efforts, and he made a notation of it in the "black book," a book filled with both good and bad notations to be used in preparing annual evaluations. But that was it. No medals, fanfare, nor passes on our next screwup, which would surely come. Just a note in a book long since forgotten, stating we had risked our lives running into a burning building. The notation didn't even clarify that we had done so several times and brought residents to safety. Firestone could be funny that way. Some of the things that occurred with regularity there would have brought media attention elsewhere. We were probably better off without it.

Emergency Operations protocol was enacted and remained in effect for several days. Many of the residents refused to go back to their homes during the following weeks for fear of buildings collapsing. The parks became campgrounds, and once the rumbling stopped, the crime resumed. Now there were more vulnerable people and vacated buildings on which the predators could prey. Which meant we remained too busy for misdemeanor arrests in the following days as well. The hypes were left to their devices, free to inject opiates and steal from their neighbors in order to support their habits. And Johnny B. was none too happy about any of it.

———————

YOU SELDOM SAW VANITY PLATES (PERSONALIZED LICENSE PLATES) IN THE ghetto.

One night on Compton Avenue, I spotted a 1979 Buick Regal with license plates that read RGL BGLE. The fact that vanity plates were so seldom seen in that area was enough to draw my attention. But a plate that spelled *Regal Beagle*, that was something you'd only expect to see in the hood stripped and burned, stolen from the west side and abandoned in an alley. I knew, long before the dispatcher confirmed my suspicions, that the vehicle had been stolen. The driver was a wild-looking cuss who strained not to look over at us when we passed each other traveling in opposite directions. It was one of those things a cop learned to recognize: the way a person looked at you or sometimes the way he wouldn't. I whipped a U-turn, and the driver of the Regal Beagle turned off Compton Avenue onto Firestone Boulevard and headed west at a high rate of speed. The chase was on.

Allow me to digress and tell you about my partner that night. His name was Steve. Unless you were from the East Coast, then it was Kenny. Don't ask me, I'm a West Coast guy, and I never understood it. But Joey and Petey and other Firestone guys who hailed from the likes of Boston and Brooklyn and other places where people talk funny, well, they seemed to get it, and they each called him Kenny.

Steve/Kenny Evers had a couple of years on me at the station. I was still fairly green, having just finished patrol training a few months before. We were partnered up for a couple of nights, and on this night, I drove. Steve/Kenny was bookman.

It was a Friday evening, and the streets were congested. We maneuvered around the traffic as we continued west on Firestone Boulevard, following the suspect who drove on the wrong side of the road to go around cars. My partner broadcast our location and direction of travel, as we would soon be leaving the county area and heading into the City of Los Angeles. At a major intersection, the suspect tried to go around the cars ahead of him, but oncoming traffic was heavy, blocking his escape. So he jumped the curb and drove down the sidewalk of Manchester Boulevard (Firestone turns into Manchester at Central Avenue, where the county becomes the city), and I followed him, making my partner a little nervous. The truth was, I, too, had some reservations about driving at a high rate of speed down a sidewalk. Fortunately, there were no pedestrians on it at the moment, but I kept thinking that a shopkeeper might step from his business right into the middle of ours.

After a few hundred yards, we sailed off the sidewalk, the radio car bouncing as its tires grabbed the pavement, and we continued chasing the suspect along the boulevard, picking up speed as we continued through the heavy Friday night traffic. And then it happened.

The suspect went through a solid red light and struck a vehicle crossing through the intersection perpendicular to our direction of travel. Before his car came to a stop, the suspect leaped out of it and ran. I followed suit as my partner broadcast the information over the airwaves. I chased the suspect through an alley and onto the next street before he disappeared into the night. This was before the days of hand-held radios, and I had split from my partner in unfamiliar turf. That was not a good idea, and it was a situation we generally tried to avoid. With the suspect now out of my view, I jogged back to my radio car, where my partner awaited, rendering aid to the motorist who had been struck broadside by the stolen vehicle. Assisting units were arriving, one after the other, and my partner utilized the help to set up a containment of the area.

Like dogs and cats, once you stopped chasing a bad guy, they usually stopped running. Most of them weren't conditioned for prolonged physical activity. With the containment set, it was likely we would find the suspect, as long as he wasn't in his own neighborhood where he might be harbored by friendlies. Given the speed he had been traveling when he hit the other car, it didn't seem that he had planned to stop any time soon. I was fairly confident this was not his neighborhood.

The helicopter circled above, its light bathing the tops of houses and trees, its blades chopping through the heavy night air as we started a foot search for the suspect with the aid of a canine unit. The dog led the way, and within two or three houses from where I had last seen him, we found the car thief hiding beneath the foundation of a home. The dog pulled him out and chewed him up quite badly in the process.

The arrestee would require medical attention, so we would have to transport and book him at the Los Angeles County Medical Center jail ward. As we headed that direction, my partner suggested we grab something to drink. After all, we were all coming down from major adrenaline rushes and had worked up powerful thirsts. We stopped at a local food joint, and my partner said he'd buy while I kept an eye on our prisoner. Before stepping away, Steve/Kenny asked the bloody man in the back seat if he wanted something to drink. "Sure," the man said. And my partner returned with three large sodas. Before continuing the journey, we propped both the suspect and his soda in a manner that would allow him to sip from a straw while we traveled downtown. (This was before those evil straws were banned in California. Today, a prisoner would be left dying of thirst, thanks to the same liberals who would complain about the treatment of prisoners.) We arrived at LCMC, where our arrestee received medical treatment and was booked for grand theft auto and evading arrest, a felony since occupants of another vehicle had been injured.

Later in court, the defense attorney walked into a trap I hadn't created but saw coming. Armed with photographs of his client, who had survived a violent car crash and then was bitten by a police dog, and who then had moderate force applied against him as he resisted arrest, the attorney began asking for details of the timeline while his client was in our custody. I concealed my enthusiasm about his direction until he asked: "When you drove my client to the hospital, did you stop anywhere along the way?" He must have believed that his client was beaten on his way to the jail, or that some other terrible thing had occurred before we arrived at the hospital. I looked the jurors in their eyes, one by one, and told how we had stopped to buy the injured man a soda for the ride to jail because he was thirsty. I glanced to see the defendant smiling at the memory, while noting that many of the jurors had watched his response as well. There were few things so pleasing as to leave an attorney speechless, if only for a moment.

NEARLY ALL OF THE UNITS AT FIRESTONE WERE TWO-MAN CARS. WHEN YOU had a great partner, there seemed to be nothing better. Pat Martin, an academy mate and friend, became my partner in the overlap car, so called because half of the shift fell during the standard P.M. shift, the other half during the "Early Mornings" (E.M.) shift. If you went into law enforcement for the action—as Pat and I both had—you couldn't beat those hours as far as the potential for blood-pumping, adrenaline-rushing action. And the underbelly of South Los Angeles seldom disappointed.

But with action came complaints, internal investigations, and lawsuits. The vast majority of complaints resulted from using force during the course of arresting felons. Amazingly, many violent felons are willing to fight or at least resist when cops try taking them to jail. Fortunately, back in the eighties, and to a lesser degree the nineties, department administrators generally understood that police work is dangerous, violent, and not always a pretty sight to the casual observer. Jurors, however, were not so empathetic.

On a hot summer night in Firestone, Martin and I were dispatched to handle a gang fight in the south end of our jurisdiction. We arrived to see scores of misguided youths fighting in the street. Our attention was quickly drawn toward one youth, in particular, Mr. Gilbert Espinoza. He was running down the road, striking a presumed adversary about the head and body with a large piece of lumber. It was an assault with a deadly weapon, an act that would have justified the use of deadly force to stop. But we arrested Gilbert with only minimal force applied while he resisted being handcuffed.

Gilbert's lovely sister, Maria, also there and involved in the melee, inserted herself into our situation by attacking us, kicking and punching us while we handcuffed Gilbert and escorted him to our car. After placing Gilbert in the back seat of our unit, we arrested Maria for interfering with an arrest and committing battery on a peace officer. She, too, resisted, which caused us to use minimal force to subdue her. Basically, she was forced over the hood of the car and held there while we struggled to gain control of her (large) flailing arms so that we could handcuff her. Gilbert began yelling and screaming from the back seat, telling us to remove our hands from his sister. He was thrashing about, alternately pounding his head against the windows and then lying across the seat and kicking the glass.

By this time, our sergeant, Joe Guzman, had arrived. He ordered us to remove Gilbert from the vehicle in order to hobble restrain him before he broke out our windows. We did, and he kicked at us violently as we handled him. A hobble strap was wrapped around his ankles and, with his knees bent, attached to his handcuffs. This was an authorized procedure used only in extreme cases of non-compliant, violent arrestees. He was then placed back into the car where he would remain horizontal for the ride to jail. He had no injuries. His sister had no injuries. Joe Guzman stated we did a great job and that we had used commendable restraint during a volatile situation. The arrest was basically rather routine, though it all happened in the midst of a melee on the streets and could have ended very differently. As mentioned, we would have been completely justified in shooting Gilbert when we first observed him attacking a man with a deadly weapon. Later, I would wish we had.

This occurred in the summer of 1988. Shortly thereafter came the complaint, alleging that Martin and I, along with two other deputies, Geody Okamoto and Brian Dunn, had violated the civil rights of Gilbert and Maria Espinoza. A mealy-mouthed, sleaze-bag attorney named Tom Beck, who specialized in suing cops, was behind all of it. Our actions that night had withstood the scrutiny of my department's Internal Criminal Investigations unit and our Internal Affairs bureau. All of our actions were ruled to be within policy, and any force that had been used was deemed justified by the circumstances.

About one year after the incident, the four of us were notified of a federal lawsuit that had been filed against us. The suit alleged that we had violated the civil rights of the gangster siblings.

Lawsuits are part of being a cop. Any cop who works the streets for any length of time—at least in any jurisdiction where there is a high rate of crime—will be sued. In the academy, the instructors warned us that it would happen. Most lawsuits are settled, and the parties being sued are never bothered with being deposed, much less brought into hearings or court appearances. As such, many cops are incensed that the county (or city or state, depending on the cop's agency) would pay off someone when the cop believes their actions were appropriate and justified. I had felt the same way until later when I would be one of a few unlucky ones to spend six weeks as a defendant in federal court. It was by far the worst six weeks of my life.

Because the county chose to defend us (and itself) in this case, it took years for it to go to trial. After receiving trial date after trial date, and as the months and years passed by, it began to feel like it was never going to happen. Then we were given another date. Though I don't recall now what that date was, I can tell you two things with certainty: the "for sure" date was in the early months of 1991, sometime after March 3, and while I watched the news on March 3, there was no doubt in my mind that the trial would go on the given date. Because that was my luck, that I would face judgment in an excessive force beef right after the Rodney King incident and when the infamous video of his beating was being played 24/7 by every news station in the country. It seemed they even kept the video going in the background during the weather reports. We were screwed.

As it turned out, Rodney wasn't the only thing that screwed us. It was also my great luck that we drew a federal judge who hated cops. The (semi-) Honorable J. Spencer Letts had been appointed to the bench by President Ronald Reagan. Letts, who had been a corporate lawyer with no practical experience in trials, now wielded unassailable powers from the federal bench. Of course, such appointments are for life, so it mattered not how egregious his conduct might have been. Our attorney, provided to us by the county, knew Letts well, and he warned us that we had a tough road ahead. The attorney told us that the judge hated deputies because he had once been issued a traffic citation by one. Letts had mailed his ticket to Sheriff Sherman Block with a note instructing the sheriff to "fix it." Block sent it back with a note explaining that he doesn't "fix" tickets. Ever since, the attorney warned, the judge seemed to have it in for all deputies who appeared before him.

We found that to be understated in our case.

During the beginning days of the trial, Letts watched us four defendants carefully as we sat solemnly at the defense table dressed in suits and ties. He glared at us as if *we* were the threat in the room, while coddling the gangbanger plaintiffs and their witnesses.

When the plaintiffs' mother testified, she told several blatant lies. In cross-examination, our attorney tore her to pieces and, while still on the stand, she ultimately admitted that her testimony had been fabricated. Letts handed her a box of tissues and told her that it was okay that she had lied. Then he addressed the jury, telling them to make nothing of her lies, that she was only a mother protecting her children. In the same breath, he straightened in his throne as a vicious scowl crept onto his long face, and he pointed his finger at the four of us who sat quietly while being condemned. "But the four of you know better!" he exclaimed to the surprise of everyone in the courtroom. "I won't tolerate any misconduct from you officers!"

The next six weeks included the judge questioning the validity of our testimony that the defendant had struck the window of our radio car with his head while wearing cuffs. He said—in front of the jury—that it was preposterous to think one would do such a thing. (Had he never watched *Cops*?) In fact, he was so convinced it was a falsehood that he ordered a demonstration wherein his court clerk would wear handcuffs and be placed in the back of a car. Our attorney objected, of course, because it is not the place of the judge to try the case. But his objection was overruled. It seemed our attorney would object a dozen times a day during the six-week trial on numerous issues, only to be consistently overruled. On many of those occasions, the judge had threatened to hold him in contempt as he tried to argue his point.

One Monday morning, little Gilbert didn't show up for court. We four presumably guilty men were snickering and passing notes to one another, questioning where the little asshole might have been. Of course, we had each concluded that Gilbert was likely in jail. During the morning recess, we made a call, and sure as hell, Gilbert was in custody at East Los Angeles Sheriff's station. He had been arrested over the weekend when an undercover narcotics deputy, while conducting surveillance of a suspected drug dealer's home, observed Gilbert commit a drive-by shooting. Remarkably, Gilbert had his infant child in the van beside him. This was after the downtrodden plaintiff had testified with tears in his eyes that he had never been involved in any sort of gang activity.

Gilbert's gang activity was a matter of record, a record which was withheld from the jurors in our case. At just nineteen years old, he had been arrested more than a dozen times. Every arrest had an element of gang activity. After one such arrest, Gilbert had been additionally charged with carving his gang affiliation and moniker on the jail wall, an incident that had been video-recorded. Yet Letts, the brilliant, unassailable, black-robed pompous ass that he was (past tense, because he is now deceased), ruled that none of the past crimes and sins of the plaintiff would be admissible, because, of course, any such information would be highly prejudicial.

"But your honor," my attorney pleaded in vain as Letts once again refused to allow pertinent testimony into the trial, "this is impeachment material! He testified before your court that he has never—"

Letts growled over the bench and told our attorney to take his seat. He went on to say something about how this drive-by shooting incident was only alleged to have happened, and then he went as far as to suggest that the entire incident had been orchestrated by us defendants in order to influence the outcome of the trial.

It was at that moment I understood why Letts had a standing order that no officer would ever be armed in his courtroom.

When the trial concluded, we were held liable (found guilty), and punitive damages were additionally assessed by the jury. It came as no surprise, given the biased position of the kangaroo court to which we had fallen victim. It also hadn't helped that throughout the trial, footage of the Rodney King beating persisted. The images of that alone would have swayed many jurors against us.

Our case would later be overturned. When an appellate court hears a case, they can rule one way or the other with or without publishing an opinion on their ruling. The Ninth Circuit Court of Appeals—the most liberal appellate court in the country—overturned the verdicts against us, and they published an opinion detailing the dastardly deeds of the (semi-) Honorable Judge what's-his-ass for his blatant prejudice against us. No jury would have rendered a favorable verdict for us under the circumstances, the appellate court stated.[2]

After the case was overturned, the plaintiffs settled with the county —for far less than they had sought—in order to avoid having to go back to court. There were two really good reasons why they chose to do so, in my opinion: first, they would not likely find another judge who hated cops as did Letts; and secondly, our precious little Gilbert was now deemed to be "unavailable." Gilbert Espinoza had been killed in a walk-up, gang-related shooting, of all things.

On another evening in 1988, Pat Martin and I were cruising Central Avenue, our western border shared with LAPD's 77th and Southeast Divisions. The areas immediately outside of our jurisdiction were cherry patches—under-policed areas wherein criminals brazenly stood on street corners selling their dope, armed and ready for conflict with rivals. In county jurisdictions, gangsters seldom held guns on their persons while stationary at their homes or hangouts; they usually hid them nearby where they could access them quickly because their chances of being jammed by the cops exceeded their chances of being shot by rivals. Though poaching in the city was generally frowned upon by our brass, closely guarding our borders was perfectly acceptable.

On this particular night, my partner and I were traveling north on Central Avenue when we both noticed a compact car that had turned onto Central from 89th Street and proceeded south. It had come from the city, which also meant it had come directly from the area of 89th Street and Wadsworth Avenue, a crack cocaine sales mecca. We both looked over and saw the "Aw shit" looks on the faces of the two occupants.

Profiling is a very useful tool for law enforcement in spite of the fact that it has become a dirty word. It has nothing to do with a person's race; it is simply a matter of knowing what criminals look like and how they react to seeing the cops. To simplify this idea, just imagine a mother recognizing the troubled look on her ten-year-old boy's face when he runs into the house after breaking something or accidentally setting the cat afire. Well, these two cats had just broken something, and we were betting (correctly, it turned out) it was one or more laws classified as felonies. We flipped a U-turn and began following them while checking their license plate through dispatch. Both occupants watched closely in their mirrors as they proceeded south on Central, then onto Clovis Avenue, taking us farther into the city.

The vehicle traveled much slower than the speed limit, and the two occupants were busy inside, moving about and looking back at us. My partner and I were preparing for what might happen next. "They're going to run," I guessed, as they turned onto Colden Avenue and significantly slowed their pace. They were barely crawling when they arrived at the mouth of an alley where there were no streetlights (or they had been previously shot out, which was often the case), and the scant light provided by the moon was shaded by trees. They had picked the perfect place to stop in the cover of darkness, and it hadn't been an accident. Suddenly, the passenger's door flew open, and a man wearing a trench coat bailed out of the car.

I was the bookman that night, meaning the passenger deputy. Before my partner stopped the car, I had bailed out and was prepared for the foot race. I was never a fast runner, so I needed a good jump in order to have a chance at catching him. Just as I cleared the cover of my vehicle, I realized something wasn't right; the suspect had only moved a few feet from the car, just beyond the beams of our spotlights that shone upon the vehicle he had left, and now he was stopped, and he was facing me. In the darkness, I couldn't see his hands. He was a mass of black clothing against the black of night, nearly invisible. We were no more than a car's length apart, and I had my gun pointed at him, the shoot/don't shoot scenario playing in my head during the nanoseconds that felt like long moments as time seemed to nearly stop. I knew something was terribly wrong, that this man who had stopped to face me, and whose hands I couldn't see, was now more of a threat than I had anticipated—much more than I ever could have imagined, as it turned out. But I didn't know for certain (at that moment) that he was armed, and I didn't want to be in a bad shooting.

But the second that something metallic hit the ground, I knew he had dropped a gun. *Don't shoot* was the thought that went through my mind at that exact moment. My brain insisted that I hold my fire because the immediate threat was gone, dropped on the ground. Though I hadn't seen him with a gun, nor had I seen a gun fall to the ground—it was too dark to see either one—I knew in that fleeting moment that he not only had possessed a gun but that he no longer had it in his hands.

Imagine another scenario: I can't see his hands. It's dark. He leaps from the car, something hits the ground just as I shoot, and the man falls dead on a cell phone or a car stereo he had stolen. These are the split-second decisions cops all over the country have to make, decisions that are second-guessed in slow motion by people who have never faced grave danger themselves. Decisions that can cost you your life on the one hand or your career and freedom on the other.

In the next instant, the suspect was running through the alley. As I gave chase, my mind raced to process what had happened. I knew then that he had tried to kill me, and I knew that I would find a gun on the ground back near the car he had come out of, back where he had made the decision to take me on, but something had stopped it from happening. He had dropped his gun. Had he fumbled with it? Did it fall out of his coat as he tried to grab it? All I knew was he had stopped and faced me, and then he had dropped a gun, and now he was running and getting away. It didn't sit well with me, to say the least. He looked back while pulling away from me in the alley, and it occurred to me that he might have a second gun and was about to shoot at me. I fired my weapon at him but missed, and the would-be cop killer disappeared into the darkness.

A fully automatic Mac-11 .380 ACP machine pistol with a fully loaded 32-round magazine was recovered from the ground where the passenger had stood facing me. The Mac-11 is an open-bolt gun, which means the bolt is always open other than when it falls on an empty chamber. The bolt on this gun was found in the closed position on a live round with a dented primer. In other words, the suspect had pulled the trigger on me with a gun I never saw, and the good Lord had allowed it to misfire. The firing pin had struck the first of 32 rounds which, on that particular weapon, can be fired with one pull of the trigger and in less than two seconds.

The driver was arrested without incident, and a handgun was recovered from his person. Several thousand dollars in cash were recovered from inside the car, along with a cell phone the size of a tissue box. Back then, only the President and dope dealers had cell phones, and this wasn't Air Force One.

Though we set up a containment and searched for the outstanding suspect, he was never found. The driver would not reveal his partner's identity, and a killer remained free to try again. This is something that has haunted me since that night, and it will likely do so until the day I die. I truly regret not shooting him when we were just feet apart, facing one another. The instincts of good guys are different from those of killers. At the exact moment that I knew the suspect had pulled a gun on me, I also knew he had dropped it, and my instinct was to not shoot as the *immediate* threat had vanished in the same instant it had been revealed. As I chased him into the alley, it occurred to me that he was still a threat, that he might have another gun, that he was a fleeing felon, but by then, it was too late. My parting shot was really nothing more than a giant fuck you.

---

1. More about the Tiki motel and *The Terminator* can be found here: https://terminator.fandom.com/wiki/Tiki_Motel
2. A summary of the Appellate Court's ruling can be found here: https://law.justia.com/cases/federal/appellate-courts/F3/48/1227/607288/

12

MARINA DEL REY

DECEMBER 1988

O n the heels of the Gilbert Espinoza fiasco, the Clovis and Colden caper, and several other incidents unworthy of mention but that led to several complaints and internal investigations, I took advantage of an opportunity to go on loan to Marina del Rey Station.

The Marina was not known for action, at least not so far as police activity went. As such, the cops who trained there were not very experienced when their six-month training programs were completed, as compared to those deputies who trained at fast-paced stations. Because of that, sometimes trainees assigned to the marina would be sent to Firestone for a few months of their training period, but only if there were deputies at Firestone who would volunteer to swap with them. At the time, my very good friend and roommate, Bobby Harris, was assigned to Marina del Rey station, having been administratively transferred out of Firestone station as part of a disciplinary action. I needed a short break from South Los Angeles, and my hope was that if I volunteered for the body swap, Bobby and I could work the same shift and carpool to and from the station. More than anything though, a few months away from the fast-paced, high-crime district of Firestone would be a smart move at that time. A cooling-off period, so to speak.

I had been at the marina for one month on the night four men jumped me and beat me unconscious.

The reason it happened could be traced back to when I first reported for duty at the seaside station. In the first few hours of my first shift as a Marina deputy, I had made an arrest of a man illegally carrying a firearm in his vehicle. Later that day, I sat in the briefing room finishing my arrest report, the evidence on the table before me. Deputies and supervisors alike stopped to ogle the gun, and nearly each of them wanted to hear the story. They acted as if I had captured Sasquatch on the beach. But I hadn't; I had only made a good observation arrest of a felon with a gun. It was police work, not magic. As I finished up, a sergeant informed me that the captain wanted to see me in his office. I assumed he was going to welcome me to the station or maybe even thank me for volunteering to come to the Marina so that *his* trainee could take a spot at Firestone for a few months and learn something about police work. Foolishly, I thought maybe he, too, had heard of the arrest, and wanted to congratulate me for a job well done.

But that wasn't at all how the meeting went. His name was Sanchez and he spoke with a heavy Spanish accent. I walked in at his direction and approached his desk, prepared to shake his hand. He didn't stand. He glared, pointed to a chair across the tidy work area, and told me to sit. The tone had been set, but I had no idea why. Was he upset that I had arrested someone with a gun? I couldn't imagine what I might have done to cause him to be angry with me—I had just pulled up, so to speak.

"You are in a fishbowl, and I will be watching you."

That wasn't the first thing he said, but those words are seared into my memory and I will never forget, nor forgive him for them. He went on to tell me that he was aware that I had an Internal Affairs investigation going at the time, and that there was a lawsuit pending against me. This wasn't something that was rare among cops from fast stations, and I was perplexed at his demeanor and attitude about it. He continued to lecture me, saying that *his* station was no ghetto, and blah, blah, blah. I stopped him. "Sir, you are aware that I volunteered to come here, right?" I had to ask, because at that point, I had to assume that he thought I had been sent there as a manner of discipline, that I had been "rolled up" from Firestone as had my roommate. Sanchez said he did, in fact, understand that I had volunteered to come to the station, but he was none too happy about me being there.

Perplexed, but also pissed, I stood up from my seat. "Well, if you don't want me here, send me back. I'm doing you a favor by being here." I walked out and slammed his door behind me. The next thing I did was call the training/scheduling sergeant at Firestone and demand that I be brought back to Firestone immediately. So much for my demand. I was told that I would remain at the marina for five months, and there was no option of coming back early. Great. I pleaded my case but to no avail.

Following that bad news, I tracked down the scheduling sergeant at Marina station and asked that he put me on the early morning shift—graveyard. With no options left, I decided I would treat this assignment as a vacation, and I would not do any police work while I was there. I would never again stop someone whom I suspected to be involved in criminal activity, and I would drive with blinders on and only answer my calls. What else could I do, being in a fishbowl and all. Besides, the graveyard shift would assure me I wouldn't have to look at Sanchez's fat face again during what I knew would be a long five months.

On the first early morning shift, a sergeant welcomed me and, during a brief conversation, asked that I impart some of my experience to others on the shift. He stated that one female deputy, in particular, who had just finished her six-month training program, had potential but very little exposure. He asked that I take her under my wing. I told the sergeant about my meeting with the captain and my resulting disposition. He was disappointed about both, shaking his head as I repeated the captain's words to me. The sergeant seemed like a good guy, so I told him I would certainly help when and where it was appropriate to do so, but that I would not stick my neck out one inch there. The captain had made it clear that he was out to crucify me, and I refused to place myself in harm's way with him being the judge and executioner of any complaints that might arise or incidents in which I might be involved.

Not a week went by before I was terribly bored. I hated not being a cop; it went against my every grain. The female deputy was, in fact, good at her job, though inexperienced. I would back her up on calls and traffic stops when possible and, when appropriate, share with her my thoughts or suggestions about how she might better handle a particular scenario.

One night she received a call of a suspicious person near a restaurant that overlooked the marina. We arrived in tandem and were able to spot the man as he had been described. As the female deputy spoke with this suspicious person, I could see that he was nervous. I could also tell that he was lying in his responses to some of her questions. She seemed to be unsure of what to do, so I abandoned my work stoppage protest, and took over. My instinct told me that the situation was not a good one, and I sensed an underlying danger to the contact. So I told the man to place his hands on the railing near where we stood, and I searched him, recovering a small handgun that had been concealed in his coat pocket. It was fully loaded. The grips had been wrapped with tape. I told my companion to be sure to handle the gun carefully as to not destroy fingerprints, and to make sure to request not only a latent print deputy to examine it, but also an ATF (Bureau of Alcohol, Tobacco, and Firearms) trace of the gun's history. I knew there was something very sinister about this man, and that contact. I even considered that perhaps I was being set up for something by the captain, as sad as that might be.

Months later, as I was recovering from a concussion and damaged equilibrium, I received a call from an FBI agent who needed more information about the arrest. He explained that the man we (she) arrested was a hitman for one of the Italian mafia families on the east coast, and he had been sent to Marina del Rey to fulfill a contract. I told the agent that I didn't have any of the details available to me, as I was home, recovering from an injury. However, everything should have been in the report that the other deputy had written. It wasn't, he said. So I told him everything I could remember and hoped it would be enough.

IT WAS ABOUT MIDNIGHT, NEW YEAR'S DAY, 1989, WHEN I WAS DRIVING past the Red Onion in the marina while on patrol with my blinders on, the ones that weren't nearly as reliable as my commitment to duty seemed to be, even at the risk of the captain's wrath. I passed another sheriff's patrol car traveling in the opposite direction and I waved to the driver. He was working my "sister" car that night, and we would be the only two radio cars in the marina. Two one-man cars, and the city was alive with the excitement of a new year. It was the end of a weekend, a Sunday night, but one on which the following Monday was insignificant to most as it would be the recognized holiday. As a result, people were partying like it was Saturday night on steroids.

The other deputy pulled into the Red Onion, and as he did, he contacted me by radio and asked if I would assist him in a bar check. The station policy forbid deputies from doing bar checks by themselves, especially at the Red Onion. It was one place in the marina where a deputy sheriff could count on finding trouble. Reluctantly, I agreed. I didn't like the idea of it, as it went against my self-initiated work slowdown, my commitment to driving with the blinders on. And I knew that no good could come from being there. But I also figured his primary reason for wanting to go there was to check out the ladies, and I didn't blame him for that, so I pulled into the lot and parked behind him.

We descended the spiral stairs together to where the nightclub sat below the restaurant, packed beyond capacity. People standing side by side yelled at one another to be heard over the blaring music. Scores of young people danced—on the dance floor or at their tables or on their barstools—hundreds of bodies moving to the thumping beat in the thick and humid air, a medley of perfumes and sweat hanging in the dim light. We snaked through the crowd, each of us noticing the scantily clad, beautiful women as they moved to the rhythm, undeterred by incidental contact with others around them. One of them bumped into me, and she smiled. We were close, looking each other in the eyes, when my attention was drawn to a commotion beyond the crowded dance floor.

A small area at the edge of the dance floor had cleared and two men stood in the center. One was punching the other in the face, repeatedly. The one being struck was mostly trying to cover up, making it clear to me which of the two was the aggressor. I instinctively went to him. As I approached, I flashed my light toward his face, cluing him in that I wasn't just another patron looking to enter the fray. He glanced at me and then continued hitting the other man, undeterred.

Sanchez was in my head: "You're in a fishbowl, and I'm watching you."

The department—at that time—trained us to use our flashlights as weapons when needed. They were more convenient than batons (which few of us at Firestone ever carried) and, if used properly, they could be more effective. This was long before cops carried tasers and pepper spray, and our tools were limited, if not primitive.

In the brief moments that passed as I went to intervene, I foolishly made the decision to only use my bare hands. I didn't know it at the time, but later I would find out that the man being beaten was the bouncer, and the one doing the damage was a trained fighter. I shoved my flashlight into my rear pocket just before reaching the man, and I grabbed him by his shoulder. My intention was to break up the fight without having to use force (beating the man with my flashlight) and chance starting a riot. *You're in a fishbowl.* He turned and drilled me squarely in the jaw with his fist.

I'd been in a few scraps. In fact, I'd been beaten, kicked, and bitten during some of the various altercations I had experienced through the years. But I had never before been punched so hard that it felt as if I'd been hit with a sledgehammer. I weakened, things went fuzzy, and before I could recover, he was swinging and hitting me repeatedly. I knew I was in trouble, but I had one thought in mind: my partner would be jumping in at any moment, so just hang on.

The trouble was, I never saw that "partner" again until later that night when he walked into the emergency room without so much as a scratch on him.

Certain that help was on its way, I held on. I had my arms wrapped around the fighter with my head tucked into his body, trying to avoid further damage until help would arrive. The first punch made it clear this wasn't the type of man I wanted to stand toe-to-toe with. Soon, I felt others around me, pushing and pulling at me, and then I was part of a group that was moved across the dance floor. I held tight. He wasn't going anywhere but to jail, no matter what.

We—me and this group of people who were mauling me while I was holding onto the one who had first hit me—continued traveling across the room until we crashed into a cigarette machine or a jukebox, some large item with neon lights glowing in the darkened room. I fell to my knees but immediately came back up, regaining my grip of the man I was intent on taking to jail. As I started to doubt that help was coming after all, and while trying to come up with another plan that didn't include boxing with the man with dangerous fists, whom I held onto with all of my might, I was struck in the back of my head by a hard object. My first thought was that I had been hit by a beer bottle. A second blow hit my head with even greater force. And then a third. I was in trouble, losing consciousness, and I knew I had to act. No help had come; I was on my own, and now I was receiving serious trauma to the head while being pushed and pulled and punched and kicked. I had but one option, and that was to use deadly force against my assailant. If I were to survive this attack, I had to shoot the man who was behind me, beating me with a hard object, trying to kill me.

I pushed away from the first man I had remained latched onto, and as I turned to my left, I drew my gun from its holster. The blows to my head continued, moving along the left side as I turned, rapid thumps from something large and heavy, bell-ringing cracks against my skull. I brought my gun up to take aim, but I couldn't see anything other than a blur of colorful clothing, flashing lights, bodies in motion, figures moving away. *Don't shoot.* There it was again. Through training we were constantly confronted with shoot/don't shoot scenarios, and the manner in which one handles these situations was closely evaluated. You had to be able to make split-second life and death decisions, unlike those who would later judge your actions. Again, I found myself in a situation that warranted shooting the SOB who was trying to kill me, but this time there were hundreds of people crowded in the bar and I couldn't identify the target among them. It was a no brainer; I couldn't take the shot.

I awoke with a man stooped over me, saying, "Stay still... don't move... you're hurt bad." The music had stopped, and the crowd was mostly gone. I then recognized the man who was with me as one of the bartenders. I had met him previously and I remembered seeing him behind the bar when we had walked in a short time earlier.

"Where's my gun?" I asked. I remembered having pulled it and that my last conscious thought had been the decision not to shoot. But I didn't know what happened after that.

"I put it beneath you," he said.

The bartender had been smart enough to secure my gun once I hit the ground, and wiser yet to not be standing over a downed cop with a gun in his hand when help arrived. I later learned through witness statements that when I had pulled my gun, I was teetering and ready to fall, nearly unconscious at that time. The crowd parted as if a shark were in the water, including the four men who had assaulted me. It explained why I couldn't see my target when I spun around to face the person who had been hitting me in the head with the heavy object; he had moved away quickly and had become part of the blurry crowd. I also learned that the suspect had removed the flashlight from my back pocket while I was holding onto the first man, and that is what he had used to hit me on the head. And the son-of-a-bitch kept it when he fled, a hundred-dollar flashlight never to be seen again.

"Help me up," I pleaded.

"You should wait," the bartender replied. "Help is on the way. Stay down."

"Help me out of here," I insisted. I wasn't going to lay there like a victim, though that is exactly what I was.

The bartender helped me up and I retrieved my gun from beneath me. As I stood, I was still unsteady, but the bartender helped me across the now-empty room, up the stairs, and outside. I still had no idea where my partner was.

A sergeant had arrived and was outside trying to get information from departing patrons when I emerged from the building. He came to me and began asking questions. I didn't have answers. Someone then came up to us and said the suspects had fled in a white Bronco and some type of sedan, two vehicles. There was a total of four men, the person said.

The radio crackled with activity, units from Lennox, Firestone, Lynwood, and even West Hollywood notifying dispatch that they were responding to the "deputy down" in the marina. I knew what they would feel; I had been on their end too. I didn't want anyone killing themselves to get to me. Rolling hard to help a fellow deputy is instinctive, nearly unstoppable, but also one of the most dangerous things we do as cops. My situation was already over, and I would survive. I grabbed the radio in the sergeant's car that sat parked at the front door, and I put out a broadcast that no additional units were needed at the location, but that we needed responding units to search for the suspect vehicles. I provided the vehicle descriptions and their directions of travel. As I finished, the sergeant hovering over me, said, "We need to get you to the hospital."

"I'm alright," I argued.

At about the same time, two paramedics appeared at my side and began trying to assess my medical condition. I told them, too, that I was fine, that I had a job to do at that moment and I would go get checked out when finished. The sergeant told me again that we needed to go to the hospital. I began arguing. Another sergeant appeared, one whom I had never seen before. He was black. He had a commanding presence, the confidence of a seasoned street cop. He was no marina cop. His eyes bore through me. He said, "Get in the car. We've got it from here." I didn't argue. He wasn't asking, and he wasn't the type to take no for an answer.

I said, "Okay, Sarge."

The black sergeant, who I later learned had responded from Lennox station, put me in my sergeant's car, and he drove me to the hospital. I sat in silence during the short drive to the local medical center, a place that deputies there referred to as the Marina Dog and Cat Hospital. It certainly wasn't the best of the best, but it had an emergency room. The hospital staff had me take a seat in the waiting room and the receptionist began asking about insurance. I couldn't believe it. The Marina sergeant tried to nicely explain how these things worked, that the county would cover everything, and he'd take care of all the paperwork. I sat dripping blood on the ground, thinking, Jesus Christ, is there anyone in this godforsaken marina who knows what in hell they're doing? Finally, I said, "Are they really going to leave me sitting here?" The sergeant tried to hush me. *Don't make a scene.*

The nurse's problem had been where to put me. The bouncer that had first been in the fight with the main suspect had arrived at the hospital before me and was occupying the one emergency room. (I don't recall for sure that they only had one room, but if not, the bouncer had been placed in the last available room.) When I found that out, I told the nurse to put me in the same room with the bouncer, because I was not staying in the lobby another minute. She did. When I walked in, the bouncer looked up at me and said, "Damn, you look worse than me." I told him that that was because I had taken his beating for him. He smiled and thanked me, and then we began recounting what had happened. The bouncer told me that he used to box recreationally, and that he had never been hit so hard in his life. Nor had I, I assured him.

The bouncer said he didn't know the men by name, but he had seen them before. The previous weekend he had tossed them out of the night-club for causing trouble. They had obviously come back looking for more. This night, the man we both had fought had captured the bouncer's attention when he began throwing shot glasses against the wall. It was as if he was begging the bouncer to take action. When the bouncer approached the group, the main instigator immediately hit him.

The deputy who had asked me to accompany him into the nightclub showed up at the E.R., though he showed no signs of trauma. The bloody bouncer and I both looked at him with contempt. I asked, "Where the hell were you?" He explained that he was trying to get to me in order to help but that he had been held back by the crowd. I said, "If you saw what was happening to me, you should have shot your way through the crowd to help me." He claimed to have strained his back in the ordeal, and he ended up taking some time off work to heal.

I was examined and sent home, even though I had made it clear to the staff that I had been knocked unconscious. Usually they want to keep you overnight and monitor you when that has happened. My roommate, Bobby Harris, picked me up from the hospital and drove me home. I was dizzy and nauseated. At home, I went to bed. But the room spun, and I got up, feeling sick to my stomach. As I went to the restroom, I lost consciousness again and fell to the floor. Bobby called the station and told them what had happened and told them he was taking me to "a *real* hospital."

Over the next few days a series of tests would show that I had suffered a severe concussion and equilibrium damage. For several weeks I was unable to drive due to dizziness. My roommate, Bobby, and other friends, Dennis Macauley and Scott Anderson, to name a couple, would help me get to my various appointments. About a month later Sanchez finally called to check on me. Any other captain would have called the next day, if they didn't drive out to your home for a personal visit, given the severity of my injuries. I took the call but was short with him, nearly biting the end of my tongue off holding back the things I wanted to say. In four months, I could return to Firestone, and my goal was to be well enough to return to duty by then, and not a moment earlier. I would not return to Marina del Rey even if I had to resign from the department.

The men were eventually identified in spite of the shabby job done by the so-called investigators at Marina del Rey station who were assigned the case. The only reason they were caught was that a young lady went to the station one day and told deputies that she had overheard her boyfriend's buddy bragging about beating a deputy. She provided the names of the three she knew—her boyfriend, his brother, and one other young man—and arrests were made. The three were rich white boys whose fathers provided high-dollar attorneys before the ink had dried on their booking slips. Almost immediately thereafter, bail was posted for each one. Not one of them ever spent a single day in jail for what they had done to me. They pleaded to lesser charges, against my protests to the district attorney's office, and essentially got off scot free. This was yet another sign of amateur police work. The detectives should never have taken a case like that to the local branch; rather, they should have gone downtown and filed the case with the Crimes Against Peace Officers Section (CAPOS) of the district attorney's office. The results would have been far different.

13

RETURN TO FIRESTONE

MAY 1989

I went back to work at Firestone station the day I would have returned from my loan to the Marina. Truthfully, I probably could have returned to duty a few weeks sooner, but I wasn't going back to that place to deal with that captain. So when my doctor and I discussed my return to duty, I gave him the very date that I was scheduled to return to Firestone, and that was the date he determined that I would be fully recovered and ready to serve.

It was great being back at Firestone, back to working with some of the finest law enforcement officers in the world.

Firestone was a place set apart from every other station in the county, much to the displeasure of some who had never been a part of it. The deputies were a tight-knit group and the overall staffing were family. Supervisors were often there by choice, having worked there as deputies, and knowing what a special place it was. We were all self-motivated, hard-charging deputies, who, in the face of mortal danger, would race to the action. I often said that if I had had *any* Firestone deputy with me that night in the marina—even if he was the worst one to ever call himself a "Stoney boy"—the outcome would have been far different.

At Firestone, and truthfully, most sheriff's stations—certainly the fast-paced ones—any assistance request from one of the units in the field would empty the station. Deputies who were off duty, having just ended their shifts or not yet begun, and detectives from the back room, and even supervisors, would all bail out of the station and jump into any available vehicle to rush to the scene of the request. Some were in uniform, some were not. Some were half in, half out of their uniforms, having run out of the locker room, and others would emerge from the gym with a gun stuffed in their sweats. Even our station mechanic, George Ramos, was known to jump in a car and roll to an assistance request now and then. When the desk announced over the public address system within the station that a deputy needed assistance, professional staff and all non-sworn personnel—and even the jail trustees—would stay clear of doorways and the parking lot exit, knowing that what would come next was not unlike the running of bulls. In some ways, that's exactly what it was.

In the eight years I worked at Firestone, two deputies were shot, one of whom died. Most of us had been shot at more than once, and many of us would be involved in shootings at one time or another. You hear tales of cops who never pulled their guns from their holsters. That wasn't Firestone. It wasn't South Los Angeles. We pulled our guns multiple times each shift and often had them pointed at dangerous adversaries. With the numbers of gang members, drug dealers, and hosts of other violent criminals that we would encounter on a regular basis, violence was always anticipated, and it often came. It was that expectancy that gave us an edge and kept us alive. Mostly.

ONE THANKSGIVING, JOHNNY BABBITT CAME UP WITH THE IDEA OF DOING A potluck for those of us who would be working the P.M. shift. He suggested we wear long-sleeve Class-A uniforms and ties for the occasion, dress usually reserved for interviews, ceremonies, and funerals. We would come in from the field and partake in the festivities, if all went well. Johnny was assigned to work inside that particular day, and most of us working the field were assigned to work one-man cars. That was a very unusual occurrence at Firestone, as generally all cars were two-man cars, but it was something that had been done to allow more deputies to

NOTHING LEFT TO PROVE

take the holiday off. (Yes, I know how un-P.C. the term "one- or two-man cars" is in today's world. But that's just the way it was, what they were called then and what I'll call them till my dying day. No disrespect of the fairer sex intended.)

I grumbled at the idea of the formal dinner. Most of my long-sleeve Class-A uniforms were well-worn, and I only maintained one for special occasions that didn't show the wear and tear of a ghetto cop's standard attire. I didn't want to wear it on patrol, but I did want to be a team player. After all, Johnny could be persuasive, usually by unleashing his sharp tongue and quick wit on any adversary, even a good friend.

Briefing ended at 1400 hours. As I headed out to my patrol car with my equipment bag and a shotgun in hand, Johnny said, "Okay, I'll see you in a while for dinner. Be safe out there." He sounded like an old salty sergeant from *Hill Street Blues*. I made some smartass comment about him working as a desk jockey, and headed for my radio car.

Minutes later I was assigned to handle a family disturbance call in the 1500 block of East 87th Street. This location is south of Firestone Boulevard and east of Compton Avenue. I had just pulled out of the station parking lot, which is only a few blocks from that location, when further detail on the call came in: the disturbing party, an uninvited, unwanted male family member, who was under the influence of PCP (Phencyclidine), was tearing up the home.

We referred to people high on PCP as "dusters." PCP, an animal tranquilizer, has an effect on humans that is anything but tranquil. In fact, its use often results in schizophrenic behaviors and superhuman strength. That, coupled with the attendant immunity to pain, can make it very dangerous to attempt to arrest someone who is under the influence of it. Tasers rarely worked. Getting onto the back of a duster in order to apply a chokehold could be like wrestling a grizzly. The "swarm technique" was about the best option, though truthfully there were never any easy answers, at least not back in the eighties.

Coordinating the call, I told my assisting units we would meet at Compton Avenue and 87th Street and roll in together. However, when I arrived at that location, I saw a CHP car abandoned in the middle of the street with both doors open. I knew its approximate location was near the call for service residence, and I guessed that the chippies had jumped our call.

The California Highway Patrol enforces traffic in unincorporated districts of Los Angeles County. Firestone chippies were a breed unto themselves, in that they too were addicted to the action and fast pace of working in a high-crime neighborhood. As such, they would monitor our radio frequencies, and it wasn't uncommon to have them show up at our hot calls.

I announced on the radio, "Chippies are 97 (at the scene), I'm rolling in. All responding units roll directly to the location."

As I approached, I could hear a commotion inside the residence. I ran in through the open front door to find two CHP officers fighting with a man, flailing about through the kitchen and dining room, knocking over furniture. Four women stood screaming and yelling for the officers to stop what they were doing. I announced my presence and jumped in to help. As I did, the women watching joined in to help the suspect. They were pulling on our uniforms and grabbing at our arms and legs. We fended them off and continued fighting to control and handcuff the suspect. It seemed like an hour had passed (though it was only moments) when additional deputies arrived to assist us. By then, the women were punching and kicking us as we fought with the suspect. The assisting deputies tried to restrain the women, which resulted in separate fights breaking out everywhere.

When things calmed down there were four women and a "duster" under arrest. The house was in shambles with overturned and broken furniture throughout.

One of my assisting units transported the suspect, who had to be restrained with handcuffs and leg hobbles, while I crammed all four women into the back seat of my car, out of spite. To say they were angry is an understatement. For the short ride to the station, the "ladies" yelled and cursed and said horrible things about my mother—of all people. I yelled, "Happy Thanksgiving," with some expletives, pissed at them and, at this point, none too happy with my good buddy, Johnny B.

When I arrived at the station, several deputies and a sergeant were in the parking lot to greet me. They wanted to see the end result of what had become quite the Thanksgiving Day event. As I unloaded the women from the back seat of my car, Johnny stood with his trademark grin. My uniform was torn and tattered and bloodstained. My tie was nowhere to be found. I marched the women past him and grumbled, "Happy Thanksgiving, pal."

Later we laughed about the incident while enjoying a nice meal in the briefing room. Being a bachelor at the time, my only contribution had been a couple of cans of vegetables. Normally, I might have felt sheepish about eating at least my share of the main course, having contributed so little. But I had paid my dues that day for sure, so I dug in, unapologetically. It turned out to be a pretty good Thanksgiving Day after all, and certainly one to never forget.

I WORKED ALMOST ALL OF THE HOLIDAYS. BEING SINGLE DURING MY PATROL days, I would volunteer to work so that those with families could have the time off. Like many cops, I loved my job and usually looked forward to each shift. The station was home, its occupants my family. At times, I couldn't believe they paid us to do the job. (Other times, it was clear they didn't pay us enough.)

As is generally the case with police work, the holidays were mostly unpredictable. Crime rates soared. Robberies and burglaries picked up around Christmas, and reports of domestic violence increased as well. Drug use remained steady, and alcohol flowed freely, fueling the violence among friends and strangers alike. There would be siblings who stabbed one another, parents who beat their children, and neighbors who fought with fists and sticks and sometimes guns. Gangsters weren't opposed to committing a Christmas drive-by shooting just to keep it real in the hood. Suicide cases were expected, and you could always count on at least one homicide scene with a Christmas tree or an inflatable Santa Claus in the background. There was nothing like yellow police tape to accent the holiday décor.

But even Firestone station had the occasional quiet and peaceful holiday, and I fondly recall one such Christmas Eve. I happened to be partnered with a station favorite, Henry Romero, a great deputy sheriff who would rise through the ranks and retire as a commander.

The cold, damp evening air drifted through our open windows as we slowly patrolled the Walnut Park district, where street vendors offered tacos, tamales, and grilled corn on the cob. Others peddled flowers for the girlfriends and knockoff jewelry for the wives. There were gifts for the kids: *piñatas*, puppets and dolls, *baleros*, and noise makers for all occasions. Many of these toys were handcrafted of wood or leather and imported (smuggled) from Mexico; others were made in China because even nostalgia wasn't sacred. Everyone—including us—was in a festive mood that night, and since the violence and mayhem hadn't materialized, Henry said he had a few stops he'd like to make.

Sure, why not?

A "few stops" consumed at least half of our shift as we visited homes throughout the area. I wondered if the people were part of his family, extended or otherwise. All were warm and friendly, inviting us in and insisting we partake of their holiday meals. There were hugs and kisses, handshakes and sincere well-wishes, and promises to stay in touch. Some filled our hands with gifts, trays of food, and beverages we would save for later. By the end of our shift, our bellies and hearts were equally full.

As it turned out, the wonderful people we visited with that night weren't family, only friends, people Henry had met and developed relationships with over the many years he worked those streets. I was still pretty wet behind the ears at the time, and it made an impression, one that stayed with me for the remainder of my career. Henry was doing community-oriented policing before it was cool—or should I say, mandated.

It wasn't long after that night when the lightbulb came on, and I realized how Henry—and the many others who worked in similar fashion—seemed to know everything that happened on the streets. He and his partners—my good friend Jerry Plent comes to mind—routinely took bad guys to jail, and it wasn't uncommon to see these crooks smiling and chatting while being booked on felony charges. It occurred to me that this was the secret of veteran cops: respect and rapport. Having fun in what many of us would argue was truly the happiest place on earth.

If you can close your eyes and feel the damp air of a cool night on patrol, maybe hear the sounds of the street or even smell the inside of a radio car, feel the stickiness of its steering wheel and armrests, then you've been there and done that, and you are likely nodding and smiling at the memories. For those who haven't been there, know that the great majority of cops are kind and caring souls, driven to the profession with the desire to help others, to protect the weak from bullies and predators, and to stand up for those who are unable to stand up for themselves. We sacrifice holidays and special occasions and sometimes much, much more to make a difference in our communities. To make a difference in *your* communities.

EASTSIDE BISHOPS ARE A CLIQUE OF THE BLACK STREET GANG, "BLOODS," and this particular clique claims as their own, in part, the geographical area of Elm Street south of Firestone Boulevard. This is the unincorporated area of Watts, located in the south end of Firestone's jurisdiction.

Alec "Mac" MacArthur had been a deputy sheriff since 1981. After a short stint working Custody, Mac transferred to Firestone station for patrol training. His six-year tenure as a street cop had been action-packed with pursuits, fights, hundreds of felony arrests, and many shoot/don't shoot scenarios. But he had never before exchanged gunfire with an adversary, and he never before had to pull the trigger on another man.

On Sunday, April 24, 1988, a cool Sunday night, Mac was working an overtime shift with his good friend Ron Duval. They wore plain clothes, jeans and sheriff raid jackets with protective vests beneath. It was attire recognized by residents of sheriff's jurisdictions everywhere as that of the gang detectives. Their call sign was 11G ("Eleven George").

That night I was stuck working the desk as the station dispatcher. It was a necessary assignment that all patrol deputies were rotated in and out of, and most of us hated it.

At some point in the evening, the station received a 9-1-1 call reporting shots fired in the 8800 block of Elm Street. Gunshots were heard almost daily throughout Firestone's district. Citizens would call in to report such activity with resignation in their voices: "They shootin' again down here on Elm Street." Desk personnel would question the caller: Do you see who's shooting? Is there a vehicle? Who are they shooting at? Without details to boost the call to a "245 Now" (assault with a deadly weapon) call, it would be dispatched as "923s" (shots fired). Many times, the shots-fired calls would develop into something much more serious. But other times, neither the source of the shots fired nor their intended target(s) would be discovered.

I sent the call to Rich Lopez, a seasoned and respected Firestone deputy, a man with whom I would work at Firestone and again at Homicide, and whom I am proud to call a friend. (In my Dickie Floyd Detective Novel series, there is a character named Davey Lopes, and that character happens to closely resemble Lopez.) Rich had handled hundreds of these types of situations, and he nonchalantly acknowledged the call.

MacArthur and Duval were both familiar with the Bishop gang members who plagued the 8800 block of Elm Street, and they knew that these gangsters would use a small dingy walkway that connected Elm Street to the alley at the rear of that location to escape the presence of sheriff's deputies driving into their neighborhood. Duval suggested to Mac that they come in through the back, covertly, while radio cars would be driving up the street. Mac turned his lights off and crept through the alley, stopping near the walkway to Elm Street. Having been nearby, they arrived in less than a minute, whereas Lopez had indicated he had about a three-minute ETA (estimated time of arrival).

Mac had recently transitioned from patrol to the gang unit. In patrol, he wore a leather duty belt with a Smith & Wesson revolver holstered on one side, and a pouch with three "speed loaders" in front. Like most other deputies, his belt included two handcuff cases worn on his back, a baton ring on the side, and he carried two "dump" pouches in the middle of his back that held additional ammunition. Speed loaders are plastic cylindrical devices designed for quickly reloading revolvers. With practice, six bullets could be loaded into a six-shot revolver in one smooth action. Dump pouches are designed to house individual rounds. When they are unsnapped, the loose rounds of ammunition fall into your hand, allowing for loading one bullet at a time, a much slower process. This event predated the use of semi-automatic pistols in our department; we were dinosaurs in the world of law enforcement. Mac had stopped carrying the dump pouches when he transitioned to the softer nylon gear belt that is commonly worn by detectives wearing soft clothes (street clothes as opposed to uniforms). Lastly, Mac always carried a backup gun, as did most street cops in violent neighborhoods. His was a two-inch .38 caliber revolver that he kept in his back pocket.

Duval broadcast on the radio that they had arrived and were planning to approach on foot from the alley. Mac went ahead through the walkway, his gun in his right hand, a radio and flashlight in his left. He stopped short of Elm Street in order to survey the area before responding units arrived in the event that there was an active shooter on the street. He paid particular attention to a known gang house located very close to the walkway, noting that it and the street were eerily silent.

A flicker of headlights turning north onto Elm Street from 92nd Street caught Mac's eye. He assumed it was his academy mate, old partner, and close friend, Rich Lopez. He knew Rich was the handling unit and would be responding. Just as the patrol car turned north, Mac heard footsteps. Somebody was running, and by the sounds of shod feet slapping against concrete, Mac knew the runner was drawing nearer. Mac's view was limited due to a market at the corner of the walkway and Elm Street. He waited in the shadows to avoid being seen. The footsteps slowed as the runner drew nearer, and suddenly, the figure of a man rounded the corner. The man was backlit by a distant streetlight, and Mac saw a gun in his left hand. The voice of Mac's training officer, Larry Swanson, echoed in his head: "Hands. Hands. Watch his hands!"

Mac processed the situation in an instant: there had been a report of shots fired, and the armed man before him had been running, apparently from the arrival of police. Now they were face to face, so close that Mac could smell the odor of Olde English 800 malt liquor on the man's breath. Mac had no place to retreat or seek cover, and his eyes were fixed upon the man's hand that held a gun.

Mac's gun was in his hand, steadied near his waist, not far from the holster from which he had drawn it. It was tucked at his side, the barrel pointed at the suspect, who raised his gun and began leveling it at Mac. Gunshots rang out, which Mac described as being "muffled." In those moments, Mac fired his gun as fast as he could pull the trigger, and the suspect fell not far from Mac's feet. Mac had followed the suspect with the sights of his gun and tried to fire again. This time, the hammer of his revolver fell on an expended cartridge; his six rounds of ammunition had been fired. It was a brief and surreal moment that Mac stood over an armed gangster in the dark walkway with an empty gun. He knew he needed to get to cover before trying to reload, so he started for the end of the alley. As he turned from the suspect, he was struck in the back by a bullet that had been fired from the downed man's gun.

Mac said the blow felt like it had come from a three-pound sledge-hammer. The impact knocked him off balance and threw him forward. He landed hard against the concrete, elbows first. His primary weapon flew from his hand, as did the radio and flashlight he had carried in the other. A sharp pain permeated his back, but he knew he had to move or risk being killed. Mac scrambled to the end of the alley and around the corner of a fence, crawling on his hands and knees. This position offered concealment, but it would do little to protect him from gunfire. He pulled his backup gun, having lost his primary weapon when he fell, and he pointed it in the direction of the suspect. Ten feet was all that sepa-rated him from the gangster who had tried to kill him. Mac knew he had been hit, but he wasn't sure how badly he was hurt. He only knew that a bullet had struck him somewhere near his spine.

Unsure if he could continue his retreat, Mac emptied his backup gun in the direction of the suspect, skipping rounds off the concrete the way we were trained to do in such scenarios. (We were trained that when a bullet is fired at an acute angle onto a flat surface, it will skip off that surface and then follow its plane until it strikes something else, or, theo-retically, loses its energy. Think of skipping a flat rock against still waters. The flatter the angle, the better it skips and follows the surface of the water. The same is true when a bullet is skipped off a hard surface. To hit a target that is on the ground, or perhaps along a wall, it is easier to aim short of the intended target and to allow the surface to assure the strike.)

After firing the five rounds from his backup gun, Mac shuffled farther back with the intent of reloading his weapon. Instinctively, he reached for his dump pouch; it wasn't there. All that remained was the ammunition for his primary weapon, which was contained in his speed loaders. It was the same ammunition he would use in both weapons, but his speed loaders were designed for the six-shot revolver, not his five-shot backup gun. Mac manually dumped the bullets from a speed loader and reloaded his backup gun with five of the bullets, leaving the sixth lying on the ground. Hunkered down with a reloaded weapon, Mac turned his attention back to the alley to assess the situation. That's when he heard Duval calling out for him. It was the first time since seeing the armed man that Mac thought of his partner. Duval announced, "He's down. He's down."

Mac responded. "I'm hit!" At that time, the thought occurred to Mac to remain still since he had been hit near his spine. He didn't want to spend the rest of his life in a wheelchair.

Duval recalls that when they had first arrived at the location, and as Mac started into the walkway, he had seen an older Hispanic male in the alley, and he thought maybe this man could provide some information about the shots that had been reported. The man didn't speak English, but when asked, he was able to understand that the deputies wanted to know where the shooting had come from. He pointed to Elm Street. Duval entered the narrow walkway and saw Mac ahead of him, nearly to Elm Street by then. Mac held his gun in one hand, a handheld radio and a burning cigarette in the other. Duval recognized the roar of distant engines to be that of responding radio cars. Immediately after, Duval heard the sounds of someone running on the street, hasty footsteps in the dark. A man came around the corner at a run and bumped into Mac, the two of them brushing shoulders. Mac and the other man ended up just feet apart, each turning to face the other as they passed. Each man was pointing a gun at the other, and Duval found himself down range from a gunfight, stuck in this narrow walkway with nowhere to go.

The gangster fired. Mac fired back, flames erupting from the gun he held low and tight to his body. Duval could see that Mac still had a burning cigarette and a radio in his other hand. Bullets whizzed past Duval as the gangster between him and his partner fell to the ground. Mac turned and ran toward the other end of the alley and suddenly dove around the corner. Duval retreated for cover at the west end of the walkway as his partner did the same on the east end.

Duval came up with his gun ready to fire at the suspect, but he wasn't sure where his partner was. He started into the walkway again, approaching the suspect, just as Mac began firing again, skipping rounds off the concrete walkway toward the suspect, who lay prone on the ground. Again, bullets hissed and snapped as they whizzed past Duval. He again hastily retreated to the alley west of the walkway for cover. Duval then went to the car to broadcast on the radio that there was a shooting. He heard Deputy Lopez's voice excitedly stating over the airwaves that there were "923s." Duval keyed his mic and corrected: "No, it's 998 (deputies involved in a shooting)! 998!"

A radio car arrived in the alley, and two Firestone patrol deputies joined Duval. The three of them entered the walkway, and Duval called out to his partner. "Mac? Mac?"

"I'm hit, Ronnie! I'm hit," Mac cried out.

As they passed the downed suspect, Duval saw that he was no longer a threat, gasping his final breaths. Duval and the two deputies got to Mac just as Deputy Magana arrived on the street. Together, they inspected Mac to find that his Kevlar vest had done its job, stopping the bullet that had struck him.

Rich Lopez was a six-year veteran patrol deputy at Firestone. That night, he was working with a trainee who had recently been assigned to him for the evaluation stage of his training program. The young deputy's name was David Powell. In 2002, Deputy Powell would be killed by gunfire. Ironically, by the time of Powell's death, Lopez was a six-year veteran homicide detective, and he was dispatched to assist with a murdered deputy investigation. He only learned after arriving at the scene that it was his former trainee, Powell, who had been killed.

Lopez recalled that the night Mac was shot, there had been several consecutive nights where 923s had been reported at the same location. Each time they had responded, the streets were empty. He suspected it was the Bishop gang members who were doing the shooting, and he further suspected they were getting away by running through the alley. On this night, he coordinated with Mac and Duval, who would come in from the alley behind the location.

Lopez recalled coming in from Firestone Boulevard, south on Elm Street. He passed by the walkway and stopped. Within seconds, shots were fired. Lopez could see muzzle flashes at the mouth of the walkway. He saw Mac come around the corner and "hit the deck" and then "buttonhook." Mac now lay prone, facing into the walkway from where he had come, and he fired again. Lopez could only see Mac on the ground, not the threat with whom he was engaged.

The shooting stopped. Lopez heard the radio broadcasts that confirmed units from stations near and far were responding to the assistance request. Lopez—believing there could be a second suspect—told Magana to coordinate the response of additional units in order to contain the area.

Mac called out, "I'm hit!" Hearing the announcement startled Lopez, and he went to where Mac lay motionless on the ground. Lopez remembered seeing that the bullet had been stopped by Mac's vest. Lopez told him so, and they stood him up. Mac's first words to his buddy and academy classmate were, "Give me a cigarette."

Magana remembered it was a cold night. He had been on some type of detail to a local hospital or maybe Lynwood station. When the call went out, he responded. He arrived and saw Mac lying on the sidewalk as if he were paralyzed. He ran to him and asked if he was okay. Mac said, "I've been shot! I've been shot in the back." Magana saw a bullet hole in the back of Mac's raid jacket. He lifted the jacket and saw a bullet hole in the vest beneath it. He looked under the vest and saw that the bullet had not penetrated it.

In addition to having been a great cop, Magana was known as a comedian. Not in the literal sense, but he was a funny man who always clowned around, laughed, smiled, and enjoyed life. Even at times of extreme duress, Magana could be counted on to be cool and offer levity. Mac remembered that when Magana came to him and checked his back, he said: "Get up, stupid, you aren't shot; the bullet is in your vest." (With Magana's Spanish accent, "stupid" was always pronounced "stupit," Mac fondly recalled.)

Relieved that Mac hadn't been shot, the two cops hugged. The bad guy lay motionless a few feet away. Sirens blared from all directions as units responded to the radio broadcasts that an officer-involved shooting had occurred and a deputy was down. Deputies from neighboring Lynwood and as far away as Carson and Lennox responded to the scene, all of them rolling hard because a deputy was down. One of the Firestone units responding had turned onto Elm Street and lost control of their vehicle, crashing into a parked car. Neither the driver nor the passenger was injured.

Paramedics arrived and evaluated Mac. His back stung, and he had scrapes on his hands and arms from crawling on the pavement, but he was otherwise in good shape. The suspect was pronounced dead at the scene.

Mac was sent to St. Francis Hospital for further evaluation and x-ray. He was cleared to return to duty. When he arrived at the station, he found it crowded and abuzz with department brass, homicide detectives, partners, and friends. Mac provided a statement and was cleared to go home. But instead, he stayed in the comfort of his partners and friends for a while, telling and retelling the story to all who had gathered to hear it. I was one of them.

At the time, Mac was thirty-one, divorced, with no kids. He found a quiet corner and called his parents in Michigan. It was close to midnight, three a.m. back east. He told them he had been shot, saved by his vest, and that he had taken the life of a 19-year-old gang member. His father, stunned, repeated "Oh my" and "Thank God" as he listened. Mac pictured his father sitting at his mother's desk in the corner of their bedroom, his mom sitting up in bed asking, What happened? Is he okay?

Alec MacArthur was okay.

Mac slept uneasily that night and returned to the office late the next morning, only to hear that another deputy-involved shooting had just occurred in Firestone. Mac grabbed a detective bureau car and rushed to the scene. When he arrived, he discovered there was no need for further assistance. Another armed gang member had been shot and killed during the execution of a narcotics warrant, and the situation was under control.

A sergeant on scene reminded Mac of his mandatory session with the department shrink as a result of his shooting the night before, and he escorted him back to the station. In the confusion, the car Mac had driven to the scene was left there. A couple of hours later, the detective's car was torched, presumably by friends of the dead man, his fellow gang members.

There were credible threats of retaliation, and deputies at our station took extreme caution to avoid being ambushed in the coming weeks and months. Mac was temporarily reassigned for his own protection. It was said that the Bishops had put a contract on his life. But soon he would return to Firestone station where he continued working as a gang investigator for six more relatively uneventful years.

Mac never received any recognition for his courageous actions during a gunfight. It seemed the department shied away from rewarding a lawman who, during the course of his duties, justifiably took the life of a bad man. Others who had been shot and saved by their vests, but hadn't taken a man's life in the process, were awarded the Medal of Valor.

For the rest of his career—and beyond—Mac would often reflect on that night on Elm Street. He is grateful that he had been able to respond as he had been trained to do during a life-threatening moment, and that in doing so, he had survived being shot. He's never been happy about killing a half-drunken 19-year-old gang member who, as it turns out, had been shooting at his girlfriend's house because she cheated on him.

Dupont, the manufacturer of Kevlar, would later have Mac appear in a commercial for their product. He was paid $11,000 for his contribution.

Mac went on to have a successful and, in his words, "wonderful career." He worked some of the best assignments in our department and ended his career with an eight-year stint at the elite Sheriff's Homicide Bureau.

I am proud to call Mac a friend, and I am honored to have worked with him at Firestone station and again at Homicide Bureau. Most of all, I am grateful that he is alive and well and enjoying retirement in an undisclosed location surrounded by water.

The reason I've included Mac's story in my memoir is because it was a memorable night for me as well. I believe our police and fire dispatchers are often unsung heroes, people who spend hours behind the scenes dealing with insanity on the phones and chaos on the radios, sometimes all at once. It is a very stressful job that requires a special type of person. That night, I had dispatched Lopez and Powell to the call of shots fired, and I listened intently as Mac and Duval arrived to assist. I'll never forget when Lopez got back on the radio and announced that there were "923s," because I knew immediately that there was more to it. Lopez wouldn't have put that out if it had only been the sounds of gunfire. He knew, but didn't have enough information to state that a deputy had been involved in a shooting. Moments later, Duval announced "998," confirming that deputies had been involved in a shooting, and that radio broadcast was soon followed by another, that there was a deputy down.

To be trapped at the station only a mile or so away and unable to assist was stressful. It seemed an eternity before an announcement was made that the deputy was okay and the suspect deceased. A short time later, when Mac arrived back at the station, I left the desk and went back to the gang office, where he was taking off his equipment. I asked if he was okay. He held up his raid jacket and stuck his finger through a bullet hole, and he smiled. "Yeah, baby," was all he said. I hugged him and went back to the desk, feeling a little choked up as the adrenaline settled and the reality of what we faced every single night sank in.

THERE WERE THREE BASIC RULES FOR SUCCESSFUL POLICING:

1) Don't Go Hungry

But far too often, we would. Not by choice but due to the level of activity on a given shift. In my day (at least), we worked eight-hour shifts on patrol. There were no scheduled lunch breaks; you ate when you could. When and if it quieted enough to do so, you stood at the hood of your patrol car and scarfed a couple of tacos or a burger at a local greasery while listening to your assigned frequency—Frequency 22, in our case.

2) Don't Get Wet

When it's raining, find shelter and a cup of coffee. Respond to calls as needed, but there's no sense in initiating your own activity in the rain. Well, that was good in theory, but we young deputies working in South Los Angeles were highly motivated and could only tolerate boredom for so long. Maybe an hour. If the rain continued, the coffee sessions would conclude, and the hunting would resume. The gangsters, pimps, and thugs might not be out on the street corners, but it was an excellent time to look for stolen cars. People didn't like walking in the rain.

3) Never Beat Rescue to a Call

This meant don't arrive ahead of the paramedics. They are the ones who have both experience and expertise when it comes to trauma and saving lives. For all of the fireman jokes I make and shots I freely take at my friends in their oversized yellow pants and suspenders, there was nothing better than turning onto a street in response to a medical emergency and seeing the firemen had already arrived. Unfortunately, that wasn't always the case.

One afternoon, Liam Gallagher and I responded Code 3 (lights and sirens) to a call of a "902R" (Rescue responding), "baby not breathing." I drove and Liam was bookman that day. We knew there was a train traveling along the tracks that divided Firestone's jurisdiction in half as we had raced to beat its crossing at Florence Avenue ourselves. Because the truth was, we never lived by any of the rules, especially Number Three. To hell with waiting for Rescue, a baby wasn't breathing. The railroad crossing gates had been lowered, and we could see the train heading south, a short distance from where we had paused but for an instant. Without conversation or consideration, I floored it, and we sailed around the lowered arms with their blinking red lights and proceeded to the call. A baby wasn't breathing.

There were three fire stations in Firestone's area at that time. The two closest to our destination were 9 and 16. Both were east of the tracks. Station 9 was north of Florence Avenue, near where we had responded from. But the firemen there wouldn't beat the train. They also wouldn't go around the arms as we had and often would whenever it was necessary. Station 16 was farther south at the time, south of Firestone Boulevard on Holmes Avenue. The tracks were elevated at Firestone Boulevard, so theoretically, they would be able to get to us without waiting out the train. The problem was that either one or the other would be dispatched, and we didn't know which. It was luck of the draw.

The radio car hugged the pavement and its tires squealed as I turned onto 67th Street from Hooper Avenue at a high rate of speed. The location was an even-numbered address in the 1100 block, which meant it would be closer to Central Avenue (than Hooper) and on the south side of the street. Two men stood marking the location, outside watching for help to arrive. Although they didn't appear anxious, they were somber. Frightened. There was no question it was the place. We skidded to a stop near the troubled men who turned and looked toward the house behind them as a manner of directing us to the problem. We abandoned our vehicle with its engine running and doors open and ran to the front door of the home, which stood open. Waiting.

The baby was blue. It may have already been too late. Liam snatched her from the mother and started CPR without hesitation, giving her mouth-to-mouth resuscitation. There was no equipment back in those days; you just did it or you didn't. Sometimes it was best not to beat Rescue to a call. But this was a baby, and she wasn't breathing.

I allowed half a second to listen in the moment of stillness. There were no sirens. No firemen in close proximity. They were probably waiting for a train to pass. I said to Liam, "Let's roll, partner."

Without hesitation, Liam ran to the car carrying the baby, continuing CPR as he did. I followed him to his open door and slammed it closed as he stepped inside. We departed the location in a cloud of smoke from melting tires while clearing the air (radio traffic) for an emergency radio broadcast.

"10-33, give me the patch."

A soothing female voice: "Firestone unit with 10-33 traffic, go; you are on the patch."

"Firestone 11 we are responding from the 1100 block of 67th Street to MLK (Martin Luther King Hospital) with a baby not breathing. I need Firestone and Lynwood units to clear intersections."

Liam worked frantically against the motion of the car jerking side to side, accelerating and decelerating quickly. The siren wailed as we reached speeds nearing 100 mph on Central Avenue. Every few seconds, I would announce our location and direction of travel. Units from Firestone and Lynwood announced their arrival at major intersections so that other units would know to go to the next one. Each major intersection we approached on our way to the hospital had been secured by assisting deputies. Most often, it would be two patrol cars, each sitting broadside with lights and sirens activated, blocking cross traffic, allowing us to sail through without even slowing for red lights. Once we cleared an intersection, the deputies at those locations would join in behind us and sometimes pass us to get to the next intersection in the event it had not yet been cleared by other deputies. This is a tactic referred to as leapfrogging, which allowed us to pass through intersections without slowing or worrying about cross traffic. Every unit from both stations had risked life and limb that afternoon in order to clear our path. A baby wasn't breathing.

We skidded to a stop outside of the E.R.—our car ticking, smoking, and smelling of burnt oil and fiery brakes—and were met by waiting staff: doctors, nurses, and hospital police. Liam ran from the car with the baby and handed her off to a nurse whose open arms signaled for him to do so. The lot of us ran inside together, passing dozens of civilians with various ailments and injuries waiting in the lobby to be seen. We continued through double doors and into the ER operating room, where life-saving efforts were continued and elevated.

Liam and I stood silently against the back wall, out of the way. Watching. Waiting. Praying.

It seemed to be hours—maybe it was only minutes—until the urgency began to settle, and the staff started shutting down various machines and devices. One of the doctors looked at us and shook his head. We walked out without saying a word.

As we walked through the waiting area, there was the family, the two men who had been outside the residence, and several women, including the woman who hadn't spoken nor protested when two uniformed men scooped her baby from her arms and fled. Here they were, with no communication between us. They had instinctively known where we would have gone; it was the nearest emergency room. All of their eyes searched us for answers, though they knew. They must've known, having seen the answer to their question written on our faces.

We stopped, and I looked into the terrified, wet eyes of the mother. I shook my head. "*Lo siento.*" (I'm sorry.)

She wept. She grabbed her mouth and stooped over, sobbing and shaking her head. One of the men embraced her. The other thanked us in broken English, somberly. We began to step away, but I stopped. "*Como se llama ella?*" (What was her name?)

"Vanessa," the man answered over the wailing of the child's mother.

We walked out and silently drove back to our jurisdiction where we went 10-8 (back in service), available to handle whatever would be our next call. There would be no counseling nor coddling nor safe spaces wherein we might gather ourselves as emotions replaced the adrenaline.

We had a job to do, so we masked our emotions and remained afield to do it. Even though Baby Vanessa had stopped breathing.

ON ANOTHER NIGHT, LIAM AND I WERE PATROLLING THE NORTH END OF Firestone when we saw a carload of gangsters slow as they rounded a corner where other gangsters loitered. What attracted our attention was one of the men in the car popped up through the sunroof and began shooting into the crowd. People went down, and the vehicle sped away. We saw the muzzle flashes and heard the shots, and as we sped past the crowd in pursuit of the suspects, we could hear yelling and screaming from those on the sidewalk. Several victims were on the ground.

We pursued the suspects until they turned onto a cul-de-sac which ended at the train tracks. We were on their bumper by then, and we skidded to a stop behind them and bailed out of our radio car, prepared for a gunfight. Guns flew from the car windows, and the gangsters raised their empty hands high into the night sky that was illuminated by our spotlights and flashing red and blues. The suspects were no longer interested in shooting now that they faced an armed adversary.

They were Blood gang members, "Blood Stone Villains" from the Pueblo housing projects just north of Firestone's jurisdiction, who had ventured south hunting Crips. The victims—this time—were a group of 59 ("five-nine") East Coast Crips. We used to say that today's victims were tomorrow's suspects. After we had taken the shooters into custody, we returned to the location of the shooting, where paramedics were attending to victims, and another pair of deputies had secured the scene. A young man, dressed in blue from head to toe, lay dead on the sidewalk. Several others had been wounded. Several of them reported that the shooter had popped up through the sunroof, said, "What that Villain like," and began firing his weapon.

Another night, we were patrolling the south end of our jurisdiction when suddenly, a barrage of gunfire erupted near us. We rounded the corner and saw dozens of gangsters running in every direction. Some of them were shooting, and others were just scattering.

No amount of academy training sufficiently prepares you for the moment you turn a corner to find yourself amid multiple shooters and scores of people running in every direction. I focused on one man who stood in the middle of the street, firing his gun indiscriminately. I aimed my car at him, hit the siren, and gave it the gas. Deadly force comes in many packages.

The suspect threw his gun and raised his hands as I skidded to stop, nearly missing him completely.

Everyone had disappeared in a matter of seconds, having escaped through the yards of houses, down the streets and alleys, and through the park. When help arrived just moments later, everyone else had vanished. Amazingly, nobody had been shot.

Grape Street is a street of infamy in South Los Angeles. The 9500 block sits north of the Jordan Downs housing project, and both are home to the Grape Street Crips. When I worked at Firestone, it was considered a cherry patch for drug and gun arrests, and it probably still is. It also happens to be in the City of Los Angeles, not the county. But only by a few inches; at least, that's how it appeared on the map.

For a few months, I was fortunate to be partners with Ernie Magana, a great street cop who talked fast and drove faster. One afternoon we were traveling east on 92nd Street when a car careened onto Grape Street. The vehicle was too far away for us to see who occupied it, but we were both inclined to find out—before they made it into the projects.

Magana floored it and didn't slow down much as we squealed around the corner. Within seconds, we were on the bumper of the speeding car, and we saw that the driver was a woman. The car was also loaded with children, little heads bopping around in the back, and we were both a little disappointed. Neither of us saw a need to pull her over. If the car had been occupied by gang members, a traffic stop would have been appropriate and justifiable, even though we were now out of our district. But we weren't traffic cops; we were hunting bad men. Yes, oftentimes, the women transported drugs and guns for their gangster men, and they were even known to conceal these items in baby car seats or diaper bags. Still, without a better reason to pull her over, we weren't going to bother finding out her story.

However, since we were "justifiably" out of our area and just a "few inches" into the city, we kept our eyes peeled for any other activity or persons of interest. After all, just down the road from where we were, on the southwest corner of 95th and Grape Streets, sat a notorious crack house. The Jordan Downs housing project was just south of that. Gangsters were abundant in this area, but on this occasion, there was one in particular who caught Ernie's attention. It was a young man of about fourteen years who dressed as if he had just left the Grape Street Crip gang emporium and spent a week's worth of cocaine sales profit on a new wardrobe. No, there was no such emporium, but this kid was "gangstered" out from head to toe with his purple cap (worn sideways), some type of jersey—that, like his pants, was twelve sizes too big for him—and matching shoelaces. (Crips wear blue, but Grape Street Crips wear purple instead.) His ensemble was completed with the very elegant Mr. T gold starter kit: thick gold rope necklaces, bracelets and rings, and matching gold earrings. He was riding a BMX-style bicycle, which, at the time, was the type of bike most frequently stolen, and there had been several recently reported thefts of just this type of bike.

Ernie swerved to the side of the road and stopped. We both jumped out as Ernie ordered the gangster to "Grab the hood."

The criminal types in Firestone's jurisdiction had been trained by the generations of no-nonsense deputies who preceded us and who had paved those streets with their own blood, sweat, and tears. The station's legendary history included the Watts Riots, the annual Watts Festivals, the origination of the Crip gang, and some of the highest murder rates in the country. It was also famous for being stocked with courageous, tough men and women who took to the streets and placed themselves in harm's way to make those streets a little safer. The gang members had a healthy respect for, or maybe fear of, those who wore the tan and green.

Thus, the miniature gangster dropped his bike and grabbed the hood of our radio car, spread-eagled as if he had assumed the position dozens of times before—he probably had. Ernie homed in on him, quick to check his waistband for weapons while asking where he got the bike. But at the same time, a man who had been walking up the sidewalk and was only a few feet from where the gangster had dropped the bike stepped from the sidewalk onto the street, moving toward Ernie and the kid. I focused my attention on him as my partner was focused on the gangster. His eyes were locked with mine, and his right hand was in his jacket pocket. Ernie had just reached the gangster—this all happened in a split-second—and his words "Grab the hood" still hung in the air. I was drawing my pistol as the man's right hand came out of his jacket. Nearly forty years later, I still remember seeing what filled his hand. I also remember his exact words: "I ain't gonna lie, deputy, it's cocaine."

He extended his arm to show a large disc-shaped object that was off-white in color, about two inches thick, and the diameter of a medium-sized skillet. I couldn't believe my eyes; it *was* cocaine! It was the biggest "rock" I had ever seen and certainly the largest quantity I had brought in from a street arrest. Most crack cocaine arrests by patrol cops are the result of finding one or more small "rocks" on a suspect, and we all made a lot of those arrests. Getting a cookie was a big deal, something to brag about. Especially on a pedestrian stop. It was a great hook![1]

The pedestrian handed me the cookie as I met him at the front of our patrol car, and then he, like the young gangster had, naturally assumed the position with his hands on the hood. My partner looked over quizzically as I placed my handcuffs on him. I held up the cookie and told Magana what we had. Ernie said, "Cool!" and sent Mr. T's mini-me on his way. The proverbial small fish released back into the murky waters of Grape Street.

On the way to the station, Ernie said, "How are we going to write this, partner?" Meaning, we were in the city, and watch commanders never seemed to appreciate us poaching LAPD's area. I was bookman that day, and bookman has the responsibility of getting the arrest approved by the watch commander and writing the report.

I told him, "Just as it happened, partner."

He argued, "Nobody's going to believe that story."

He wasn't wrong. It would sound like a tall tale. But I told it just like it happened, and the watch commander approved the arrest, albeit with a slight grin on his face. It was as if he were skeptical about the story, so I encouraged him to go to the booking cage and ask the suspect what had happened. He said he didn't need to do that, that he trusted me, but I insisted. The arrestee was actually a bit of a character anyway, so I knew the conversation would be entertaining. The lieutenant acquiesced, and the two of us left his office for the booking cage.

Through the mesh cage, my lieutenant asked the man how he was doing. He was okay, he said. Then my boss asked the man why he was in jail. This was the type of question that would oftentimes put smiles on our faces, creativity never lacking in such situations. There were the usual, "Man, I gots no idea. I di'n't do nothin'!" Or, "They *say* I had a (insert item: gun, dope, bloody knife) on me." Or, "I guess they found dope in my pocket, but these ain't even my pants." This time, our arrestee smiled and said, "It was just a routine roust. I was walking up the street with my cocaine, and the poh-lees said to grab the hood. Like I told them, I wasn't gonna lie; it was cocaine. It was too big to eat, and I ain't runnin' from Firestone."

AFTER THREE YEARS AT FIRESTONE, I WAS ASKED TO BECOME A TRAINING officer. Reluctantly, I agreed to it. There were others who had been there longer, but the training staff selected me, and I wasn't going to turn them down. It was in the fall of 1989, and I was at the top of my game. I knew the streets. I knew the crooks. I had handled dozens of murders, hundreds of robberies and deadly assaults, scores of rapes, and a smattering of kidnappings. I used to joke that the only thing I hadn't yet handled as a patrol deputy was an airplane crash, and I would be comfortable leaving that one out of my curriculum vitae.

Before promoting to detectives in 1991, I would be at least partly responsible for the training of nine newly assigned deputies. I took the responsibility very seriously and went out of my way to expose my trainees to every possible scenario, crime, and type of criminal they might ever encounter. It wasn't uncommon to make two or three felony arrests per shift. We would bring in dope, guns, stolen cars, wanted fugitives, and an assortment of predators. The vast majority of all of our activity was self-initiated, not the result of responding to calls.

During the time that I was a training officer, I had an occasion to pair with a young woman who had just finished her six-month patrol training period. After briefing that day, we inspected our vehicle and shotgun, and had a quick chat about tactics and expectations in given situations. It was just past two, and we would work until ten p.m. She insisted that I drive, even though I urged her to do so. When you are fresh off training, you haven't spent much time behind the wheel. Conversely, as a training officer, you drove ninety percent of the time. But she was adamant that I drive, so I wheeled us out of the station parking lot and headed south. "What do you want to do?"

"What do you mean?" was her reply.

"Well, is there anything you didn't get a chance to do or see as a trainee, something you had hoped to experience but haven't?"

"I'd like to get a gun."

Shocked, I glanced back and forth from the road to my partner. "You haven't made any gun arrests?"

She forced a smile. "No sir."

"First, drop the sir. Second, who the hell trained you?"

She went on to say that her training officer—who hadn't been trained at Firestone himself but had transferred in from another station—was the type who liked making dope arrests, and that is what they had focused on. She'd made hundreds of them. She'd already testified as an expert in the field of narcotics during preliminary hearings. She could write a dope report in her sleep, and she could spot a junkie at a hundred yards. But never a gun arrest while working patrol in South Los Angeles. I was stunned.

I said, "We'll get you a gun tonight."

Some people had referred to me as a bit of a shit magnet. It was true. I seemed to stumble upon really bad men doing really bad things at just the right—or wrong, depending on your perspective—times. I used to say I'd rather be lucky than good, and that seemed to be the case for me.

Case in point: Not five minutes had passed since this conversation about making a gun arrest when I spotted a carload of parolees headed north on Compton Avenue. Okay, we're not supposed to profile, so let's just say there were four assholes in the car, and all of them appeared to be fresh out of the pen at worst, or at best, street gang enthusiasts. They were unfortunate enough to be riding in a vehicle with expired tags, which I happened to notice at some point after flipping a U to get behind them. There was my probable cause to make a stop.

I hit the overhead red light, but they didn't yield. I politely tooted our siren to get their attention, and it seemed to work; all four looked back, the driver through his mirrors, and his passengers by craning their necks to show us wide eyes, the looks of surprise and concern. Yet on they traveled. I ran the plate over our radio, but before the dispatcher could provide us with the details, the driver turned into a parking lot and stopped. We were not far from the Pueblos, a notorious housing project that was home turf to the Pueblo Bishop Bloods. I was glad they pulled over before getting there, which is where I assumed they were heading. I told my partner to be ready, these guys were dirty.

"Let me see some hands." It was a standard order when approaching carloads of hoodlums. In Firestone, many of the locals would have their hands up and even outside of the windows before we were out of our cars, knowing the drill. All but the driver complied with the order. He leaned forward and appeared to be stashing something under the seat. I drew my gun and made the announcement again, zeroing in on the back of his head and issuing a friendly warning of what might happen if he didn't obey the order. He brought his hands up.

I holstered my weapon and ordered the driver out of the car. He complied. I patted him down for weapons while keeping an eye on the other occupants. The driver didn't have any weapons on him, so I instructed him to go back to my partner at the hood of our patrol car. I then ordered the front passenger to slide over and exit via the driver's door. He did. As he unfolded himself from the car, I was surprised at the size of the man. He stood close to six and a half feet tall, and he probably weighed in at a solid two-fifty. There was not an ounce of fat on his body, and his arms were as big as my thighs. I told him to turn around and place his hands on the top of the car, which he did. I began patting him down and felt the grip of a gun in his waistband. I jerked my gun from its holster and put the barrel of it at the back of his skull, telling him to freeze. I then yelled "four-seventeen" (man with a gun) to alert my partner.

I glanced over to see apprehension on my partner's face. She was lost, unsure of how to react. She hadn't been exposed to such situations in her six months of training. But she was a hell of a dope cop. I yelled at her: "Pull your gun out and point it at this asshole!"

She did. She pointed it in our general direction and held it there, its barrel bouncing around uncontrolled.

Before going any further, I calmly told the big man at the end of my barrel, "You're too big to fight, and you've got a gun in your waistband. I'm not playing any games with you, got it?"

"Yes sir."

"You're going to leave your hands on the top of the car, and I'm going to take that gun out of your waistband. Then I'm going to handcuff you. Understood?"

"Yes sir."

"You see my partner?"

"Huh?"

"My partner. Look at her."

He carefully glanced in her direction, and no doubt saw that she was pointing her gun at us, the barrel visibly shaking. I said to the big man, "If you so much as flinch, I'm going to tell her to shoot, and she's going to kill us both."

"Yes sir."

"I don't particularly want to die today. Do you?"

"No sir."

"Okay, good."

I removed from his waist a six-inch Smith & Wesson .357 Magnum revolver and stuffed it into my belt at the small of my back. If you don't know guns, this is a big one, not the type many men could conceal. Then I reminded the big man of my partner in the event he forgot how dangerous this situation had become. He assured me he was still cool. I hooked him up and then used him as a shield as I kept the two remaining suspects—still seated in the back seat with their hands up—in my view while retreating to our patrol car.

The troops had arrived, but I had barely noticed. Someone yelled out to me, "Got him," and the big man was whisked away as I kept my focus on the two remaining suspects. Now that we had plenty of assistance, we extracted the other occupants using high-risk, felony stop tactics. Each of them had guns concealed in their waistbands as well.

With four in custody, we searched the car and found the driver's gun concealed beneath his seat, right where he had reached during my initial approach. The question will always remain: was he concealing it or attempting to retrieve it? Sometimes you never knew how close you had come to killing or being killed. Other times you did.

All four suspects were parolees fresh out of the joint. (It turns out that profiling thing works pretty well.) Gun arrests of convicted felons are at the top of the gun arrest food chain, an automatic felony charge and a trip back to the Big House. We also recovered a large sum of cash from the trunk of their car, about twenty thousand, as I recall. When it was all said and done, my partner that night proclaimed me as the greatest street cop ever. I didn't bother correcting her, though I wouldn't honestly agree. The truth was I just seemed to get lucky sometimes, especially when it came to making gun arrests. But you didn't get lucky unless you were trying hard, too.

My partner that night turned out to be a good street cop, respected by her peers at Firestone station, and someone I consider a friend.

———

EVERY NEW YEAR'S EVE IN SOUTH LOS ANGELES THE SKIES RAINED LEAD. Over the years, there have been varying strategies as to how deputies would be deployed during such dangerous hours. We still had a job to do, and all of us were there to do it. Nobody liked being called in from the field to shelter during the height of celebratory gunfire, but that is what they generally had us do. Every year many of the cars in our parking lot would be damaged by bullets that had fallen from the sky, emphasizing the point. The other reason the shelter policy was implemented was in an effort to minimize deputy-involved shooting situations. But whether or not we sheltered for a half hour or so at midnight, the hours before and after were just as dangerous. Gunplay was the norm throughout South Los Angeles, especially on New Year's Eve, and we were tasked with combatting it safely and, preferably, peacefully.

The year I became a training officer, we hadn't been ordered to shelter at midnight on New Year's Eve. We were going to stay out in the field, so I warned my trainee: "You *will* see people shooting guns tonight.

You *will not* shoot them for doing so." The truth is, anyone who worked in the ghetto long enough would see people shooting their guns in the air as a way of celebrating, and each time, the vast majority of us would put ourselves at additional risk by not being quick to shoot them for it. On New Year's Eve, these contacts would be unavoidable, and I prayed that nobody was just so drunk or stupid—or both—that the muzzle of said gun would be allowed to swing in our direction if and when we confronted them.

As predicted, shots were fired all night long, and on many occasions, we would be close to the source. Several times, we observed a shooter but chose not to pursue them onto private property or into the residences to where they fled. Again, it was a different type of night.

But gangsters were always fair game. When you could take a gang member to jail and get another gun off the streets and out of their hands, you were saving lives. Also, every gun taken off a gangster had the potential to solve murders. So when I looked down a side street while driving past it and noted there were a number of gang members gathered in front of a known hangout, I knew they would be worthy of a closer look.

I turned onto the next street and parked our radio car in an alley beyond their view. We then snuck by foot through the alley and worked our way to a position directly across the street from where the gang members had gathered. All along, we heard gunshots coming from where they stood. The shooting continued with breaks between volleys. From what I could see, there was only one gun in play. I knew it could be otherwise, but the job was full of risks. We made our way to within twenty yards or so of the group, staying concealed behind a row of parked cars as we watched one of the gangsters empty the gun into the air and then reload it. I smiled at my trainee, whose eyes were wide with anticipation. "Be ready," I whispered. "The next time they reload, we're going to rush them."

Another six shots were fired into the sky, and the revolver was empty. "Now!"

The group scattered as we ran toward them, pointing our guns in their direction and yelling for all to stop. Their fleeing during our approach wasn't unexpected, so I remained focused on the youngster with the gun and didn't worry about catching the others. They were the smaller fish (that night) going back into the pond, and I'd be back to fish it again many times in the following years.

The shooter froze and dropped his gun, which we recovered after handcuffing and searching him. It was a great arrest that was a lot of fun to make, and I was proud of our accomplishment. I had told my trainee earlier that night that if you had to shoot someone on New Year's Eve, everyone would doubt the necessity of your actions. Justified or not, there would remain a stigma about the shooting. The last thing I wanted to do was to shoot someone on New Year's Eve.

When we recommissioned our patrol car from the alley, prisoner in tow, I read a message that had come in on our recently provided mobile digital terminal. A friend of mine who worked at another station had shot and killed a man. Without knowing a single detail about what had happened, I knew it would be viewed as controversial, at least by the brass and probably the media too. Regardless of whether it was justifiable, and no matter how good the shooting might have been, I feared it would be the end of a good man's career, and it was.

MY TRAINEE AND I, WORKING UNIT 15A ("FIFTEEN ADAM"), HAD JUST handled a burglary alarm call on Central Avenue north of Florence Avenue. Our shift ended at 2:00 a.m., and we were close to getting off. We had been assisted on the call by an early mornings (graveyard) car, Unit 12, a pair of heavyweights, literally and figuratively, Frank "Sonny" LaFlamme and Joe "Bobo" Barbosa. When we cleared the call as a false alarm, we pulled our radio cars side by side and sat in the middle of the otherwise vacant boulevard for a chat. We were discussing where to grab a cup of coffee since the night was slow when the procession of a brown van and two LAPD cars passed by.

The trio crossed Central Avenue and continued east into Firestone's jurisdiction, the cops with their red and blue lights flashing but the driver of the van oblivious to them.

"Doesn't look like he's going to stop, does it?" Frank said.

"Nope," I said. "Let's go."

The four of us deputies, in our two sheriff's radio cars, trailed along to see what might happen next. This is called "monitoring," a common practice that makes sense to every cop on earth other than the captain we worked for at the time and one arrogant LAPD lieutenant.

The van traveled at a speed below the posted limit, as did the LAPD cars with their flashing lights, and we followed from several hundred feet behind with neither emergency lights nor a sense of urgency, the four of us chatting from car to car as we slowly trailed them. The driver of the van would stop for red lights and proceed when they turned green, obeying all the traffic laws other than pulling over for the cops. It was an odd situation that captured our interest on an otherwise boring night.

We switched to a car-to-car frequency and alerted the other units in our area and our desk that LAPD was following a failure to yield through our jurisdiction. We advised that we were monitoring this situation and would continue to do so until they cleared our area in the event they needed our assistance.

After about a mile or so, the van turned south, remaining in our jurisdiction and actually going deeper into it. Shortly thereafter, the van turned onto Leota Street, which we knew dead-ended at the railroad tracks. This was, in fact, the street where my trainee and I had arrested the gang member shooting his gun on New Year's Eve. LAPD wouldn't know that it was a dead-end street, nor would they know that it was gang-infested, a place where stolen cars were often dumped and from where violence was routinely reported. For the first time during this event, I began feeling an intensity about the situation.

I turned onto Leota and stopped. Sonny and Bobo pulled alongside our car. In a quick assessment of the situation, we all agreed that there was a good chance the driver would bail and run across the tracks and that LAPD would need us to help set up a containment. Again, they were unfamiliar with the area—of this, we were certain. Just as we finished making our plan, there was a commotion at the end of the street. The van drove over the curb, kicking up a cloud of dust, and then turned and drove directly at the LAPD cars that were pursuing it. Tires squealed and motors raced and suddenly there were flashes of light as the sounds of gunfire echoed through the night.

I saw the van coming at us, this time with a level of urgency, speeding down the street directly at us and still being pursued by LAPD units.

There was no way for them to pass by us due to how our two radio cars were situated on the narrow street. From where we sat, it appeared the van had rammed into one or both of the LAPD units as it drove through the cluster of radio cars, and now it was coming at us. To avoid being rammed ourselves, I accelerated forward and swerved to the side of the road in one of the few spaces available in a long line of parked cars. Bobo, however, could only retreat rearward, so he did. But the van bore down on his car as he raced in reverse to avoid the suspect. The van caught up to Sonny and Bobo's vehicle and rammed them.

More shots were fired as the driver of the van continued to use his vehicle as a deadly weapon. Sonny and my trainee both fired at the suspect while Bobo and I took evasive driving actions. Bobo lost control of his vehicle and struck a parked car. The suspect continued past them, and LAPD continued their pursuit. We fell in behind LAPD as the suspect now drove at a high rate of speed, fleeing the scene. I announced over dispatch radio that we had been involved in a shooting and were pursuing the suspect. As we quickly departed our area and found ourselves headed north toward downtown L.A., a timid watch commander insisted that we return to the scene of the shooting and allow LAPD to continue their pursuit without our assistance. We did as we were ordered, though I was none too happy with the command.

We would later learn that the van had crashed shortly after we had terminated our involvement in the pursuit and returned to the scene of the deputy-involved shooting. LAPD captured the driver, and they had apparently used physical force in making the arrest. They brought him to Firestone station, where they dropped him off, telling our watch commander that the suspect was all ours since, after all, we had used deadly force against him—meaning that we had fired our weapons at the suspect.

This LAPD lieutenant went on to deny that any of his officers had fired at the van while expressing some displeasure with our involvement in their pursuit. Never one to remain silent when speaking up is the right thing to do, I challenged this LAPD lieutenant, telling him we heard and saw his officers shoot their weapons. He continued to deny that they had, and he became even more indignant about our participation in the entire event, implying that everything would have gone smoother had we not interceded. I countered that he and his men were in *our* jurisdiction and that we would be remiss in not monitoring their activities in the event they would need assistance, which clearly they had. He seemed unimpressed, so I took the opportunity to explain to him that although his department was large and that the city they patrolled was expansive, that truthfully, LAPD was just one of more than forty such departments within *our* county. The lieutenant didn't like that too well, but I really didn't care. He was lying about what happened out there, and LAPD was washing its hands of it all. Sometimes you just had to piss on another dog's fence, and I never hesitated to do so.

The four of us deputies were subsequently disciplined by our station captain for being involved in an unauthorized pursuit and for unsafe operations of our vehicles. I contested my suspension and written reprimand. When my captain learned that I was fighting the discipline, he summoned me to his office to discuss it. I asked him rhetorically why we bothered to patrol the streets of our jurisdiction if we weren't expected to observe and monitor any activity that could bring trouble to its citizenry. Why not have us play cards in the station until the bell rang? We could slide down a pole and go to work the way our friends with the shiny helmets do, then come back to the station for movie night.

The argument didn't work either time, when I pleaded my case to the captain or when I fought him all the way to an arbitration hearing before a judge. There, the LAPD lieutenant exacted his revenge when he testified against us. Under oath, he swore that only "the sheriffs" had fired their weapons that night on Leota Street. It was a bold and brazen lie. He knew it, I knew it, and at least three other sheriff's deputies and a couple of LAPD officers knew it. But the son of a bitch lied under oath about what happened that night, and I sat at the table next to our counsel, seething.

After the hearing, our gazes locked as I walked past where he was standing with the representatives of our department who had been our adversaries in the hearing. We were in the hallway, just outside of the courtroom, and I struggled to hold my tongue as Barbosa and I passed by them. Quite honestly, it wasn't like me not to pop off, but I was so angry it would have been easy to provoke me beyond the exchange of words, and nothing good could come from that. The lieutenant was first to look away because it isn't easy for a liar to look an honest man in the eyes.

Barbosa was driving us back to the station when I began wondering if I was having a heart attack. There was a tremendous pain in my chest, one which was only exacerbated by taking deep breaths. Joe noticed that I wasn't feeling well, and I told him my chest hurt. He asked if I wanted him to take me to the hospital, and I said no. A few minutes later, I was clutching my chest, thinking, yes, that's what I need to do, go to the hospital, but when he asked again, I again declined. This is why men die of heart attacks, by the way. Joe said, "Too bad, we're going," and he drove me to St. Francis Medical Center and marched me into the emergency room. After a series of tests and a period of monitoring my vitals, they concluded that I hadn't had a heart attack, but not from a lack of trying. My blood pressure hovered in the red zone, and they kept me there until it subsided. "You need less stress in your life," a doctor had concluded. I laughed at the ridiculousness of that and went back to work.

APPARENTLY, I WAS, AT LEAST IN PART, RESPONSIBLE FOR THE CHANGE OF A department policy with regard to "no-hit" deputy-involved shootings. When a deputy is involved in a shooting that results in death or injury to any person, Homicide Bureau investigates the case and presents its findings to the district attorney's office. Up until the night I chased and tried to shoot a guy who had car-jacked and shot a man before I happened on him, no-hit shootings were simply reviewed by the station watch commander. That is no longer the case.

My trainee, Dana Duncan, and I were traveling south on Compton Avenue when I saw three obvious gang members riding in a car that was traveling north at about 88th Street. The occupants all appeared nervous when they saw me watching them, and the driver made a quick turn onto 87th Street as I began to turn around to get behind them. We came around the corner quickly, in time to see them bail out of the car and start running. I gave chase to the driver, who, as he rounded the corner into an alley, was grabbing at his waist. A gunshot rang out in the night, and I instinctively fired my weapon at him in response. The suspect disappeared into the alley.

I heard my partner yelling commands, and I turned back to see he had his gun trained on the car that the gangsters had occupied. He told me there was a suspect still inside, in the back seat. It was dark, and I hadn't seen him, in large part because I had focused on the driver when he bailed and ran. I returned to the cover of our radio car, where we waited for assistance from other units before extracting the suspect from the car.

When we commanded the suspect to exit the car, he cried out that he was unable, stating that he had been shot. I thought, Oh Jesus, did I hit this guy? How bad a shot am I? The car sat between me and the suspect when I had fired my weapon at the runner, but I remembered having a clear line of fire as the suspect rounded the corner into the alley. There was no way I could have shot this guy in the car—or could I have? Either way, the suspect continued his refusal to come out on his own, citing he was too badly injured to move. Once assisting units arrived, we approached and recovered a gun from the gunshot suspect before removing him from the vehicle and allowing the paramedics to work on him. I was relieved to know that he had a gun, just in case it was my bullet that found him.

As it turned out, he had shot himself while pulling his gun out of his pants when he and the other suspects had decided to bail out of the car. It was a relief knowing I wasn't *that* bad a shot and a bit amusing that this idiot had shot himself. But now we needed to find the other suspects, and I wondered if the one I had shot at would be found somewhere bleeding or dead.

The outstanding suspects were found during an intense search that involved canines, and each was arrested. None of them had been hit by gunfire, and I was a little bit disappointed. Especially when we learned that these gangsters had just shot a man and robbed him of his car minutes before we saw them. The suspects had assumed that we knew what they had done, and they apparently were prepared to shoot it out with us, if need be, in order to escape.

John Martin was our watch commander, and he came out and took my statement about the incident and the shooting. He searched for and recovered a bullet from the tree that stood where the suspect had been when I fired. Martin reminded me, with a smile on his face, that you have to "lead" a running suspect, much the way you lead a bird in flight or your receiver when throwing a pass. That was it, as far as any review of my actions was concerned.

A couple of weeks later, Martin told me that the department executives were having debates about the lack of investigation that accompanied no-hit shootings. Because there had been someone injured by gunfire during my "no-hit" shooting incident—though it clearly hadn't been my shot that injured him—that event had drawn the attention of our department administrators. Policy was rewritten, and from that time forward, station detectives would investigate any such "no-hit" deputy-involved shooting, and their investigations would automatically be reviewed by our Internal Affairs division.

"So much for the good times," Martin had said.

Interestingly, Lt. John Martin was later "rolled up" from his assignment as the early morning watch commander. The captain—the same one who had disciplined me and three other deputies following the pursuit and shooting on Leota Street—had called him in to ask why there were so many pursuits, shootings, and uses of force on the early morning watch. In response, Martin had shrugged and told the nervous captain, "Shit happens." The captain didn't care for his response, suffice it to say, so we lost a great man to political maneuvering. On the last night of his assignment to our watch, we brought in a cake that had "Shit happens" written with white frosting across the top, along with our station logo, *FPK1* (Firestone Park, Station 1), in a diamond.

THERE WERE MANY GOOD PEOPLE WHO LIVED IN FIRESTONE'S AREA, BUT they weren't the ones with whom we often interacted. Rather, they were the parents and grandparents and innocent children who lived behind bars, unable to escape the violence that plagued their community. They were the business owners, the caregivers, the laborers who feared for the safety of their families.

Bob Youngblood was the owner of Bob's Tires on Firestone Boulevard, and he was my friend. When I was new at Firestone, I had heard that Bob would give the local cops a discount on tires, so the first time I needed a set, I went to see him. I immediately liked the big man—*how could you not?*—in his overalls and with his contagious smile, one that came from somewhere deep inside and couldn't be helped nor faked. He had big dimples, and his eyes glimmered when he talked about fishing in his slow, southern drawl. After the first time we met, I would stop and visit with him often, usually while on patrol. He and two or three other old men would sit on metal folding chairs in the shade outside of his shop when there weren't customers, and he was never ashamed to have a deputy sheriff pull up a seat alongside him. We would talk about hunting and fishing, good women and dogs, and the south, from where both of our families hailed. Sometimes we'd even talk about crime and bad people in the neighborhood. It came up once when I was there, and a man walked onto his property trying to sell him something. Bob's smile disappeared, and an authoritative business owner commanded this scoundrel, "Get out of here with all that! Go on, now." The man shuffled on, and Bob said to me, "They steal from you at night and come around trying to sell you your neighbor's shit during the day. If nobody bought what they was sellin', they wouldn't be out at night stealin' it." It was a simple philosophy, one that was lost on many.

Bob got sick and spent his final days at a hospital in the nearby city of Downey. When I heard the terrible news, I went to see him. He couldn't talk, and his smile was gone, and his eyes no longer glimmered. Rather, they conveyed the fear and apprehension of a dying man, and it broke my heart to witness this. I said a few words, all I could think to say, among them that I knew he was a good man and that he would always have a special place in my heart. I left him that day with tears in my eyes, and the next day Bob was called home by his Savior.

South Los Angeles needed more Bob Youngbloods in it. The truth of it is the world needs more men like him in it.

May he rest in peace.

---

1. Cocaine is "cooked" during the process of making crack. In the disc form—straight out of a skillet—it's called a cookie. The cookie is then cut into smaller "rocks" for individual sales.

FIRESTONE DETECTIVE BUREAU

SEPTEMBER 1991

A fter losing the Espinoza federal lawsuit and being told that I was to give my hard-earned money to the gangster siblings as a result of the punitive damages awarded to them, I had lost my love of the job. I would regain it in later years, but as a patrol deputy —at that time—I found myself with a gigantic chip on my shoulder. It felt as if, on the one hand, the public expected us to put ourselves in harm's way to protect the innocent, and on the other hand, they were willing to crucify us for doing so. This was still before the four Los Angeles policemen would be sent to prison for doing their job exactly how they had been trained to do it. (What most people don't know is that LAPD had restricted their officers from using far more effective tactics, such as the application of carotid restraint holds, and in doing so had left them with few alternatives to the use of batons, which are oftentimes— as in the case of the Rodney King incident—ineffective.) When those officers were retried in order to appease the loudmouth critics, that changed a lot of us in law enforcement—dare I say it sucked the life out of some. My good friend Frank LaFlamme had suggested that we release the criminals from prison and take their places until the public has had their fill of political justice, see just how long it would take for them to beg us to come back. Now, as I write this memoir, society is at a new level of stupidity with politicians pushing for defunding the police while simultaneously supporting the release of violent offenders from jails and prisons, and pushing for no cash bail systems, as the entire system is, of course, racist. There is no way possible I could be a cop today, and I pray for those who continue to hold the thin blue line between a civil society and chaos, to the extent that they are allowed.

Back to thirty years ago in Firestone. After the trial I was patrolling the streets with a terrible attitude and a great partner, Dana Duncan. He had been my most recent trainee and we remained together because I so enjoyed working with him. Dana had been a cop at Culver City PD before being hired by the sheriff's department, so he came with plenty of experience. He had also been a Green Beret in the Army, though he never bothered telling anyone that. I found out one night during a traffic stop when the person we stopped claimed to have been one, and Dana challenged the man with an intensity anyone rarely saw from him. At any rate, Dana and I were partners, and I will always appreciate those few months when he endured my new bitter view of police work.

Not long after the trial, Jim Lally, one of our detective sergeants, pulled me aside in the parking lot and said he wanted me to apply for a position in the detective bureau. A year or so prior, I had done a short stint "on loan" to the detective night car, and although I had enjoyed the experience, I still preferred working uniformed patrol. I told him as much, and he leveled with me. "Everyone has noticed how you've changed since the lawsuit. You're a great cop and you need to come back to DB before you ruin that reputation."

After careful consideration, I realized he was right. Maybe DB was just where I needed to go. I applied, interviewed, and in September 1991, I was promoted to station detectives at Firestone.

At first, I had difficulty embracing the new job. However, like any new job, there was a lot to learn about the basics of being a detective. There was more to it than just interviewing witnesses and solving crimes, such as writing and executing search warrants, filing criminal complaints at the courthouse, and a whole new spectrum of paperwork that accompanied all of it. The best part of the job was the people I worked with and for. To name a few, Jim Lally, who as I mentioned had been instrumental in my becoming a detective, and Dan Gayhart, were our detective sergeants. Russ Owens, and later John Martin, were the DB lieutenants. I was broken in by two of the best detectives in the bureau, Scott Fines and Stacy Silva. The bureau was full of great people: Chuck Norris (not the martial artist/actor, but somewhat of a legend himself in our department), Joe "The Moe" Martinez, Ozzie Newsom, Rudy Schaap, Bob Pettit, Phil Martinez, Maria Serrano, Paul Brown, and Greg Nelson. And of course, one of my favorite partners of all times, Joe Sheehy.

The real fun began when I was assigned to the detective night car with Sheehy. "Chicks dig the night car," he would say. And, "Chicks dig shoulder holsters." "Chicks dig station dicks." Et cetera. Joey was like a big dog with his head out the window, drinking up the wind. He literally loved everything.

The best part of the night car was we didn't have to wear slacks and ties; we wore jeans and raid jackets as we spent much of our time out in the field doing follow-up on cases and assisting patrol. In Firestone and areas like it, you would be foolish to not wear a protective vest. Since the vests would essentially destroy dress shirts, and since the other essential equipment typically worn in the field (duty belt with accessories) was harsh on any sort of dress clothing, the more relaxed attire was permitted. The next best part was that we were back to doing police work rather than spending the bulk of our shifts inside, buried in paperwork. Oh, and chicks dug us, apparently.

Sheehy, also known as Shamu—thanks to our good friend, Chuck Norris—was a big guy who had been blessed with speed. You would never expect it, but the man moved his large frame as quickly as any lightweight, though he was anything but that. Joe also played hockey. When we were partners, he still played as a member of the department's team, and in his early days he had played professionally on a minor league team. There he had been used as an enforcer, the guy who was sent onto the ice to take out a player from the other team, the hard way. He was a tough guy, strong as an ox, and he knew how to box. He made a great partner.

One night we were in the field when a disturbance call came over the radio. We were right around the corner from the location, and the address was one with which we were both familiar. The family there included two very large, very belligerent brothers, who, when drinking, were known to become violent. We turned the corner, planning to wait for the assigned patrol unit to arrive so we could back them up, but our plans quickly changed when we saw the two men fighting in the street—two water buffalo locking horns. Joe was driving, and he accelerated toward them, nonchalantly saying in his thick Boston accent, "Uh, we better break this up before one of these dummies gets hurt."

Joe hit the siren as we skidded to a stop for effect. We bailed out of the car and yelled some of that magical police shit at them: "Stop, freeze, break it up..." They turned and looked at us as if we were aliens. One of the two began walking directly at us. He veered in Joe's direction, which didn't disappoint me at all. This was about three-hundred pounds of pissed off drunk coming our way, and it wasn't going to end well. He was walking fast, at the verge of breaking into a trot. Joe hastened his pace, going directly at him—two bulls coming at each other with their heads down. When they were about six feet apart, Joe lunged forward with one arm held out straight like a running back pushing through the defense, and he planted the palm of his hand on the man's chest to stop him. He did so with so much force, and so quickly, that the huge, charging man was lifted from the ground, his feet coming out from beneath him. He landed flat on his back, his head hitting the pavement with an audible thwack. It was truly a thing of beauty, something you might see the actor Chuck Norris do in a movie.

Joe yelled, "Get up," and the moment he said it, he seemed to reconsider the order. "Stay down!" he commanded next. Then, "Turn around!" By now, we were all confused. Joe looked at me and grinned. He was always a joker, and even at a moment like this, he was able to have fun. He added—for my entertainment—"Now, uh, do the hokey pokey," and we both laughed heartily.

The two brothers were arrested for disturbing the peace and being drunk in public. Such an arrest would seldom occur in our jurisdiction without some other factor, in this case my partner having had to put his hands on one of the two drunks. Any hands on by then was considered a use of force, and the best practice in any such scenario was that the disturbing party went to jail. If Joe hadn't had to put one of the "dummies" on his ass, they likely would have only been issued a warning:

"Knock this shit off and go back in your house. If we have to come back, you're going to jail."

THERE IS ANOTHER STORY THAT WARRANTS TELLING THAT INVOLVES THAT big goon friend and partner of mine, the lovable man named Joey.

Before either of us were detectives, we each responded to a call early one afternoon in Firestone. Joe was working with Scott Fines. I can't recall who my partner might have been, though I clearly remember the details of the incident. The call was an assist DCS (Department of Children and Family Services) with the removal of children from an unfit home.

The mom was a crackhead, and her "baby daddy" was in jail. There were five kids, aging from a few months to about seven or eight years old. The mother of these terribly neglected children protested mightily—as any mother would—to the children being taken away from her, and my partner and I were dealing with her in the living room while Joe and Scott were in an adjacent bedroom tending to the kids. The small ramshackle home reeked of dirty diapers, stale beer, cigarette smoke, and body odor. Scott walked out of the room, shaking his head in disgust. He stopped near the threshold and lit a cigarette. I heard a baby crying and stepped over to see what was going on in the room, seeing the anger in Scotty's eyes as I moved past him. In the room, Joe stooped over a filthy mattress, changing the diaper of a terribly neglected infant. The diaper appeared to have not been changed in days.

When we walked out of the home, Scott said to his partner, "Don't ever change, Joey. You're a beautiful human being."

ON A SUNDAY NIGHT, MARCH 29, 1992, JUST TWO MONTHS BEFORE THE L.A. Riots started, Firestone Patrol Trainee Nelson Yamamoto was gunned down by an illegal alien. He had responded to a man with a gun call, accompanied by his training officer and two other deputies. They located two armed men in a detached garage at the location of the call.

The suspects emerged, and a fierce gunfight ensued. One of the two suspects was killed. Deputy Yamamoto was gravely wounded, and two days later he succumbed to his injuries. The suspect who shot him was able to escape, though he was later tracked down in New York where he was, thankfully, killed while trying to flee a state trooper.

This day was among the darkest in my career. Nelson Yamamoto, a 26-year-old with only three years on the department, was an enthusiastic, cheerful young man who was well on his way to making a terrific deputy sheriff. I will never forget the smile that seemed to always be on his face, even while he was being hazed as a trainee at Firestone.

My wife, Lesli (fiancée at the time), came to the station with me that night. All of us detectives were called in to assist in the manhunt. Several spouses had arrived, as had people who had previously worked at the station, and others who worked nearby. Lesli also attended the memorial services with me and experienced her first and only department funeral. Though there would be more, I didn't take her with me after her first. It was enough for her to see what she was getting herself into while there was still time to get herself out of spending her life with a cop. I knew she wouldn't, and she didn't.

In a matter of weeks, Lesli would be further burdened with fear as Los Angeles burned and violence spread throughout the southland, knowing I was in the thick of it all. To say she was baptized by fire might be one of the most appropriate uses ever of that cliché. She was obviously sent from heaven to be a cop's wife, because she endured more than her share and has stood with me through all of it. I happened to be that lucky cop. I am part of a minority of cops who can brag that they have had just one spouse, and that they are happily married after all these years. I am, indeed, blessed beyond what I deserve.

A few years later, May 12, 1995, another dark day came when Deputy Stephen Wayne Blair was shot and killed by a gang member in the city of Lynwood. By then, Firestone had merged with Lynwood to create Century station, and I was assigned to the Century night detective car and Crime Impact Team.

Whenever a colleague is killed in the line of duty, it affects the entire law enforcement community. The closer it hits to home, the greater the pain and grief. The death of any officer across the country brings sadness, sorrow, and reflection. When it happens in the same state or county where you work, there is an intensified effect. The death of a member of one's own department is similar to the death of a family member, and when it is someone with whom you had worked it is like losing a parent, a sibling, a child.

The night Steve was killed came at the end of a long stretch for me and my colleagues working on the Crime Impact Team, where we maintained somewhat of a flex schedule because of the nature of our investigative work. That Friday night, I headed home a couple of hours earlier than usual, having put in many more than 40 hours that week without compensation. I had just walked into my home north of Santa Clarita when my partner, Jeff Leslie, called to tell me that Steve had been shot, and that it didn't look like he would make it. I walked into the nursery and kissed the head of my sleeping daughter, the only child we had at that time—and choked back an emotion that suddenly welled up inside me. My wife saw me to the door and kissed me goodbye, grief in her eyes. She knew it would be a long night, a long weekend, a long month. She also knew the pain I would endure, and she would share in the grief as well. She had already seen much of the darkness that shadows the blue line.

By the time I arrived at the station, it had been confirmed that Steve had died. I rushed up to my office and put on my vest and raid jacket. Jeff came in from the field to pick me up, and drove me out to the scene. Steve had been transported to a hospital, but the evidence of his death remained on the filthy street where he had fallen. Jeff and I would later assist in collecting these things as the scene investigation wrapped up, and as I did—as I collected items that were stained with Steve's blood— the immensity of this tragedy consumed me, and those feelings and images have never subsided.

The rest of the night and into the next day, my teammates and I saturated the area in search of the suspect or anyone who might be harboring him. Others were doing the same. Soon the streets were empty, and that part of Lynwood was eerily silent, everyone staying indoors to avoid the cops. But that didn't deter us; we hit the homes of known gang members, motel rooms where we knew some stayed, crash pads where others could always be found. No member of that gang (which I will not acknowledge by naming it) was safe from our wrath that night, and many of them were snatched from the streets or their hideouts, and dragged to jail.

For the next several days, my partners and I worked around the clock, sleeping a few hours here and there at our desks or in the station bunk room. We were on the hunt for Steve's killer, who, by then, had been identified and named. We conducted surveillances, interviewed gang members and their affiliates, worked our informants, and did whatever the homicide detectives asked of us. At one point, we developed information about where the suspect might have been, and we immediately established a surveillance of that location while notifying Homicide about the development. The detective who was notified dismissed the notion, saying they had better information they were working on, and they needed us to assist them with it. Several days later, their information took them to that place we had told them about, and the resident admitted that the suspect had been there for several days—he had likely been there when we had pleaded with Homicide to hit it. The suspect was eventually captured, tried, and convicted of murder.

Steve was a well-respected deputy, a husband, and a father of three boys, and his loss—like all line-of-duty losses—was a tragic one. One of his sons would later follow in his father's footsteps and join the ranks of the Los Angeles County Sheriff's Department.

15

CENTURY STATION DETECTIVES
AND THE CRIME IMPACT TEAM

1994 -1996

W hen Firestone and Lynwood stations first merged, and before the detective night car became part of the Crime Impact Team, Bobby Reed and I were teamed up as the first Century detective night car. We had known each other since our days working in Custody, he at the Inmate Reception Center while I was assigned to Men's Central Jail next door, and we were friends. While I worked Firestone, he had worked at nearby Lynwood station. Once again, I was blessed with a great partner, one whom I would always consider a good friend, and whom God called home far too soon.

When the night car became part of the Crime Impact Team, Bobby and I not only handled the duties of a night car; we also, with the team, investigated everything from narcotics to vice laws, robberies and burglaries, and all violent crimes. We worked undercover arresting prostitutes, buying drugs, and doing surveillance. Eventually, Pat Tapia would become my partner in the night car as Bobby returned to day shift.

One afternoon, Pat and I learned that a car, stolen during the course of an armed robbery, had been located outside of an apartment complex in the south end of Firestone's area. The particular location was a stronghold for the Bebop Bloods, a black street gang. It wasn't an area where undercover cops could easily fit in to do surveillance, so we drove there in an undercover vehicle to see where the stolen car was parked, and to try to get some ideas of how we might be able to set up on it and wait for the bad guys to return.

When we arrived, we were pleased to see a county maintenance crew fixing something on the road north of the apartments. We hurried back to the station and scrounged up some hardhats and orange vests. We had a closet full of props for various situations, and somehow, we even came upon a can of orange spray paint. Pat and I drove an undercover Chevy Blazer to the location and parked on the sidewalk adjacent to where construction was underway, and surrounded our vehicle with orange cones. The "real" workers up the street watched us carefully, wondering who we were and what we were doing, but all of the residents of the area ignored us. We walked around in hardhats and orange vests and sprayed paint on a couple of curbs the way we had seen other workers do. Who knows what we might have screwed up by doing so. The real workers were frowning at us, but nobody ever said anything to us. They seemed to be confused by what we were doing and who we were, but with our confident demeanors, they might have been apprehensive to check. They probably assumed we were management—after all, we were at least that incompetent.

Meanwhile, our team members waited a couple of blocks away for something to happen, staged to respond when we requested them. Eventually, two thugs came out and loaded up in the stolen car and departed without a single glance in our direction. We tossed our paint and threw the helmets in the back, drove over the cones and off the curb, and the chase was on. With the help of our assisting partners and nearby patrol units, we were able to capture the crooks and take them to jail.

———

DURING A PERIOD OF NEARLY A YEAR, I DRAGGED MY TEAM MEMBERS ALL over Southern California in pursuit of a band of gypsies. The case had begun with a simple fraud report where a couple had agreed to rent a home and provided a deposit, only to find out that the family who rented them this home—a home that by then stood vacant, only a Christmas tree with fake presents left behind—didn't actually own it. In the first days of this investigation, we came upon dozens of others who had fallen victim to these gypsies, some who had also provided deposits to rent the home, and others who had been swindled out of their life savings by the woman who last lived there, a fortune teller. Her gimmick was foreseeing danger or bad health in store for those who sought her counsel, and always, evil money was determined to be the root of their problems. But fear not, if cash was left with her for several days, she could bless it and remove the evil spirits and return the cleansed money minus a very modest stipend. Though by the time the money was clean enough to be returned, the gypsies would have run their various scams on enough people that they could leave in the night with suitcases full of cash. It amazed me how many people fell victim to these thieves.

In pursuit of this band of gypsies, I had written no fewer than twenty search warrants, and we had served them at various homes, businesses, and storage facilities all over Los Angeles, San Bernardino, Riverside, and Orange Counties. But the suspects seemed to always be one step ahead of us, willing and able to walk away from anything at a moment's notice. We recovered thousands of dollars worth of stolen or embezzled property (upwards of $100,000 as I recall), and we had identified numerous others involved in similar scams, from various branches of the tribe. In the end, our tenacity paid off when we finally found the primary suspects and were able to place handcuffs on them. Though these people fit the definition of career criminals, literally being raised—and raising their offspring —in the arts of deception and fraud, none of them had criminal records. The problem (for law enforcement) was that their crimes were too small for us to routinely commit the attention to apprehending them that we had this time, and they moved so quickly that nobody could keep track of them. Another problem was that few of the victims would ever report these crimes, as many of them were undocumented themselves. Our efforts were rewarded with one felony filing that was quickly reduced to a misdemeanor, and the gypsies were free to continue bilking the public.

If not for the love of the hunt, an otherwise sane man might wonder why he worked so hard to make a difference in an ungrateful society and within a dysfunctional justice system.

A MOTHER AND DAUGHTER DISAPPEARED FROM THEIR HOME IN THE CITY OF Lynwood, part of our jurisdiction at Century station. I took the lead on the investigation and was assisted by my teammates, Jeff Leslie and Mike Arriaga. The mother had uncharacteristically missed work the day before, and likewise, the daughter hadn't shown up for school.

The protocol for handling missing person cases could seem strange to those outside of law enforcement. Without compelling reasons to do so—mental health, suspicious circumstances, et cetera—reports of missing adults were not taken until the adult had been missing for 72 hours. The reason for this is simple: adults are allowed to disappear if that is what they choose to do; there are no laws forbidding it. If an adult is at risk, say someone with Alzheimer's, that is a different story, and we not only take the report immediately, but a tremendous effort is put forth to find them. With missing juveniles, a report is taken in any circumstance, and the efforts to locate them begin right away.

In this case, it was immediately apparent that something terrible had happened. Two newspapers lay on the walkway to the front porch, that day's and the previous. The young girl's schoolbooks and backpack sat on a table inside, and the mother's personal belongings were left behind, items she would have taken with her on a planned trip. There were more than enough clues to warrant treating this as a possible worst-case scenario, a kidnapping or homicide. We sealed off the home and the alley behind it and called for a team of forensic investigators from the sheriff's crime lab. We also notified Homicide Bureau of what we were working on.

Not long into our investigation, we learned that an adult son of the missing woman had a criminal history involving drugs—possession and sales—so we began working on the theory that the victims (the mother and young daughter) may have been kidnapped for a debt that was owed. Kidnappings are handled by station detectives; kidnap for ransom cases are handled by the Metro detail of our Major Crimes Bureau, then known as the Special Investigations Bureau. So I made the notification, reluctantly, not wanting Detective Division to come in and take our case away from us. I was told to keep them posted and to be sure to let them know if a ransom demand was made.

The remainder of our team got involved, and soon we were interviewing relatives and friends all over the county. We established surveillance of places of interest where further crimes or contact might take place, and we placed recording devices on the phones of two relatives in the event that they might receive a call. At the crime scene, we collected numerous items of evidence, and the crime lab had collected fingerprints from inside the home and tire impressions from a patch of dirt in the dilapidated alley behind it. But now things were slowing down, and we found ourselves waiting for something to happen. That is when Metro called back to check on how things were going.

It was Dennis "Deac" Slocumb, the lieutenant in charge of Metro, a man whom I had worked under when he was a lieutenant at Firestone station. "Danny, what do you guys have going on down there?" He wanted a firsthand account. When I had made the notification, I spoke to one of his sergeants and provided the details known at that time. Deac called for an update and also to make personal contact, likely because he already knew me. It was then that he told me he was going to assemble his team and respond to Century station. "We'll monitor the case in the event it ends up coming here (being reassigned to Metro), and we'll be at your disposal in the meantime, available to assist you with whatever you need."

It sounded great, but still, I feared they would take the case away from me. This was an interesting case—potentially a very tragic one—and I didn't want to lose it. They arrived a short time later, Slocumb and one of his sergeants, along with five or six investigators who wore jeans and boots, beards and ponytails. Their arrival was on par with that of *The Magnificent Seven* if only the theme song had been played over the loudspeaker. These were the big leaguers, Detective Division—SPI/Metro! Fears of losing the case to them aside, this was going to be a great experience. Though I had no idea, at that moment, just how great it would be.

We were several days into it when a call came in demanding a payout. Now we had a kidnap for ransom case, and it would no longer be mine to handle. Deac broke the bad news that my case was being reassigned to Metro, but then he told me I would be staying with it. Deac had told his captain that none of his guys knew the case as intimately as I did, having taken it from the first steps, and that it would be beneficial to have me go on loan to Metro until its conclusion. Their captain made the arrangements with mine, and on to the big leagues I went, if only for a few weeks.

The case had a successful conclusion that made department history. The mother and daughter were safely recovered after being held captive for 64 days, thanks to the great work of Metro. I had only stayed on loan to them for a couple of weeks before my captain wanted me back, but my good fortune had just begun. At about the time I was preparing for my return to Century, Slocumb told me they had an opening coming up, and he hoped I would apply to come to SPI. I was flattered, honored, and beyond excited. I had just recently put in my first application to Homicide Bureau, but everyone knew it took several attempts to get there, if you ever did—because they were the elite of the elite. So going to SPI would put me in Detective Division (rather than being a detective in Patrol Division), and it would give me that much more of an edge in getting into Homicide someday. At least, that's how I saw it at the time.

What I hadn't expected was that all of my stars seemed to be aligned and shining at once.

I applied to SPI and went through the process, which included an oral interview, something I seemed to always do well at. I was comfortable and confident, and at one point, I had the interview board laughing. One of the interviewers noted that on my application, I had indicated that I spoke "some" Spanish, and he asked how fluent I was. I looked each board member in the eye and said, "Do any of you speak Spanish?" Each shook their head. I said, "Then I'm fluent."

Not long after, I received a call from the operations lieutenant at Homicide, who informed me I had made the list of ten candidates to go to Homicide. I couldn't believe it because, as I had said, it was very unusual to make the list for Homicide on your first application. But there was more. He said, "You're also on the list to go to Special Investigations." I hadn't yet heard that news and it was almost unbelievable. But what would I do? This was terrible because I now would be faced with a decision. What a great mess to be in! Before I could spend much time pondering this dilemma, he told me they had already worked out a solution. The lieutenant from Homicide said, "It takes us a year to get all ten people here off a list, and the list expires in one year whether or not all ten are transferred in. Why don't you go to SPI for a year, and we'll put you at the bottom of our list. You'll come in a year, or the list will expire, and you can apply again. Then we'll put you first on the next list."

I was stunned. I didn't know what to say. So he added another detail. "We've already worked it out with Slocumb."

It seemed almost too simple for the gigantic, cumbersome machine that is the Los Angeles County Sheriff's Department. Nothing was that easy. I said, "You can do that?"

I could almost hear him smiling through the phone. "This is Detective Division. We can do whatever we want."

16

SPECIAL INVESTIGATIONS BUREAU METRO DETAIL

SEPTEMBER 1996

My first day at the STARS Center office in Whittier was spent completing administrative paperwork for my new assignment, "a job so secret"—as one logo t-shirt professed—"even I don't know what I'm doing."

They assigned me Bureau number 558, and informed me that I would no longer be listed in the department personnel records due to the undercover work done there and the sensitivity of some of the cases investigated. If someone were to call sheriff's headquarters to verify my employment, the person who answered the call would not be able to find me in their database, and the caller would be told that no, I do not work for the sheriff's department. The way around that was to list the unit commander's direct number on any such application where verification of employment would be required. This was something that was unique to Special Investigations Bureau, and perhaps a nod to the unit's acronym: SPI.

I was directed to an old metal desk, one of about eight crammed into a relatively small space that was our primary squad room. They issued me a handheld radio and a take-home car, a 5.0 Mustang that had red and blue lights hidden behind the grille, a siren, and a hardwired sheriff's radio concealed in the glove box. I had never felt cooler in my life.

Special Investigations Bureau comprised several details: Metro—where I was assigned—Prison Gangs, Surveillance, Organized Crime, and Vice. There were close to a hundred total personnel, and at the end of that first week most of us gathered for a bureau meeting in what might have been called the quad, when this particular campus was Whittier High. Chief Helena Ashby—who was greatly respected by the bulk of Detective Division personnel—led the meeting with an award ceremony. Those in the bureau who had worked on the famous "Ruby" kidnap case —the Century case that had been mine until a ransom demand caused it to be taken over by Metro—were called to the front where they joined the chief and had bestowed upon them grandiose awards and commendations for their great work on that case. And they deserved it, but I have to be honest and tell you how disappointed I was not to be included. My pity party was short lived, however, as I remembered that my efforts had been recognized by those who mattered, and I had been duly rewarded by an assignment to Metro, something for which hundreds strive but never attain.

FUGITIVE APPREHENSION WAS FILLER WORK FOR THE METRO DETAIL. TO ME, there was nothing worse than sitting around the office waiting for something to happen; I wanted to be busy. The nature of our work at Metro, in large part, was responsive. The cases we handled were all "in progress"—murder for hire, kidnap for ransom, life-threatening extortion, escapes from custody, and threats against public officials. Someone was kidnapped, we'd go to work. Bad guys escaped from custody, we'd start hunting. A judge was threatened, we'd set up around-the-clock protection while investigating the source and credibility of the threat. And so on. But also, Metro detail had absorbed the duties of the then-defunct (due to budget cuts) Fugitive detail. There were file cabinets full of felony arrest warrants to be served at will, and I always kept a dozen or so in my briefcase for fun and adventure. I lived in the north part of the county, and SPI was headquartered at about the worst place it could be, Whittier. (You couldn't get there from anywhere!) So I would generally take warrants for north county fugitives which would allow me to start my time early in the morning with warrant service close to home, or give me a reason to head north earlier in the afternoon.

The funny thing about police work, though, is that sometimes those "adventures" could be more than one bargained for.

There was a warrant for a doper who lived near Gorman in the far north part of our county. It was up in the mountains where sometimes I'd take my dog to go hunting, though I hadn't done so for quite some time. But I knew the general area and thought it would be a nice way to spend the afternoon, a little mountain drive and a fugitive arrest. On the map, it seemed to be just a short distance from civilization. The map had deceived me.

Two hours after leaving Whittier, I was checking my cell phone every few miles, hoping I would again see a signal as I snaked through the mountain on roads that hadn't been maintained very well over the years. I checked my handheld radio too, but nobody seemed to pick up my transmissions. I had climbed in elevation for thirty minutes when I began thinking I was lost. There couldn't be any homes this far out in the middle of nowhere!

The pavement ended, and I continued driving on a rough gravel road in my county-issued Ford Mustang, an undercover cop car that was good for speed, cornering, and looking cool, but not for mountain driving on dirt roads. I stopped as a six-foot rattlesnake crawled across the road in front of me, accentuating the absurdity of my being there. Though I have a fear of rattlesnakes, I am fascinated by them too, and I like to watch them from safe distances. And as I watched this giant rattler slither away, it occurred to me that this whole trip may have been a mistake.

However, anyone who knows me at all knows that once I've set my mind to something, I'm hard to stop. So on I went, and finally I rounded a corner and came upon a two-story house standing on a flat lot, nestled in the tall pines atop the rocky mountain. Gravel crunched beneath my tires as I inched toward the home, checking my warrant once more to remind myself of the name and physical description of the wanted man. Scanning the home and its surroundings, I noticed two children staring from an upstairs window. They were probably five or six and both had snow-white hair and expressionless faces. Neither wore a shirt. It was difficult to say what gender they were, which mattered back in those days. It was creepy, like something out of a Stephen King novel.

My attention was drawn from the strange children when a pack of dogs—there were a dozen or more, some breed of hounds—ran off the porch and surrounded my car, barking viciously as I came to a stop directly in front of the place. The front door flung open and a woman ran out screaming at the dogs. She was the age of a young mother, fairly attractive—in a white trash tweaker sort of way—and stark naked.

Suddenly she noticed my presence and froze for a long moment. Maybe not long enough. But time seemed to stop or maybe it only felt that way, and eventually, she seemed to realize a man was sitting in his car staring at her. They apparently weren't accustomed to visitors dropping in on them at their remote mountain home, even in the middle of the afternoon. She turned and walked back into the house, but in no real hurry. The door closed behind her and I glanced up to see the mannequin-like children hadn't moved. The dogs had followed the naked woman to the front door, and it seemed like a reasonable course of action for me, too. After all, I was committed at this point, and quite curious now too—though still a little creeped out about the whole affair.

The dogs were sniffing at me as I stood to the side of the front door and knocked. In a moment, the woman answered it. She was blonde. I hadn't noticed that before. She was now wrapped in a red checked flannel shirt that was too big for her. Too big for Shaq, to be honest about it. She asked what I wanted, so I flashed my badge and mentioned the fugitive by name. She was shaking her head to indicate she didn't know him as a voice boomed from behind her, "Who the fuck is that?"

The thought went through my mind that this was exactly how cops got themselves killed, getting in over their heads when nobody knew where they were and having no way to call for help, just as the man with the booming voice appeared at the door. He stood behind her, though it would have taken six of her to conceal him. He was wider than she was tall, and the top of his head was above the frame of the door. He had long straggly hair and a wild beard, a mountain man-outlaw biker hybrid. He glared at me with his beady eyes as she finally answered him, saying, "It's the cops." *Plural.*

What a great idea, I thought. She thinks there's more than one of me, and I sure wished it were the case. But either way, she thought so, and I hoped he would too. I raised my handheld radio that was of no other value to me than a bluff, and said, "It's code four up front, guys, just hold your positions."

The mountain man was saying, "What the fuck does he want?", talking to *his* woman but glaring at me. I was working on an exit strategy, which by then had become the single most important thing to me in the world. I wanted to be off the mountain and back in civilization, home with the family I might not ever see again. Suddenly it seemed I heard banjos playing, and this big asshole in front of me was now pushing the woman aside and taking over, his presence alone demanding I answer the question that she hadn't.

The description of my suspect was 5-07, 140 pounds. This wasn't him —thank God!—and I figured the odds were the man on the warrant didn't even live there. And that became my first strategy in the leaving-here-alive plan. If the description on the warrant had been "big as a house and ugly as an ape," I would have lied and told him I was looking for Peter Pan. I surely wouldn't have suggested I was there to arrest *him*. I mentioned the name on the warrant and said, "Obviously *we* have the wrong address, so me and the troops will leave you fine folks alone." I mean, it was mid-afternoon and everyone here was naked. I didn't care what they had planned for the rest of the day, as long as I wasn't included in those plans. My legs bumped dogs to clear a path as I retreated, thanking the meth cook for his time and wondering what good my nine-millimeter would do if he charged.

When I started the car, I noticed the two children still gazed from the upstairs window. The mountain man stood watching from his porch. The woman was no longer in sight, and the dogs meandered about, having lost interest in the whole ordeal. I turned the car around and started driving away, envisioning crosshairs on the back of my head until I made the corner and hit the gas. Gravel flew and a cloud of dust accentuated my departure. I began laughing as I raced off the mountain, feeling good to be alive. That short time with the Clampetts had been an exhilarating couple of minutes.

The next morning, I told the story to the team while sipping coffee in the comfort of our office. My lieutenant, Deac Slocumb, grinned while listening to the details, and I knew he'd have something entertaining to say about it once I finished.

He didn't disappoint. "You do know," he said, in his methodical manner of speech, "that if you would've gotten yourself killed, the whole department would wonder what the fuck you were thinking by going up there alone. I'd just shrug and say I had no idea."

Fugitive work also included extraditions. We would fly around the country to pick up prisoners and bring them back to L.A. County. Usually, the person had absconded or violated probation or parole. Sometimes it would be for cases that hadn't yet been adjudicated. On one occasion, my partner and I flew to the maximum-security federal prison in Colorado to bring a mafia hitman back to testify against his former colleagues. It was considered an extremely high-risk transportation for a number of reasons, primarily due to the threat of a hit against him while he was in our custody. He was an older gentleman, late sixties, who was polite, cooperative, and intelligent. Truthfully, he was one of the more pleasant prisoners I ever transported.

We flew commercial on these trips, yet none of the other passengers ever knew what we were doing. Most airlines wouldn't allow prisoners to be handcuffed during a flight, so we would place on them either a leg brace—a mechanical device that would lock when they stood, designed to slow them down if they ran—or a high-voltage stun belt, operated by a remote control that either my partner or I would carry. Since we were armed, we would be pre-boarded and seated in the very last row, and never served alcohol. Most of us would explain to our prisoners that if they caused any problems on the plane we would be forced to rent a vehicle and drive them back to L.A. This was something we never wanted to do, as you had to map your trip to stop every eight hours and spend the night somewhere with a jail that would hold your prisoner overnight. Because that was the last thing we wanted to do, I would threaten the prisoner that if we had to drive rather than fly, he would ride in the trunk of our rental car the entire trip.

Thankfully, the only trip I ever made where we had to drive the prisoner back had been a turn-around trip to Vegas. Three of us flew out to bring two back, one of whom was a former deputy sheriff who had been convicted on a charge of rape under the color of authority after using his badge to get sexual favors from prostitutes. He had been given probation but had absconded to Nevada for work in the construction field. Now he was facing serious jail time.

The other prisoner, a young black man facing dope charges, had protested at the idea of being flown back, stating that he couldn't fly. There were people who had never been on a plane before and were terrified because of it, the type more likely to use buses to move around the country if they didn't have their own transportation. They would make up a dozen reasons why they couldn't fly, or they'd tell you straight that they were scared to death to get on a plane and there was no way they were going to. We gave this guy the standard warning about riding in the trunk, but he was adamant that he couldn't fly. He said, "I ain't even playin', man—I can't even go on rides at Magic Mountain without passing out." That's when we knew he was serious.

So we rented a van and hauled both men home from Vegas. The black guy was fast asleep in no time, so we got to hear the whole story about the deputy sheriff with a thing for prostitutes and who had been too stupid to keep it in his pants and too cheap to pay for it.

One thing about traveling on the county dime, you didn't have much time to see anything. But cops are cheap, so we would try to do as much as we could in the few short hours we had available to us. Most trips were overnighters, so if you flew out early one day, you'd have a few hours that afternoon and evening for sightseeing. Occasionally, we'd even take a red-eye to give us more time, a whole day to see the sights. I saw the Grand Ole Opry in Nashville, and though it was closed, we were able to go inside and see the stage where many legends of country music had performed. I visited the Rodeo Hall of Fame in Colorado (while there picking up the mobster), drove through the Chesapeake Bay Bridge tunnel in Virginia, and walked around the perimeter of Wrigley Field in November when the ground was covered with snow, and the Chicago winds blew through every layer of clothing I wore. I visited AT&T Stadium in Dallas and a rattlesnake museum in New Mexico. I've mentioned my strange fascination and fear of snakes; well, the snake museum tour was creepy and also enchanting. I must have spent two hours there. On one trip, I went for a jog without the benefit of knowing the neighborhood through which I would run, and I found myself in the middle of a housing project, the only white person in sight. Two-thousand miles from home, yet the residents were saying, "Five-oh" while their children said, "Hi Poh-lees."

THE ONE MEMORABLE ESCAPE FROM CUSTODY CASE WE HANDLED WHILE I was assigned to Metro was that of an accused murderer who broke out of the maximum-security housing unit at the Peter J. Pitchess Detention Center in Castaic. The desperado had, over time, bored through a concrete wall, and on the night of his escape, he and three others made it out of the building and across the field. However, only he, the most desperate of the lot, made it over the twenty-foot, razor-wire-topped chain link fence to freedom. We would later learn from him that while the search teams were ramping up, he had traveled through the rugged country surrounding the facility until he reached the truck stop located several miles north. He stowed away inside one of a dozen cars loaded onto a carrier, which ended up taking him 200 miles north to Fresno. There he called his sister and asked her to come get him and take him to L.A. to see his woman. The sister pleaded with him to turn himself in, fearful that he would be killed during his capture.

There are several things that happen during an escape: the custody facility goes on complete lockdown and an inmate count is initiated while searches and a variety of other processes begin. All local law enforcement agencies are alerted. An intense search is undertaken involving SWAT, canine, and a plethora of various deputies, officers, and agents. Our job at Metro was to take an investigative approach to locating the fugitive. While cops with dogs and guns and flashlights were beating the brush, my partner and I scoured the escapee's jail records, including his approved visitors list, his criminal history report, and any other data we could research that might reveal associates and family members. We interviewed the others who had attempted to escape with him, and those who hadn't but were housed with him or near him in the custody facility.

We contacted LAPD, the arresting agency in the murder case of which he was charged, in order to obtain details that might help us determine where to look for him if he wasn't caught on or near the grounds.

We learned that the escapee had killed two bikers in the San Fernando Valley and that the motive had involved drug sales. It was said that he was a very dangerous man who wouldn't be taken alive. Judging by what he endured to make his escape we believed it, and we were prepared for a violent conclusion.

It had to be the girlfriend. That's what my partner, John Loftus, and I concluded would be the key to finding and apprehending him. There was one woman who was a regular visitor, and she would be our target. She lived in the south bay area of Los Angeles County, an hour's drive south of the jail and four hours from Fresno. We hadn't been set up at her house for long when a car arrived, driven by a woman and with a man sitting low in the passenger seat. The vehicle slowed, and then the man seemed to have identified our surveillance of his girlfriend's house, as he suddenly ducked down in his seat.

The woman tried to drive away, but we quickly boxed her in with a tactic—not often used nor likely authorized today—called a flying angels maneuver. One of us went ahead of her vehicle and stopped her forward movement while others pulled along both sides and also blocked the back. They had no place to go—now we just hoped he hadn't had a chance to arm himself since his escape. The downside to the maneuver was setting yourselves up in a crossfire configuration. But we moved fast and aggressively, four men in jeans and ball caps with vests that identified us as cops and guns that accentuated the point. He gave up without any resistance whatsoever, and within hours after he had escaped, Metro had the killer back in custody.

The driver turned out to be his sister, and she told me that her brother had called her from Fresno and asked for a ride. She said she had begged him to turn himself in, and he assured her that he would after seeing his girlfriend just one more time before spending the rest of his life in prison. The suspect hadn't heard his sister's statement to me, yet he told me the same story when I interviewed him next. The sister worked as a paralegal at a law firm, was educated, had no prior brushes with the law, but now she was going to be arrested for aiding and abetting her brother's escape. It wasn't my decision—in fact, I had argued against it.

This fugitive may have been the second coolest killer I ever met—the first, of course, being the mafia man whom I had brought down from a federal prison in Colorado. As I transported the suspect to jail, he chatted with me as casually as if we were seated at a bar. He thanked me for our professionalism in how we treated him and his sister, and he asked only for leniency for her. I told him that it was out of my hands.

Later I would be called to testify in the trial of his escape and the sister's aiding and abetting, the two siblings as co-defendants in the case. The escapee's murder trial was yet to be held. When I met with the prosecutor that morning to discuss my testimony, I told her that I thought it was chickenshit to prosecute the sister. I felt that this was exactly the type of case where the spirit of the law should have taken precedence over the letter of the law. Prosecute the actual escapee and give the sister immunity if she testifies against her brother—that was my suggestion. But the prosecutor would have none of it, and I knew then that this prosecutor was trying to make a name for herself. I wasn't surprised to see her rise through the ranks and eventually run for the office of District Attorney. She lost her bid for the top seat, but I have no idea if she won or lost her overzealous prosecution of the killer's sister. I wasn't about to stay around after testifying, given the looks she gave me as I stepped down from the stand. She had been careful to ask only those questions of which the answers would establish that the killer had indeed escaped from custody, and that we had arrested him after seeing his sister driving him to his girlfriend's home, and not toward a jail or a police station to turn him in. But the defense attorney—apparently operating on good insight—asked me about the sister's intent. The prosecutor objected, but the defense attorney rightly argued that both she and her brother had told me what their intentions were that day. The judge allowed me to answer, and I did. I told the details of their separate statements and concluded with, "She didn't do anything my own sister wouldn't have done for me."

172

Sheriff Sherman Block received a call from a personal friend of his, an attorney named Joe, who told the sheriff that his life was in danger. The attorney's business partner had hired someone to kill him, and this hired killer was trying to extort money from Joe to keep him from fulfilling the contract. In other words, the hitman was working both sides for cash. He was doing so because he was no killer at all, just a two-bit hustler and wannabe pimp. Joe had first called LAPD's Pacific Division, the police responsible for the jurisdiction where his office is located, and wherein the hustler had contacted him personally. The officer he spoke with told him he would need to speak with the detectives, who were gone for the day and wouldn't be back until Monday. Joe, a bit incensed by LAPD's lack of concern on the matter, called his friend, Sheriff Block. The sheriff assured him that his department would take care of it. *The bear goes everywhere.*

Metro got the call, and our team was quickly assembled on a Friday afternoon. We worked through the weekend, first interviewing Joe, the would-be victim, and then devising a plan. Joe would set another meeting with the hustler, and we would be waiting in the shadows, watching, listening, recording. Once he demanded money again, we would pop him for extortion. And that's exactly what we did.

Then it was time to turn this pimp into a snitch because it was the attorney who hired him that we wanted most. Pimp-daddy said the man who hired him had contacted him through a friend and offered him ten thousand to murder his former business partner. The pimp was no killer, but he knew a good hustle when he saw it. The attorney was old and naive to the ways of *the street,* and the hustler figured he could easily play him. But now Pimp-daddy was going to play with us, having quickly rolled over and agreed to set up the attorney who hired him.

With the help of a makeup artist, we staged a death scene on a brushy hillside. Joe was pictured sprawled among the weeds with gunshot wounds to his chest. Polaroid photographs were taken and would be provided to Pimp-daddy at the time of the next act, along with Joe's wallet for added proof and authenticity. But this wasn't all done in an afternoon; it wouldn't have been realistic to do so. We set up in a hotel and had to babysit the hustler while the wheels of our plan turned slowly. The dude started asking for special meals, room service, conjugal visits—the works. I wasn't the only one who was ready to throw him out the window by the time we finally had an appointment with the dirty attorney.

The attorney chose the meeting place, a restaurant on Larchmont Street in West Los Angeles. It was close to his home, and apparently, he didn't want to be inconvenienced by having to travel far away. Or perhaps he wanted to remain in a safe part of town so that his hired killer couldn't do him in too. Larchmont Street was a lofty little region full of boutiques and trendy restaurants with patio dining and blue-haired women with thousand-dollar purses. The attorney, clearly an educated man, apparently didn't think about standing out in a crowd when he met up with a dude from South Los Angeles who drove a lowered Lincoln town car and wore a burgundy-colored sharkskin suit. But as if that didn't parade the attorney's stupidity, when he met with the hustler, he paid him in cash, discussed the case, and accepted as proof the photograph of his business partner posed as dead. The attorney was elated with the job he believed the hired killer had done. The hustler offered the attorney Joe's wallet, and the attorney told him he could keep it. This man had practiced law for fifty years, yet he was going to allow a hustler to run around using a dead guy's credit cards, never considering that he would eventually be popped and the case would unravel and land on his doorstep—if it had actually happened. The attorney would be found in possession of photographic evidence linking him to the murder.

During the meeting, the hustler was wired for sound and surrounded by undercover deputies. I had to stay in the surveillance truck because, as my lieutenant would say, I looked too scary to fit in at a place like that. He had once said of my undercover facade that I appeared more like someone who should be walking the yard at San Quentin, than some of them who actually were. From inside the surveillance truck, the entire meeting was videotaped, and we were able to watch it unfold on a monitor therein. Arresting the attorney was one of the most enjoyable busts in which I had ever participated. A close second might have been when, right after handcuffing the attorney, we hooked up Mr. Pimp-daddy. He protested mightily, nearly crying about the situation, as he had mistakenly thought we were all on the same team and he was going to walk away unscathed.

THE YEAR FLEW BY, AND BEFORE I KNEW IT, I WAS ON MY WAY TO HOMICIDE. I left a great crew behind, some of the best guys I had ever worked with, many with whom I am still close friends: Deac Slocumb and Bobby Waters, to name two of my favorites. Paul Larson, one of my sergeants, always took good care of me, and I was humbled when he tried to bribe me with a brand new (county) car to stay at SPI rather than go to Homicide. But Homicide had been calling my name for many years, and as much as I loved Metro and Special Investigations Bureau, I had to go.

I have often said that I left the best job in the county to be a homicide detective.

PART IV

HOMICIDE BUREAU

THE BULLDOGS

17

BACK TO BEING A BOOT

SEPTEMBER 1997

Before I had a chance to grab a cup of coffee or find my desk, I received my first assignment as a homicide detective. A 16-year-old boy had been struck and killed by a train in the City of Industry.

It was a chilly fall morning, and I had made the mistake of arriving at the office at seven, long before most homicide detectives would stroll in. At Special Investigations, we started early; six was the norm. When my soon-to-be partner at Homicide told me to come in around nine, I thought he had either misspoken, that I had misheard him, or that he was setting me up. There was no way I was going to come in late for work on my first day at Homicide Bureau. *Nine o'clock?*

As it turned out, most of the detectives assigned to Homicide show up at the office between eight and nine, some later. There are many reasons for it, but the biggest one by far is that you never knew when you'd be out all the next night. That extra hour or two in the morning can make a difference with the fatigue factor.

But taking no chances, I walked into the bureau early on the first day of my new assignment and was greeted at the front desk by Paul Delhauer, a deputy I had known from Century Station. He said, "Are you here now?" meaning had I been assigned to the bureau. He had likely known I was on the list to come there, but he wouldn't have known when I was to start. I told him I was and that it was my first day. "Good," he said, "I need you to roll out to Industry on a train versus ped (pedestrian)."

I knew how to investigate crimes by the time I walked through the back door at the Los Angeles County Sheriff's Homicide Bureau; it was why I was there. But this was a case involving the death of a young man, and I'd be lying if I said anything other than that it felt overwhelming at first to be the only one handling it. There's a homicide creed which states, in part, that no greater honor or responsibility is bestowed upon a detective than to investigate the death of a human being. Truer words have never been spoken.

"Paul, I don't have a clue how to handle something like that. I just drove up, man. I don't expect my partner to be here for another two hours."

He smiled and said, "It's no big deal. You can handle it. And it would be a big help because I have nobody else to send—I'd have to call someone in from home. My partner's out on another suicide."

"Is that what this is, a suicide?"

"I don't know. That's why you're going out there, to figure it out."

Great, I thought. But I was never one to shy away from a challenge, and I wasn't about to say, "I can't." In fact, I had long before stricken that phrase from my vocabulary. So I jotted the address on a piece of scratch pad and went right back through that door where my personal vehicle awaited me. I sat in my car and transferred the notes I had scribbled on scratch paper into a brand-new Homicide notebook—my first of many. I wrote down the address of my destination, the time I received the call and from whom I had received it, and every word Paul had told me about the case. Then I made a notation of the time I departed the office, and off to Industry I went.

When I arrived, the Industry station patrol deputy who had handled the call briefed me on his actions and observations preceding my arrival. I took copious notes as he told me what time he had received the call, when he had arrived, and what he had observed upon his arrival—parts of the decedent's body and his personal property strewn a quarter mile along the tracks. He turned and pointed to a distant landmark. "There's a shoe with his foot down there. That's the farthest body part we've located. I think we've found all the pieces," he said, absent emotion as if talking about parts of a wrecked car. Reflecting back, it amazes me that we (cops) held all of our "pieces" together as well as we mostly did. I nodded, jotted some notes, and went on as if it was just another day at the office, or perhaps it was a wrecked car rather than a young teenage boy that had been scattered about.

There were several witnesses, including the train's conductor, all from whom the deputy had obtained brief statements. The witnesses said the deceased teen had exited a city bus with his backpack and walked directly from the bus across the tracks just as the train arrived. The boy had ignored, disregarded, or somehow been oblivious to the warnings of the crossing gates with their flashing signals and loud bells and the train's ear-piercing whistle. It was either a fatal, tragic mistake or a sad and desperate way to end a life.

I met with the conductor and played it straight, telling him I'd been a homicide detective for about—I glanced at my watch—forty minutes, and I knew less about trains than I did about investigating death. "So," I told him, "you're going to need to tell me everything about this machine you drive, including the length, weight, number of cars, speed traveled, distance it took to stop, all operator protocols and procedures for approaching intersections, your experience, time behind the wheel today, destination, where your trip began, the distance you've traveled, amount of sleep you had last night or whenever it is you last slept, and everything you saw and did here this morning. Then I'll want to speak with the copilot."

First off, there is no wheel. Secondly, the "copilot" is called the engineer. After we got that out of the way, I learned more about trains than I ever needed to know. The conductor was a bundle of shattered nerves, and it seemed that talking about his beloved train helped him through the moment. I noted everything he said in excruciating detail.

A couple of hours later, I had finished with the scene investigation and now had the somber duty to notify the dead boy's parents. As a patrol deputy, I had borne this burden on several occasions, but this would be my first as a homicide detective. The first of many more to come—more than I could count—where I would stand in someone's living room with a blue notebook in my hand to first deliver the horrible news that they had lost a loved one—suddenly, often violently—and then to ask the questions that needed to be answered for my investigation. It was difficult then, and it never did become any easier.

This case was ruled an accident. There was no information or evidence to suggest it was suicide. That seemed to make it easier for the family; nobody wants to think a loved one killed themselves because then a search for blame would necessarily follow, even if only silently. But I've always questioned the final ruling of that case. How much could be going on in a teen's life that the entire outside world would be tuned out to the point he wouldn't see nor hear a train? But sometimes, you don't need all the answers to move on. This was one of those times.

MY NEWLY ASSIGNED TRAINING OFFICER SET THE TONE FOR HOW THE NEXT several months would be when I returned to the office later that day. In short, he chewed my ass and told me I wasn't to do anything without his direction or approval. Here I had thought my efforts might have been appreciated and that the job I had done would have served as an example of my investigative skill. Sure, there were things to learn with death investigation, but I had a foundation when I arrived—as all investigators did—and that foundation was a solid one. This new partner of mine had a reputation for being difficult to get along with, and I had to remain humble and play his game in order to survive. For the third time in my career, I was a "boot" on training status again.

The cases came quickly at the bureau, the county handling between 300-500 homicide cases each year, and many more non-criminal death investigations: suicide, industrial, recreational, and accidental deaths. There were approximately 80 investigators to handle the caseload, divided among six teams. Each team comprised five to six pairs of partners and a lieutenant. Unlike some departments, and unlike the way most homicide units are portrayed on film, the lieutenants at our homicide bureau were administrators. Some of them had no investigative experience, and they didn't need it; they were not there to tell the detectives how to investigate their cases.

Los Angeles County encompasses 4,751 square miles and is the single most populous county in the United States with its ten million residents. There are 88 incorporated cities within the county, 42 of which contract with the sheriff's department for their law enforcement needs. In other words, the sheriff's department not only polices all unincorporated areas within the county, but it also handles all of the functions of policing for those 42 cities. Compton, Santa Clarita, Industry, Lakewood, West Hollywood, Malibu, Marina del Rey, Palmdale, and Lancaster are just a few of the cities that contract the services of LASD.

There are 23 sheriff's stations spread across the county. Each has its own captain who essentially acts as a chief of police for that jurisdiction, though he/she falls under the command structure, which is, in ascending order: the area commander, a division chief, the two assistant sheriffs, an undersheriff, and the sheriff of the county. Each station is staffed by patrol deputies and station detectives; however, Homicide Bureau handles all unnatural deaths and deputy-involved shooting cases within those jurisdictions.

There are also cities within L.A. County that have their own police departments, complete with patrol officers and detectives—El Monte, Monterey Park, and Pomona, to name a few—yet who still rely on the sheriff's department to investigate some of their murders and their officer-involved shootings.

So as one might see, the centralized Homicide Bureau and its 80 detectives can be spread thin throughout the county. Some might argue that a decentralized bureau would be more effective; however, homicide investigation is best handled by the most experienced detectives a department has to offer. The combined knowledge and experience among this pool of 80 detectives is unmatched, and that is how the above-average detectives who are fortunate enough to be assigned there often become among the best detectives anywhere. You didn't have to be so great yourself when you worked in a place that was saturated with such greatness. Sometimes you would learn more in an hour-long conversation with a guy like Mike Bumcrot, who spent four decades at Homicide and investigated thousands of cases, than detectives elsewhere could learn in a lifetime.

Following the train vs. pedestrian case, I was detailed to spend a week at the coroner's office. That was a great learning experience but also a long, miserable week. My hat is off to the coroner's investigators, who see a hundred times the death that homicide detectives see, though their participation in each case is far less extensive and more narrowly focused. At any rate, that first week provided me the opportunity to see firsthand coroners' investigations at a dozen or more death scenes, and it allowed me to observe scores of autopsies. As a homicide detective, you attend the autopsies of your murder case victims, and you stand tableside to closely observe all aspects of the process. This benefits the investigator with intimate knowledge of his case, but it can also be a crucial part of the medical examination. For instance, there were times when the examiner would be trying to determine the origin of a particular wound, and the investigator would have knowledge gained from the scene or from eyewitnesses that allowed him to answer those questions.

With that first week behind me and now already with dozens of deaths under my belt, it was time to start working on cases.

OVER THE NEXT FEW WEEKS, MY PARTNER AND I INVESTIGATED SEVERAL murders, an inmate death, an officer-involved shooting, a couple of suicides, and a natural death. It was the latter that topped them all in the Most Memorable category. Up to that point in my career I had seen scores of death scenes, but I had never before experienced the stench of a decomposing body that had been undiscovered in a home for several weeks. The neighbors called the police only after they could no longer bear the odor.

The stench gagged me and stole my breath. Who wanted to breathe anyway? Not me. Not then. Not in that place at that time. I went outside a few times during the course of our investigation to catch my breath, but each time I did, it made it that much more difficult to return to the body to continue the investigation.

The decedent was a homeless woman who had sought shelter in the corner of a barren room at the back of a vacant home. Maggots surrounded her bloated body, and when the coroner's investigator turned her over, the floor became a sea of white waves rolling outward, away from the corpse and toward me. I stood my ground, though I seriously contemplated doing otherwise.

We were issued breathing apparatus at Homicide to be used at these types of scenes and also while on the service floor of the coroner's office. My partner had told me to keep cheap perfume on hand for just these types of occasions (though I'm not sure my wife fully bought into that scheme), but it didn't work. The idea was that you would spray a few shots into your mask before entering such a scene, hoping to override the assailing odors. Some detectives would smoke a cigar or rub Vick's under their nostrils, but I don't think anything would have masked the smell of that bloated, rotten corpse. Since then, I have been in the presence of hundreds of corpses, including those in various stages of decomposition, but I have never since endured such a horrific odor while processing a crime scene, one that literally gagged me.

The worst part of it is that I sometimes involuntarily recall the smell of decomposing flesh. As my daughters grew up and became fascinated with shows like NCIS, I could hardly bear to watch certain scenes, especially the ones that showed autopsies. People who watch these shows consider these scenes merely a part of the entertainment, but to those of us who have known death intimately, such scenes—as accurately as many are now depicted—often cause us to recall horrible experiences. My father, a war veteran, could never enjoy war movies. I finally understood the reason for it.

I HAD BEEN AT THE BUREAU FOR ABOUT A MONTH WHEN A DEPUTY SHERIFF was killed by gunfire as he attempted to stop a suspicious man on a bicycle in the City of Lynwood. It was October 30, 1997. I was not part of the team that was up for murders that night, but as often is the case—and it was on this occasion—many homicide detectives respond to these types of callouts without being assigned or asked to do so. I don't remember now how I heard the terrible news, but I responded to the scene to see what, if anything, I could do to help with the investigation.

Though I had worked at Century station for two years, most of my colleagues from the two stations that had combined to become

Century (Firestone and Lynwood) were no longer working patrol assignments. Most had either promoted or moved to other assignments, and very few remained working patrol by then. For that reason, I hadn't expected to know the deputy who had been killed. I didn't know who it was before I arrived at the scene, and I hadn't really given it much thought.

But as it turned out, I did know the deputy who was killed that night, and it seemed surreal to me that I was now involved in the investigation of his death.

Not long before I was promoted to Detective Division, and while still working as a detective out of Century station, Jeff Leslie and I had been out one afternoon in an unmarked detective car, dressed in our green Sheriff raid jackets tucked into our jeans, topped by Sam Browne belts which carried traditional patrol equipment. We were in the City of Lynwood, not far from where Deputy Hoenig would be killed just over a year later, when we spotted a young Hispanic gangster, gun in hand, moving quickly along the sidewalk.

The chase was on, which meant our usual questionable tactics were immediately employed: Leslie bailed out of the car and began chasing the kid with the gun, and I drove ahead to cut him off. The gangster was on the sidewalk to my left, so I accelerated past him and nosed across the sidewalk. Before I had come to a stop, my door was open, and my pistol was leading me out of the car.

This armed gangster darted across the road behind me. My partner was still in a foot pursuit but some distance behind him. I ducked back into the car, and, with my gun in my hand, keeping an eye on the bad guy over my right shoulder, I backed my vehicle away from the curb and sidewalk with the intent of continuing my pursuit. In all the excitement, I hadn't bothered to bring my other leg into the car and close the door; I had anticipated getting out again in the very near future. The door caught the bumper of a parked car and bent backward against the hinges.

Meanwhile, my partner had cut an angle at our gangster that would seal his fate, and the bad guy saw it coming. He turned to see me coming toward him from the other direction, the crunched car now parked and waiting behind me. We both had our pistols leveled at him, commanding him to drop the gun or die of lead poisoning, or some such nonsense. He did as he was ordered and was taken into custody without incident.

Our first instinct in such situations as crunching a car was always, "We can fix it" (as opposed to reporting it). But as we stood staring at the crinkled door, our hope of getting away with this one quickly diminished. With my clean driving record, I would have likely only received a written reprimand for the damage, and my transfer to Detective Division —which was already locked in—wouldn't have been affected. So we called for a supervisor and a traffic car, someone who, unlike us two Neanderthals, knew how to write a vehicle collision report. Deputy Michael Hoenig, assigned as a Lynwood City traffic car, responded.

I hadn't spoken to Deputy Hoenig much beyond a few passing greetings in the hallways of Century station. It was a big place where patrol deputies and detectives didn't interact as much as they might otherwise have, owing solely to the station design. (Detectives were secluded on a second floor, away from patrol.) On the occasions I had encountered Mike, he always had a smile on his face and warm eyes that telegraphed a friendly disposition.

That afternoon in September of 1996, Mike looked at the crunched door of our "slick" car and frowned. He then glanced at the gangster sweating in the back seat. He smiled and said, "At least you caught him."

Deputy Hoenig listened as I told him the circumstances of how I had managed to back my vehicle up with the door wide open while pursuing the pint-sized killer who now sat in the back seat. Hoenig nodded. "Not a problem, sir. Shit happens. I'll write it up the best I can."

And he did. He wrote as favorable a report as could be written, given the circumstances. I thanked him for his work, shook his hand, and we went our separate ways.

The next time I saw Deputy Hoenig, the sparkle in his eyes was gone, and his smile had vanished. Both were taken from him in a vicious, deadly attack, something we (cops) are always aware can happen, yet are always surprised when it does. I had fourteen years in the department at that point, and I had, in various roles, been involved in close to a hundred death cases. I had attended half a dozen cop funerals, and I had made several death notifications. I was no stranger to death, and I had learned to compartmentalize the emotional component of it from the business at hand, at least until the appropriate time to mourn would come. And I knew going in that working Homicide would mean that sooner or later, I would be called upon to investigate the death of a fellow officer, but I hadn't imagined it would be of someone I knew. Nor could I have imagined that it would happen so soon.

There wasn't much a newbie at Homicide could do on his own when a cop was killed. I was given a detail to handle, something so minor that I can't even recall what it was. I completed it and returned to my duties at the bureau, concealing my heavy heart from my new colleagues. My lieutenant asked about the experience, and I told him I had known the deputy who was killed. He asked if I was good, meaning was I coping with it okay, and I assured him I was—that I was fit for duty and ready to move forward. Like when a baby dies while you and your partner risk life and limb to save her, and thirty minutes later, you're handling calls for service, dealing with adults who can't get along with their spouses, or neighbors who are ready to fight. Like in war, there is never time to regroup from one tragedy before plunging into a new one.

The next day, I accompanied several others from the bureau to Deputy Michael Hoenig's postmortem examination. I stood tableside at the autopsy of someone I had known, a person with whom I had interacted and whose company I had enjoyed in the relatively short time I had known him. This would elevate the death business to a new level that perhaps I hadn't anticipated. I had now entered, for me, uncharted territory, the type not many would care to explore.

Welcome to the big leagues.

Many friends, colleagues, loved ones, and maybe even family members of Deputy Michael Hoenig will read this book, and for that reason, I will not describe his autopsy in any detail. But what struck me most was the reverence of the event. As mentioned, I had viewed many autopsies by then, and I've viewed hundreds since. Most autopsies are performed in gruesome fashion with no reverence for the dead. Sometimes a dozen autopsies would be going at once between two rooms separated by only two pairs of solid double doors, which were scarred from the battering of stainless-steel tables carrying the patients to their final examinations. The tools used to remove rib cages and skull caps are harsh but efficient. At times, the rooms would be full of idle chatter, sometimes laughter, all standard coping mechanisms in the business of death.

But that wasn't the case during the examination of a law enforcement officer killed in the line of duty. The room was hushed, the autopsy scheduled late in the day when no others would be taking place. No one spoke without absolute necessity, which boiled down to questions and answers between the primary investigators and the medical examiner. Many were in attendance: department executives, representatives from the district attorney's office, the chief medical examiner, and numerous homicide detectives, all of us dressed in blue paper gowns, paper shoes, rubber gloves, respirators and eye protection, blue hairnets on our heads.

The process of the examination was delicate, with respect for the deceased and consideration of the audience. The medical examiner used surgical scalpels, not the usual tools that resembled those used for gardening and carpentry. Even the standard and frequent spraying and washing to keep the work area clean was subdued, which was very different from most autopsies where observers learned to back away when the coroner's tech reached for the hose. It was oddly soothing. The work of a surgeon, not a butcher. A finish carpenter, not a framer.

But in the end, all of the tranquility in my world came to an abrupt stop when Deputy Hoenig's uniform was brought in for gunshot wound analysis. His badge and name tag remained intact and in their proper places, although stained by the volumes of his lifeblood that soaked his shirt.

The memory of his uniform has stayed with me, along with the image of his lifeless eyes, because it was these things that represented the entire story of his death. Michael Hoenig, a young man of only 32 years, died violently, ambushed as he exited his car, struck multiple times by a hail of bullets in the dark of night because—and *only* because —he chose to wear the uniform, the same uniform many of us have worn. He had assumed the same risks all of us had, and he paid the ultimate price while serving and protecting the citizens of a troubled society. It was something he had done for many years and almost always had done with a smile on his face.

THE HITS KEPT COMING.

At about the same time, while I was still new at the bureau and trying to keep up with everything coming at me, my partner plopped a file box onto my desk and said, "Do you know about George Arthur?"

Did I know about him?

As mentioned earlier in this book, when I was assigned to Men's Central Jail, George had been my sergeant. He was a mentor to me and to a few of my buddies. Having been a gang cop at Firestone before my time, George took a particular interest in us, as he knew we were set to go there ourselves. Not only had I worked for Sergeant Arthur, but I had had drinks with him on a couple of occasions at a local cop bar. He was a great man whom I admired and whose murder had shocked me.

It was a warm night in June of 1985 when George was murdered shortly after he departed the jail facility after his evening shift. I had visited with him not long before he left work that night, and I was sitting outside waiting for a friend when Lieutenant Brad Welker ran past me, headed toward the parking lot, fear and intensity on his face. "George Arthur has been in a bad accident," he puffed out as he ran past, answering the question that must have appeared in my expression. I learned the next day that George had been murdered in his vehicle just a short distance from the jail. It had shocked our department, and it had put us all on a heightened sense of self-awareness and reinforced the idea that officer safety didn't end with one's shift. Nobody knew who had killed George or why. But it happened just blocks from the jail, minutes after he left work. Worst of all, his killer had been lying in wait in the back of George's van.

The murder happened in the city, so it was an LAPD handle. However, when a deputy sheriff is killed outside of our jurisdiction—or even if one is involved in a shooting but survives—our Homicide Bureau sends a team of investigators to monitor the investigation. LAPD's Robbery Homicide Division (RHD) investigated George's murder, but the case went unsolved for more than a decade.

"Yes," I told my training officer, "I knew George. I worked for him at the jail."

He told me he had "reopened" the investigation that had gone cold, and he believed he had identified George's killer. He indicated the fully stuffed file box that now sat on my desk and said, "We'll be working on it in our spare time, so I want you to read everything in there and come up to speed."

I took the file box home (because there was no "spare time" during our working hours), and I read everything inside it: the first report, the homicide report, the follow-up investigation reports, forensic reports, and dozens of interviews of witnesses, friends and family of George, and deputies who had something to report, however remote. I also viewed all of the photographs, including those from the autopsy. Once again, I found myself staring into the clouded dead eyes of a friend and viewing the results of his postmortem medical examination.

My partner's theory on the case was that the killer had been a gangster from the Aliso Village housing project near where the murder occurred. With the company of an LAPD detective, we went out and re-interviewed a few witnesses who had reported seeing a man run from George's van after the crash. (George was shot while driving, and he had tried to save himself by accelerating and driving directly into a large concrete road barrier.)

The problem with my partner's theory was that these interviews weren't going the way he had hoped, and the witnesses' statements didn't support his theory of who it was they saw running that night. At one point, I asked my partner why we weren't going after the killer himself—this person my partner was convinced had done the killing—as the man was, by then, incarcerated, doing life on another murder charge. We could go interview him in prison, obtain his DNA, and perhaps resolve the case once and for all. Or at least eliminate that individual as a suspect. My partner said that's not how you do things, and I pondered this for a very long time.

The other problem was that my partner couldn't get along with LAPD any better than he got along with many of his colleagues at work. But LAPD was not obligated to put up with his shit, and they didn't. The captain of RHD finally came to our captain and said there needed to be a change. There was a rather heated meeting that included their captain and ours, my partner, me, Mike Bumcrot, and his partner, Sean

McCarthy, and a couple of LAPD detectives. After LAPD stated their grievances and made it clear they could no longer work with my partner, our captain took the case away from him and gave it to Bumcrot and McCarthy.

A few nights later, the two of them were working the desk as it was their turn in the barrel. I was working late and passed through the front desk area with a cup of coffee and greeted them both. I hadn't known Bumcrot before I got to the bureau, but I knew of him and had tremendous respect for him, and I had conversed with him by this time on several occasions. McCarthy and I had been academy mates, and we had worked at Firestone together. Bummer, as most called Bumcrot, said, "Hey Danny, you got a second?"

For Bumcrot, you bet I did. I leaned on the counter and waited while he checked his surroundings before posing the question to me. "What do you think of your partner's theory on Arthur's murder?"

There were files from the Arthur case on the desk, and I knew they were actively working on it now and likely still reviewing files and coming up to speed on it. I told him I thought my partner had been on the wrong path and that the witnesses weren't saying what he hoped they might. I mentioned my thoughts on interviewing this suspect of his and eliminating him through DNA, and how he had scoffed at the idea. Bummer didn't say much, just nodded along and made some mental notes. I asked how it looked to them. He said they were going in a different direction with the case, and that was about all he had to say on the matter at that time. I figured it might be the right direction.

Not long after, Bumcrot and McCarthy solved George Arthur's murder. A former deputy sheriff named Ted Kirby had worked at the jail at the same time I was there and while George was there as a sergeant. He had come under suspicion for a number of reasons that should have been clear to all of the investigators who had looked at this case previously. Homed in on him, Bummer and his partner went to Washington, where Kirby had retired, and they asked him for his DNA. Kirby refused, so they obtained a court order, and Kirby complied. The results linked Kirby to the murder. Before the detectives could arrest Kirby, he had disappeared into the nearby woods and shot himself in the head. Some of us believe that by doing so, he took a few secrets to the grave with him.[1]

CRIMSON ROSE GATES WAS 22 YEARS OLD, SINGLE AND VIVACIOUS, THE daughter of perhaps the most forgiving woman I've ever met.

Her sin had been breaking up with her boyfriend, a macho sort who often boasted of his combat experience as a paratrooper during Desert Storm. Which, as it turned out, was a lie. He wasn't a paratrooper, he hadn't seen combat, and he had been dishonorably discharged from the United States Army for misconduct.

On the afternoon of January 30, 1998, shortly after the breakup, Crimson Rose went to Derek Barboza's apartment to collect her personal belongings. A neighbor spoke with her before she went inside, and that same neighbor spoke with Barboza a short time later when he left the apartment. He told her goodbye and said he wouldn't be coming back. He didn't mention that Crimson Rose lay dead on his kitchen floor before departing alone in Crimson's car.

Barboza had a roommate who was home when Crimson Rose came over. From his room, he heard the two arguing. Then he heard a fight, a substantial commotion in the living area of the apartment. But the roommate was no match for Barboza—he knew this, and he was afraid of him —so he remained behind his closed door; he had no intention of intervening. The roommate huddled in the corner of his room and listened to the sounds of violence in the other room. After a period of complete silence, the roommate ventured out of his room. Barboza was gone, and Crimson Rose lay dead on the kitchen floor, her battered and bloodied face nearly unrecognizable.

Barboza fled to San Diego, where he had planned to cross the border to avoid prosecution. But he inexplicably returned and ultimately turned himself in to the Los Angeles police several days later.

My partner and I sat down to interview him, hoping for a confession. It was never easy convincing a killer to talk to the cops, but we always tried. Not surprisingly, Barboza told us he had nothing to say. We presented a photograph of the crime scene, hoping to stir an emotion or get some type of response. It showed Crimson Rose lying in a pool of blood. He just shrugged with a smirk on his face, no reaction and no comment. Barboza was big, tall, and thick, naturally strong. His hands were large and powerful. I watched as he moved them about, rubbing the stubble on his face, scratching his arm, pushing his thick, dirty fingers through a mass of black hair. He folded his hands on the table between us and left them there—the hands that had killed a young lady just a few days earlier. I detested him.

On the day of the trial, my partner and I sat with the victim's mother and father in a private room to prepare them for the exhibits and testimony that they would see and hear in the courtroom. We showed them photographs from the scene and autopsy. They wept, they gasped, they fell apart. They always did.

The smug asshole was convicted and sentenced to 25 years to life in prison. During the sentencing phase, Crimson Rose's mother addressed him in an open courtroom. She looked him directly in his eyes and spoke with resolve as she forgave him for what he did to their daughter. She then gave him a Bible. He had no response and showed no emotion.

I found this remarkable. I wanted an eye for an eye. Haul him out back and beat him to death or draw and quarter him. Hang him from a high tree or a light pole for all I cared. Assemble a firing squad; I'd volunteer. That's how I felt about it. I wasn't the forgiving type. To this day, I can see Crimson Rose Gates lying on his kitchen floor, brutally murdered and left there. And I think about the smirk on his face when we showed him those gruesome photographs of that scene. I had not then—nor do I now—have the capacity to understand such forgiveness. Apparently, I'm an Old Testament type of Christian.

Several months after the sentencing, I received a package in the mail. It was from Crimson's mother, and it contained a wooden cross necklace and a handwritten letter. In her letter, she spoke of the blood of Christ and redemption and forgiveness. She asked that I always remember Crimson Rose. That was the easy part, also the hard part. The memories are the part of the job that contribute to the wear and tear on homicide detectives. Police work is difficult enough for patrol cops, given the people they deal with and the things they see every day. But only homicide detectives become intimately involved with those whose lives have been stricken with unimaginable tragedy, and that is a burden beyond what most know, and it is one we forever carry.

Tragically, I have to add more to this saga: In April 2021, while editing this memoir, I learned that Barboza was being considered for early parole. That didn't surprise me entirely, given the revolving door that is the California Department of Corrections—now known as the more politically correct California Department of Corrections *and* Rehabilitation. But when I learned that he had committed another murder while in prison, yet they were still entertaining the idea of setting him free, I understood fully what happened to that once-great state and why much of its law-abiding citizenry is fleeing to more conservative states.

Barboza had killed his cellmate in prison, but he was not charged for doing so. He was segregated from the rest of the population so that other prisoners would be safe. Think about that; they kept him away from the other predators so that he wouldn't be able to harm them, but they want to set him free on the streets to live among you and your families and friends.

This is part of what I wrote in a letter I sent to the parole board to be considered in their deliberations:

And not only did he take the life of a precious young woman, but he murdered again in your own house, killing his cellmate. Yet no legal action was taken against him for that murder, only segregation to keep him from killing again. Isn't that the point about keeping him in prison, also?

At the time of this writing, I've been retired from law enforcement for 17 years. It's been 23 years since I investigated the murder of Crimson Rose Gates, yet this case, and many others, is still a part of my life. That's something few people would ever know about the life of a homicide detective.

THE CASES CONTINUED COMING IN. THAT WAS ANOTHER THING ABOUT Homicide in L.A., you never had much of a break before finding yourself standing over another body. After Crimson Rose's case, we handled several more murders, a few more suicides, a deputy-involved shooting in Palmdale, and the accidental death of a toddler who drowned in a pool in Lancaster. Nothing is worse than murdered children, but all child deaths are tragic, heart-wrenching, and impossible to forget.

Then we were given another officer-involved shooting case, and this one was a cluster for the record books. Four law enforcement agencies were involved. Twenty-two shooters fired hundreds of rounds of ammunition from an assortment of weapons, and a man lay dead with a pellet gun that was indistinguishable from a semi-automatic handgun in his hand. It was a case of suicide by cop, and apparently before the concept of designated shooters took hold. The autopsy took three days. On the first day, the examiner did nothing other than chart gunshot wounds, of which there were more than a hundred. On the second day, he began removing and cataloging evidence, expended projectiles and parts thereof. On the third day, the final examination took place, and when we left the coroner's office that day, we carried with us a box containing more than 300 pieces of ballistic evidence removed from the decedent's body: parts and fragments of 9mm, .40 Caliber Smith & Wesson, and .223 projectiles, and an assortment of shotgun pellets. The death of a small forest followed, necessary for the paperwork required for that case alone.

Following that fiasco, we handled another deputy-involved shooting, this one in the high desert town of Acton, then two suicides, one each in Cerritos and Industry, and then a fire death investigation. Any case involving fire requires the expertise of our department's Arson Explosives Detail investigators—otherwise known as the Bomb Squad. It was interesting to learn some of the basics of arson investigation as we sifted through the charred remains of a small home in Bellflower. Essentially, their primary goal is to determine the cause and origin of a fire. In this case, it had been a faulty wall socket. There were no accelerants used, and arson was not suspected. The victim was found in a fetal position in a corner by the door, burned to death. She had tried to escape, but the fire was too intense, the smoke overwhelming. The arson investigator explained to me that people stay low and crawl along walls trying to find their way out of fires, and often it is in a corner that they'll succumb to the intense heat and smoke.

Slogging through the soaked scene reminded me of a horrific event from my patrol days, one that is never far from my thoughts, although I never talk about it. We were dispatched to a fire one night and arrived to find a neighborhood market fully engulfed in flames. Like most businesses, the exterior of the corner building was fortified by steel scissor gates. The owners would lock it up at night when they closed, locking inside the hired help who worked through the night, cleaning and restocking shelves, et cetera. Apparently, the worker wasn't fully trusted. Several units had arrived, and we could all hear the man screaming inside. Those are sounds that never go away.

The fire department arrived moments after we did—before we could come up with any idea of how to save the man inside. Truthfully, there was no way that we could have. Even the firefighters couldn't approach the building with their cutting tools due to the intensity of the flames. Rather, they stood back and aimed their hoses at the building and drenched the fire as quickly as they could. But it was too late for the man inside.

I have always questioned my own actions that night—or perhaps, inaction would be a better way to put it. The one thing I could have done but didn't think of at that moment was to crash my radio car through the wall. It would've required the commitment of hitting the building at a high rate of speed and likely traveling deep inside, given how it was fortified by the security gates. It is very likely that I would have ended up trapped in the fire myself, and the structure would probably have collapsed around me. But we'll never know because I didn't think to do that in the instant when it might have mattered. And I question myself about it still, thirty-five years later.

At the fire in Bellflower, where a forty-year-old woman died in the corner of her living room, our focus had been to make certain that the fire hadn't been set in an attempt to disguise a murder. Had the victim been found in her bed or prone on the couch, there would have been greater concern. But much like the young man in the liquor store, she had died trying to escape the intense heat and flames while inhaling the toxic fumes of combustion, the most common cause of death by fire.

Though the evidence at the scene indicated to us that this case was a non-criminal death, it is ultimately the medical examiner who determines the manner and mode of death. The Bellflower case was ruled to be an accidental death caused by smoke inhalation.

It was during this scene investigation that I learned why my training officer had told me to keep a change of clothes and rubber boots in the trunk of my car.

SIX MONTHS HAD COME AND GONE, YET I REMAINED WITH MY FIRST training officer. The program at Homicide was designed so that new investigators would be on training for one year—six months with the first training officer and then six months with another. Apparently, my model conduct had backfired on me. I had tolerated his constantly belittling me in front of colleagues, his talking down to me in front of civilians, and his lying about me to our lieutenant. But I had kept my mouth shut, and my attitude checked. Colleagues who had known me from Firestone joked that they had bets on when I was going to lose my cool and drag him out into the parking lot. And I came close the day he walked over to my desk and, in the presence of a former gang detective, asked me what I knew about "street gangs."

"Which gangs are you referring to?" I asked. "I know a lot about the Hispanic and black gangs of South Los Angeles since I've spent my entire career there, but I don't know much about white or Asian gangs."

"I'm talking about the *Eme*," he said.

La Eme is a notorious Mexican prison gang, not a "street gang." In fact, they are the most powerful and influential gang in the California Department of Corrections system. From prison, they control the activity of street gangs through the use of extreme violence. One such activity they control is the sale of narcotics. All Hispanic street gangs in Southern California are to pay taxes to the Mexican mafia lest they find themselves on a list (*la lista*) that calls for all other gang members to assault and/or kill the offending gang's members. Most gang members will end up in prison, so it behooves them to be in good standing with the Mexican mafia when they get there.

I said, "Oh, you mean prison gangs. You said, 'street gangs.'"

He about lost his mind. But rather than saying he misspoke (I gave him the benefit of the doubt that he had and that he wasn't so naïve as to call the Mexican mafia a street gang), he doubled down, shouting at me:

"They're a prison gang when they're in prison. When they're on the streets, they're street gang members."

He was dead wrong. The other detective shook his head to gently let him know it. But still, he went on, getting himself more worked up as he did. He tossed a file folder full of papers across my desk, scattering its contents and disturbing other documents I was working with before his pigheaded intrusion. He shouted, "You think I don't know what fucking street gangs are?"

It wasn't too long after that argument when we were in his car, on our way to follow up on a case, and he said, "You know, I've been waiting a long time to have a guy like you come along, someone I'd be willing to partner with until I retire." I cringed. He said, "You're the best trainee I've ever had, and on our next case, I'm going to let you take the lead. After that, I'll sign you off training early, and we'll stay together as regular partners."

At this point, I realized that he thought I'd be a subservient little bitch who would continue putting up with his obnoxious personality and bad behavior. He didn't know me. Because once I was signed off training and made a permanent part of that bureau, there was no way I would allow anyone to speak to me in the ways that he had, nor treat me the way that he mostly did.

That next case came on a Sunday morning when Marcos Juarez was gunned down in front of a liquor store in the city of Industry. Juarez and others would show up early and begin drinking their cheap booze on the sidewalk near the front doors, where they didn't have far to go to replenish their drinks. There were a few witnesses who provided vague descriptions of the suspect, who had himself gone into the liquor store before confronting Juarez outside and shooting him dead.

True to his word, my training officer followed along but allowed me to handle the case as if I were alone. I interviewed witnesses, coordinated the crime scene investigation, collected evidence, and, before departing, obtained the surveillance video from inside the store.

The next day I was headed for STARS Center with the surveillance video when my control freak of a partner called and asked what I was doing. I told him where I was headed and that I planned to have the tech crew make still photographs of each male who entered the store an hour prior to the murder and who also matched the general description of our suspect. He wanted to know what I was planning to do with the photos. I told him I was going to show the photographs to the witnesses so we could identify the suspect.

He raised his voice. "You can't do that! We don't know who he is. You can't just show photographs to people without knowing who the person is. Also, it has to be in a six-pack."

A six-pack is a folder with six photographs, one of which would be the suspect and the other five depicting people who were similar in appearance and not related to the investigation. Although a six-pack was the preferred method for photographic lineups, the courts have ruled that it isn't the only method by which suspect identifications can be made. In short, I could absolutely hand a stack of pictures to a witness and ask him if any of the men in those photographs was the one who shot Mr. Juarez. I tried to explain that to my training officer, but he would have none of it.

"You don't know what you're talking about, and you better get in here. You don't just go running off doing whatever you want without talking to your partner."

By now, I was tired of his shit, and I knew for sure it was now or never that I needed to take a stand. Otherwise, I might be stuck working with him for a long time. I came into the office as he ordered me to do, and I immediately went to our legal resource book, where I found several citations of case law that proved I was right about the photograph identification process. I photocopied and highlighted the applicable sections that proved him wrong, and I handed them to him. After perusing the documents briefly, he threw them at me, and then he yelled and screamed and told me that I had an attitude problem and that he could no longer work with me. He said that I was bullheaded and I was nowhere near ready to be off training, so he was going to send me to another team and recommend that I receive a new training officer who could evaluate whether or not I even belonged at the bureau.

Later that same day, my lieutenant summoned me and said that my partner had told him the same thing, that he could no longer work with me, that I didn't know what I was doing, and that I needed to go to a new training officer and probably have my training period extended. The lieutenant said, "It's so strange, too. Just last week, he was telling me you were the best trainee he ever had." Well, that was before I stood up to him.

I was sent to Team 2 and partnered with Rod Kusch, and I was so happy with the new arrangement I could have kissed him and every other detective on my new team.

---

1. There are numerous articles with details about the murder of Sergeant George Arthur that can be found with a simple google search. Here is one report by the Associated Press: https://apnews.com/3de69b9344911o7ecd1o3367a6fa51of

A NEW TEAM AND PARTNER

R od Kusch was a terrific partner. The change made a difference in my daily disposition, as duly noted by my wife. It's one thing to be worn out from hard work, and quite another to be sick and tired of putting up with a difficult partner. Rod was a good cop with a great sense of humor and a terrific perspective on life as a homicide detective.

MY FIRST CASE WITH ROD CAME ONE AFTERNOON WHEN WE WERE ASSIGNED to the barrel. A deputy from Marina del Rey called it in as a suicide, telling me that a man had tied himself to the hull of a yacht and sunk it. I pulled the phone from my ear and looked at it, then asked the deputy how the man had sunk his own boat when he was tied to the hull. The deputy said the man shot holes in the boat until it sank. I tried picturing this scene, and it didn't make sense. Why would anyone go to that much trouble to kill himself? Why not just shoot yourself in the head since you have a gun? I had a vision in my head of a man bound to a boat that had sunk because *someone else* had shot holes in it, and I couldn't see how the drowned man might have done it himself. This case had the makings of a nightmare, the type that could come back to bite me and Kusch in the backside if not handled properly. That was no way to endear myself to a new team and a new partner.

Rod stayed at the office to man the phones, and I headed west. There were worse places to spend an evening than Marina del Rey, though I also had a sliver of anxiety about going there. I hadn't been back to that station since the Red Onion beating incident a decade earlier.

At the marina, I met with a crew of seagoing sheriff's deputies who were assigned to the Los Angeles County Sheriff's Department harbor patrol. They were the navy of LASD, men and women who were well versed in the operation of sea vessels and who were equipped, certified, and anxious to dive into murky waters when the need arose. The deputies explained that they had responded to a call of a sinking vessel, dove into the sea, recovered the victim, and attempted to resuscitate him. Once ashore, the victim was transported to the hospital, where he was pronounced dead.

We boarded a harbor patrol boat and headed out to sea. Once we were moving across the choppy waters, I was glad to have worn my London Fog raincoat over my suit; it provided some warmth and protection from the winds and ocean spray. We went out half a mile and stopped, the heavy boat sinking into the waters as we powered down and then popping up onto the surface once we settled. I looked over the edge, but there was nothing there to look at other than the deep blue sea. I moved across to the other side and looked down. Same thing. I looked at the deputies. "Where's my crime scene?"

"Down there," one of them said.

I looked again and shrugged. I had expected to see something, maybe part of the boat above the water or the whole boat not far beneath the surface. But there was no part of anything visible to me. I said, "So, what now? Does someone bring the boat out, or does it stay down there, or what?" I had no idea, a fish out of his water. One of the deputies explained that the boat would be recovered, but not on that day; there wasn't enough daylight to begin such an endeavor. One of the deputies said, "Would you like to see a video?"

Wait, what?

"The dive was recorded by our underwater video cameras. You can see everything, the man tied to the boat, the bullet holes, all of it. You'll see us cut him loose and bring him up."

Now we were talking!

With a review of the video, I was able to see how the man had tied himself to a ladder affixed to the cabin of the boat and how the bullet holes were near where he had stood. I also learned that the victim had made a call to his daughter to say goodbye shortly before the incident. That little bit of knowledge helped tremendously.

The kicker was the boat wasn't even his own; he had borrowed it from a friend.

I left the Marina that evening with a broadened—if not renewed—sense of pride in my department and its members. Law enforcement in Los Angeles County is a multifaceted endeavor. The vast and varied talents of the nearly 10,000 sworn sheriff's deputies in Los Angeles County cannot be overstated. And those harbor patrol guys, the ones we flippantly called "boat deputies," have one of the coolest jobs in law enforcement.

ONE OF THE MORE INTERESTING CASES KUSCH AND I HANDLED WAS THE first murder we were assigned, the day after the Marina del Rey suicide on a yacht. Joshua Marchesano, a 14-year-old boy, was shot as he stood on an outside staircase that led to the second floor of the apartments where he lived in the city of Covina. The shooter was unseen.

We recovered a rifle scope in the far corner of an adjacent property, which is where we believed—based on witness statements—that the shot had been fired from. The scope, if it was indeed from the killer's rifle, might have been knocked off its mount as the suspect made his escape from the overgrown cluster of trees and brush where he would have been concealed.

We were able to determine that the rifle was a .22 caliber, probably a 220 Swift or something similar, as opposed to a more common .22 Long

Rifle. This caliber is popular with varmint hunters and sport shooters alike, and it can be accurate out to 400 yards in the right hands. The scope we recovered would be a good match for such a rifle.

The residence where the rifle scope was recovered was a rental property. There were several people inside the home, all of whom had had previous brushes with the law and several of whom had been affiliated with gangs. One was on parole. He was our most likely suspect; however, we never recovered the rifle nor found any evidence linking him to the killing. We had scent taken from the scope and later used scent canines to compare it to the parolee's scent, but the dogs didn't alert on it. There were no fingerprints found on the scope, though a source of DNA was recovered from its eyepiece. The contributor of that DNA source was never identified. Rod and I pursued numerous leads in the case, and we searched firearms databases, trying to identify the owners of similar weapons within that neighborhood. There were a couple of other suspects that we never could link to the murder, and eventually, we ran out of leads to follow. The case remains unsolved as of the writing of this memoir.

We believed that Joshua might have been mistaken for his older brother, whose appearance was very similar to his and who had dabbled in the gang culture himself. Otherwise, it might have been a thrill kill, a random target, the victim of a soulless lowlife. Either way, it was a tragic case and one of the unsolved cases I often think about and wish I had another chance at.

ONE CASE, MEMORABLE BECAUSE IT WAS SO UNCANNY, INVOLVED AN INMATE, a large black man who died after he had been involved in a physical altercation with deputies at the Twin Towers jail facility. It turned out that he died of heart failure, the episode triggered by the physical exertion of fighting with the cops. These things happen, and it doesn't mean the cops killed him, contrary to the popular view of such matters in the singularly bizarre year of 2020 as I write this memoir.

The odd part of the case, though, was that the dead inmate's name was Danny R. Smith. Most people called Danny are Daniels, but not me and not him; each of us was named Danny by our parent(s)—in my case, my father—and it is so indicated on our birth certificates. Danny, not Daniel. His was indicated as such on his death certificate as well, and I suppose someday mine will be too.

Kusch wisely suggested that I conceal my Homicide name tag that displayed "Danny R. Smith" when we notified the next of kin.

———————

ON AUGUST 10, 1998, ROD AND I WERE SENT TO PALMDALE TO investigate an attempted murder/suicide. A man had shot his wife several times and then turned the gun on himself. She lived; he didn't. We interviewed her at the hospital, and it was sad to hear her story. The two had been married for forty years, had children and grandchildren, and appeared as content and happy as any two people could be.

That morning, the poor missus was sitting at the table having her coffee when her husband, Dick, walked in and pointed his gun at her. She said, "Why, Dick, what are you doing with your gun?" He shot her. She said, "Dick, why would you shoot me?" He answered with another gunshot. Two shots had been fired, and he wasn't finished. The missus got up from the table and ran down the hall and into the bathroom. He chased after her, firing three more times before she reached her destination, and then he cranked off a sixth round into the door as she closed it behind her. She had been struck by several bullets.

The poor gunshot woman huddled in the corner of the bathroom, confounded by the conduct of her husband, a man she had known so well for half a century. But she didn't know him at that moment, and he had offered her no explanation for what he was doing, no words at all. She waited in the bathroom until she heard a final gunshot farther away. He had gone to his room, reloaded his gun, and shot himself in the head.

The victim had been hit multiple times and was in critical condition. We believed this was going to be a murder/suicide, which, of course, we would handle. But she didn't die—amazingly and thankfully—so we were back in the rotation for murders, being credited only with handling a suicide.

It turned out the husband had been diagnosed with terminal cancer and decided (for her) that she couldn't live without him. He was wrong.

———————

THE NEXT NIGHT ROD AND I WERE DISPATCHED TO EAST LOS ANGELES FOR a gang-related murder, a drive-by shooting. We arrived at the mountainous neighborhood known as the "Mexican Alps," a historic community that offers breathtaking views of downtown and all of South Los Angeles. On a clear night, you can see the lights glimmer all the way to the coast until they or you are swallowed by blackness.

That night, darkness had come for a man named Magdaleno as he and his brother, Gilbert, found themselves on the receiving end of a drive-by shooting.

When we arrived, we found gang detectives already on scene, there to assist us as needed. With our bureau being centralized, it was imperative to work with detectives who were assigned to the local stations. They knew more about the various conflicts on their streets, and they often knew the players. The detectives told us that Gilbert was, in fact, a hardcore gang member and likely the intended target. His brother, the victim, Magdaleno, was not involved in gangs.

Gilbert told us that when the suspects drove past and began shooting, he and his brother both ducked behind a parked car. Once the suspects were gone, Gilbert saw that his brother was on the ground. He had been shot. The evidence at the scene was consistent with Gilbert's description of the action, that he and his brother had used a parked car for cover when the suspects drove by and began shooting. There were numerous bullet strikes in that parked vehicle, the trajectory and pattern consistent with someone having fired from a passing vehicle. However, there were also bullet strikes on the other side of the parked vehicle— the passenger's side—that revealed *someone* had returned fire at the passing vehicle.

As we examined the scene, we began to suspect that Magdaleno might have been hit by "friendly fire," given the location of his body and evidence that someone had shot from behind him. During the initial interviews, Gilbert denied shooting back at the vehicle or even being armed. Eventually, after a series of lengthy—and dare I say, crafty—interviews of the young gangster, Gilbert admitted to both and provided us with the gun he had used that night. The odds of that happening with a guy like him are low.

The postmortem medical examination of Magdaleno confirmed our suspicions: the victim had been shot in the back. The bullet that killed him was of a different caliber than those recovered from the "street side" of the parked car, and they matched the gun that Gilbert ultimately provided to us. Gilbert had killed his brother.

We would later learn from Gilbert that when the suspects began firing that night, it was actually only Magdaleno who took cover behind the parked car. Gilbert, an experienced gunfighter, had stood his ground and returned fire. As the suspect vehicle continued traveling, so did Gilbert's line of fire. Apparently, at one point, Magdaleno was between the two as he ran forward and ducked behind the car.

At that time in California, when a person was killed during the commission of a felony, the law allowed for the person(s) who committed the felony to be charged with murder, even if they did not directly kill the victim. This was referred to as the felony murder rule. One example of the law's application would be when two people robbed a bank, and during their escape, the police used deadly force to apprehend them, that the surviving offender(s) could be charged with the murder of his crime partner. This was a great and sensible law, yet another one that has been repealed under the guise of "justice reform."

In Gilbert's case, he had acted in self-defense when he returned fire at those who were trying to kill him. It mattered not that he was a gang member nor that he had unlawfully possessed a firearm. Legally speaking, all that mattered was that Gilbert had not initiated the felony crime that led to his brother's death. Though it was he who killed Magdaleno, we would charge the occupants of the suspect vehicle with Magdaleno's murder.

When we broke the news to Gilbert that a bullet fired from his gun had killed Magdaleno, he was devastated. He had no idea that that had been the case.

We explained to him how the felony murder rule would allow us to hold the others responsible for Magdaleno's murder even though it had been Gilbert's bullet that killed him. Though it was little consolation for the grieving gangster, it was something for him to grasp onto. Gilbert then decided he would cooperate with us by providing more detail about the men who did the shooting that night—again, another rare thing for hardened gang members. It was this information that led us to a shirtless man with a Mustang and eventually to the identification of that man's relative, who was, in fact, the primary suspect.

Over the days and weeks of investigating this murder, we spent many hours with Gilbert, driving to and from his home and East L.A. Station or to our office in the City of Commerce. There were times when we would drive him to certain locations and ask him to tell us about persons who might be related to the case. He was quite a character with a good sense of humor, and we would joke with him about his criminal activity. On one occasion, while driving through a rival's neighborhood, Gilbert leaned up from the back seat and gleefully said, "We used to drive through here shooting people all the time."

Not a big deal. Life in the barrio.

This case was featured on A&E's *L.A. Detectives*, a series that was hosted by Bill Kurtis. The film crew had been riding with the East L.A. gang detectives that night and were with them at the crime scene when we arrived. As such, we spent the next several weeks working this case with a camera crew in tow. At times, it felt awkward to have them there. Like on the day we contacted a man at his home in East L.A., someone we believed might have information about one of our suspects.

The man we spoke to was a robust Hispanic who stood unapologetically shirtless beneath the morning sun while cameramen zoomed in on him, hanging their boom mics over our heads as we tried to conduct an interview. We were there in search of a Mustang with a particular set of custom wheels, a vehicle that belonged to our suspect in the drive-by shooting. The man denied any knowledge, but a few feet from where we stood in his driveway was a set of new stock tires and wheels from a late model Mustang. He didn't have a car to match them. Eventually, we were able to identify the suspect through this lead, and we recovered the suspect vehicle. But the suspect was gone, likely back in Mexico.

Months later, while previewing A&E's documentary, Rod and I chuckled over the footage of our interview with the bare-chested *hombre valiente.* We were none too slim ourselves but not as robust as he. Yet neither of us would be caught dead shirtless on TV. We laughed at the idea of all three of us enjoying a warm morning in East Los Angeles, shirtless for the cameras while talking about murder.

KUSCH HAD SIGNED ME OFF TRAINING AFTER OUR FIRST CASE TOGETHER. Over the next seven months, we would handle 17 cases, 11 of which were homicides. According to homicide investigation expert Vernon Geberth, the man who literally wrote the book on the processes of homicide investigation, "Any city that has a homicide detective handling more than five cases is kidding themselves. Even the best detective can't handle more than five cases." He was referencing the time frame of a year.

During the years I was assigned to the Los Angeles County Sheriff's Homicide Bureau, we routinely handled upwards of 15 homicide cases each year, not to mention other death cases such as accidental, recreational and industrial deaths, and suicides. When your caseload is that overwhelming, something has to give. Cases suffer, investigators suffer, personal relationships suffer, and often fail. The key to surviving such a workload is to establish a triage of sorts, to prioritize some cases over others. The popular book and TV series homicide character, Harry Bosch, has a credo, "Everybody counts or nobody counts." Well, that may work in Hollywood, but in real life, a dead kid trumps a dead gangster every time. If you can't accept that, you have no business doing the job.

In the midst of this barrage of cases, four-month-old Venessa Nichols was murdered by her biological father and Kusch and I were assigned the case. The father was the sole caretaker at the time of her death, and he was the one who had reported her as being unresponsive in her crib. The medical examination would conclude that she had suffered broken ribs that were consistent with injuries that are commonly found in shaken babies. She also had a skull fracture, something that is often found in shaken baby cases. There were additional fractures discovered that were in various stages of healing, meaning she had suffered more than one traumatic injury in her short life, likely several. This was exactly when other cases take a back seat if they remain in the car at all.

Venessa's mother had come from Mexico and met Christopher Nichols at the grocery store where they both worked. They married, and she became pregnant, though he had not wanted a child. In order to take care of the baby while both continued working, they took opposite shifts, the mother working days and the father working nights.

On the day Venessa died, we interviewed Nichols at length in a private room at the hospital. He denied any wrongdoing and stuck with the story that he had no idea what had happened to her, that she had just stopped breathing. He suggested that she had suffered from a cold, but the truth was she had difficulty breathing because of her broken ribs. We were able to lock him into this statement, along with the fact that there had been no visitors that day. Simply put, he was our only suspect.

Nichols had never been in trouble with the law. He was quiet, withdrawn, maybe, a loner whose world was turned upside down by the addition of a child. His routine—prior to the childcare disruption—was to work at night, sleep most of the day, and watch movies from his notable collection of videos. He was also a neat freak, maybe a bit obsessive-compulsive. He apparently didn't respond well to crying babies, and his baby would have cried incessantly, given the horrible injuries with which she had lived.

Christopher Nichols was convicted of murder and sentenced to 25 years to life, thanks in large part to one of my favorite prosecutors, someone I have remained friends with for many years beyond my career and with a thousand miles separating us, Los Angeles County Deputy District Attorney, Margaret "Maggie" Moe.

―――――――

IN OCTOBER OF 1998, TOMMY HARRIS AND I WERE TEAMED UP IN THE rotation for murders, as we were on the same team and both of our partners were unavailable. I had known Tommy for a long time—everyone knew Tommy—and we had worked around each other a lot. However, this would be the first time we were partnered during an on-call period, and I was really looking forward to it. Tommy, a former powerlifter, a former bodybuilder, and a great cop who had spent many years working as a gang detective was a fun guy to spend time with. He was also a bit of a ladies' man, and he enjoyed his cocktails. It was only fitting that we would catch a case that involved a former stripper and cocktail waitress named Veronica.

Veronica's boyfriend was killed by a single gunshot wound to his head inside the makeshift garage apartment where he lived in Whittier. Veronica was certain that her former boyfriend, Tom—who was insanely jealous—had killed him, as he had said he would. Since their breakup, he had stalked Veronica, broken into her home, installed cameras on her property to spy on her, configured a wiretap for her landline, and he had physically assaulted her on multiple occasions.

However, the new boyfriend had also been a small-time drug dealer, complicating the case by putting himself into a high-risk category. A locked filing cabinet drawer had been found open in the garage, the victim's keys dangling from the lock. Blood spots were on the concrete below the opened drawer, indicating that before he was shot and killed, he was beaten and forced to surrender his stash. This didn't eliminate Tom as a suspect because he was a user of drugs, too. In some ways, it strengthened the theory that it was he who had killed the victim, as the victim was known to be a tough guy. Tom had a reputation for being one of the toughest men in town, someone whom everyone feared, someone who had put tough men in the hospital with his bare hands numerous times.

Tommy and I went and knocked on Suspect Tom's door with the intention of questioning him about the murder. A male of the approximate age and physical description of the Tom we were looking for answered the door. We asked if he was Tom, and he denied that he was, but he also refused to identify himself to us. He seemed nervous, his eyes darting around while he licked his lips and fidgeted and demanded to know who we were and why we were there. Though he was anxious, he was also strangely aggressive, even confrontational. He claimed he was Tom's friend and said that Tom wasn't home at that time, that nobody else was there. Believing he might have actually been Tom, we demanded that he produce an identification for us to see. As he turned to go inside, leaving the front door open, we followed him in, concerned for our safety. At this point, we still believed him to be Tom, a murder suspect, and we were fearful that he might arm himself if allowed out of our view. Inside, the man retrieved his wallet and reluctantly provided his ID to us. He was not Tom, the man we were looking for. Tommy saw a parole officer's business card in the man's wallet and asked him if he was on parole. He confirmed that he was.

I continued the conversation with him about where Tom was and why he was at Tom's house alone while Tommy used the landline to call the parole officer listed on the card. The officer told Tommy that the man we were speaking with was a parolee at large, that there was a warrant for his arrest, and he asked that we arrest him. When Tommy hung up the phone and turned to face him, the man must have known what was coming because he bolted. This parolee decided he wasn't going back to prison, or, as I have often said, his agenda was suddenly very different from our own.

Mr. Parolee's path to freedom first went through me, and he came directly at me like a charging bull. When he hit me, we went to the ground, and I was able to quickly get on top of him. Tommy had chased him from behind and was on him, too, as soon as we went down, but the parolee was still very much committed to his cause. As he continued to try to free himself while we worked to get control of his arms in order to handcuff him, he threw an elbow at my face. I jerked my head back to avoid the blow, effectively giving myself whiplash. An electrical shock shot down my spine, but I continued fighting to arrest the man. Tommy was able to get his other arm under control, and we handcuffed him.

When we stood up, I turned my head, rocked it each way, shrugged my shoulders, and stretched my back. The shock was gone, and there was no pain, per se, just an odd feeling. Tommy asked if I was okay, and I told him about the electric shock. He frowned, demonstrating his concern, but we both wrote it off as an odd occurrence, nothing to worry too much about.

In the following days, pain presented in my right shoulder. I had no idea why and never considered it had anything to do with the altercation we had had. Shoulder, neck—two completely different muscle groups, or so I assumed. The pain continued over the next few days, eventually radiating down my arm until most of it was numb and my fingers tingled. A week or so later, I finally went to an orthopedic doctor and complained about my shoulder. After his examination and a review of X-rays that showed there was no damage to the shoulder, he sent me to a nerve specialist. She examined me and was certain that I had a herniated disc in my neck and that it was compressing my spinal cord. An MRI confirmed it. One disc ruptured, another bulging. I was referred to an orthopedic surgeon.

I remained working for the next month or so until the pain became unbearable, and I was forced to take a maximum dosage of pain medication to tolerate it. I have a high pain tolerance, but I had never before experienced the excruciating pain I felt from this nerve damage. To give an example of my pain tolerance, after I had the first neck surgery wherein a plug of bone from my hip was used to fuse two vertebrae together, I was told that in two to three weeks, I was to begin tapering off my pain medication. I never took another pain pill once I left the hospital—at least not at that time. Later in life, I ran a half marathon with two broken ribs. I had trained all year for the event, so when I came off a horse five days before the race and cracked two ribs, I decided I would still run. It was excruciatingly painful at first, but eventually, the pain subsided, or I got used to it; either way, I finished the race, beating the time goal I had set for myself. However, the nerve pain I experienced when my spinal cord was compressed was not tolerable even for me. I eventually had to take a medical leave of absence, and I sat at home eating pain pills like they were M&Ms. (Not really, but I was using the maximum dosage that had been prescribed.)

It took several months for the county to approve my surgery, and it may have taken longer had the surgeon not told them that I would have permanent, irreversible damage if the spinal cord remained compressed. I had lost nearly all strength in my right arm by then, which had atrophied almost two inches in a few short months. When I woke after the surgery, the pain was gone. It was replaced by stinging pain where the plug of bone had been taken from my hip and dull pain in my neck from the surgery, but there was no more pain in my arm, and the terrible nerve pain was absent. I was outfitted with a plastic neck brace that I had to wear around the clock for eight weeks. Two weeks after it was removed, I was back to work, though the doctor had recommended I remain off for a couple more months. Truthfully, I could have medically retired then, but I never considered it.

I knew there was a risk in returning to work, and I was willing to accept that risk because I loved my job and I had much unfinished business. Seldom do homicide detectives find themselves in brawls, so I felt the odds were in my favor that I wouldn't re-injure my neck. The downside was that the range of motion in my neck had been significantly reduced, which isn't necessarily the best thing for a cop. However, again, I accepted that risk. What I hadn't calculated was how much damage stress does to a body. In the coming years, I would see firsthand.

Tommy continued working on the Whittier case during my medical leave, and I rejoined him in the effort once I returned. Before I had left on leave, we had found the suspect, Tom, and we hauled him in for questioning. He lied and denied, but for some reason, he agreed to take a polygraph. Before the test was completed, Tom flamed out at the polygraph examiner and stormed out of the office, literally running away.

We were able to prove that his alibi of being at work was a lie. His union brothers had covered for him and altered the handwritten sign-in sheets, which we were able to prove through scientific handwriting analysis. A friend of Tom's eventually admitted to us that he had driven Tom to the victim's house that day, but he later recanted his story, clearly out of fear of Tom. In my absence, Tommy did a great job of compiling circumstantial evidence and putting a solid case together against Tom, but he was turned away twice at the prosecutor's office as they felt the case wasn't strong enough and that witnesses were unreliable; the latter part they likely had right.

EVENTUALLY, ROD KUSCH WAS ASKED TO TAKE ANOTHER NEW INVESTIGATOR as his partner, and I was partnered with Pam Schrick. She was near the end of her career, so perhaps not as energetic as I was. Our backgrounds differed significantly, but we made good partners, and I enjoyed working with her. She was also the only woman I ever had as a regular partner throughout my career.

Pam and I stayed busy over the next year, handling nine murders, two officer-involved shootings, and eight trash runs, the term used at the bureau for death investigations other than murder cases. We were twice as busy as Vernon Geberth recommends but not as busy as I had been at other times before and after my time partnered with Pam. Our cases included a double homicide in South Gate in which a gangster committed a "walk-up" (rather than drive-by) shooting of two rival gang members, capping each of them in their heads and casually walking away. Though we had a suspect in the case, we were never able to develop enough evidence to charge him, and that case remains unsolved.

Another case we were never able to solve was a Lennox station murder wherein two Crips were walking down the sidewalk after a trip to the liquor store when one of the two was shot multiple times. He died, and the other would never provide information on the shooters. We determined early on that it was an "in-house" murder, meaning that the victim was shot by members of his own gang for whatever reason. The second man either knew who the shooters were, or he may have been involved in setting up his friend. But he would never admit to either, and without sufficient corroborating evidence, we were never able to file a case against him. Such goes life in the ghetto where the investigators sometimes care more about solving the murders than do the victim's family and friends.

An interesting side note on that case: we had served a search warrant at the home of the "friend" who was with the victim when he was killed and who we believed may have been involved in some fashion in the murder. He had a very unusual and memorable last name. Not only had we served a warrant at his house, but on another occasion, we picked him up and hauled him to the station for another interview, a more intense one than we had had with him previously. By then, we were out of clues that could help us solve the murder, and we felt certain he knew exactly who had pulled the trigger. Both times we were at his home, he was there alone. We had not met his father.

After the last interview, where we had picked the witness up and hauled him to the station, the father called and ordered me to stop harassing his child. He said he was an ironworker, and, as an iron worker, he proudly announced the union of which he was a member. His voice was extraordinarily deep, and his words were on the edge of threatening. I pictured this union iron worker as a big man with anvils for hands with which he would El Kabong me on my head if given the chance. Nonetheless, I assured him that I would do whatever it took to solve the case and hung up as he continued ranting into the phone.

A year or more later, Tommy Harris and I were following leads on the Whittier murder of the stripper's boyfriend. The suspect in that case, Tom, was also an ironworker, and his alibi was that he was at work during the time of the murder. We went to the work site, a towering mass of steel being cobbled together amongst the other high-rises in downtown Los Angeles, and while waiting at a crosswalk to proceed across the busy street, we found ourselves surrounded by these union brothers. A tiny man caught my eye as he was so different in stature from the others, and I about choked when I spotted his last name printed on the sides of his hard hat. You guessed it; he was the father of the little gangster from Lennox. I addressed him by his first name to get his attention. He turned to face me, skeptical and curious. "Who are you?" he asked, with a little less bass in his voice than what he had had on the phone. "Danny Smith, L.A. Sheriff's Homicide," I said, smiling widely as I stepped in close, towering over him. I offered my hand, and we shook hands firmly. I said, "You sounded much larger on the phone." I left him there as the signal changed, and it was time to cross the street. After standing frozen for a moment, he proceeded across the street behind us, keeping a safe distance. Tommy smiled and said, "I can't wait to hear the story about that."

Some of the other cases I handled with Pam included another child murder, which we solved, a child death, of which we were never able to determine the cause, and a SIDS death. We sent a couple of killers to prison, and there was one who pleaded to involuntary manslaughter and received a three-year sentence, of which he probably served half. Sadly, life is cheap in Los Angeles.

THE LAST CASE I WORKED WHILE STILL ASSIGNED AS PAM'S PARTNER WAS A shooting in Carson that left one person dead and another critically wounded. Pam was off for some reason, so Joe Martinez and I were paired together for that rotation. Joe had worked at Firestone when I had, so we had known each other a long time, but this was the first and only homicide case we ever worked together.

The murder happened at the busiest intersection of Carson at the busiest time of the afternoon and was witnessed by dozens of people who had arrived in a city bus just as the shooting went down. The suspect had gunned down one of the two victims and then chased the other down the block, firing at him all the way until he reached a gas station at the corner, where he collapsed. The suspect fled in a black SUV driven by a woman, and, amazingly, several witnesses recorded its license.

The vehicle was registered to a woman who lived in an apartment in San Diego. But before we would be able to go down there, we needed to interview the dozens of witnesses who waited at Carson station for us as soon as possible. We also had a large, expansive crime scene to process, so we asked for two additional teams to assist us. My former partner, Rod Kusch, and his new partner, Randy Seymour, processed the scene, while John Laurie and Steve Davis helped me and Joe wade through witness interviews at Carson station. Meanwhile, I called the surveillance detail at Special Investigations and asked them to assist by conducting surveillance of the San Diego apartment where the vehicle was registered.

It was a Wednesday, which meant we had started early at the office that day for the weekly bureau meeting, where cases would be briefed, and the captain would bore us with administrative announcements. The callout came in the late afternoon, just when I was contemplating whether I should head home for dinner and get some rest before being called out or hang around the office to see if someone died early in the evening. It was always a gamble, and this time, my not leaving early had paid off as I was still at the office in the late afternoon when the murder happened, and I didn't have far to drive.

However, by the time we finished with interviews and the crime scene investigation, it was midnight. Meanwhile, the suspect's vehicle had arrived at the San Diego apartment, though occupied only by a female. Since our shooter wasn't with her, we had surveillance stay on the location until we could get there, and we finished our interviews before heading south.

In the early morning hours of the following day, we arrived at the apartment in San Diego and contacted the female who had driven the getaway vehicle. She denied any involvement and would tell us nothing about who the male suspect was, so we arrested her, impounded her Escalade as evidence, searched her apartment, and spent the next couple of hours scouring through property and documents we believed belonged to our shooter. The man had multiple identities and life stories, but what seemed to be consistent was that he had come from New York. We took all of the items that were attributed to him—papers, letters, miscellaneous identifications, and photographs—and we held those items and their containers as evidence, hoping to identify the suspect through fingerprints left behind.

A new day had dawned while we were still inside the apartment, and it was midmorning before we were able to head north. Joe said, "I'm hungry. How about we have breakfast before heading back."

I didn't like it, and I told him so; breakfast would put me to sleep. We had been working more than 24 hours straight at this point, and to say we both were tired is an understatement. But Joe insisted, so we ate before getting back on the road.

My rule was always that the bookman (passenger) stay awake in order to keep the driver from dozing off. But Joe put his head back and closed his eyes in spite of my many protests during the first hour of the drive. The next thing I knew, horns were blasting, and Joe and I both shot straight up in our seats to find that we were traveling diagonally across the northbound lanes of the always-congested San Diego Freeway. I had been sound asleep—not just dozing—for who knows how long. I jerked the wheel, and the tires of my Crown Vic grabbed the pavement violently as we straightened into a lane. Once I had things under control, I glanced over to see Joe braced in his seat, his eyes bulging like he had seen Mother Mary in a tunnel of light. I said, "Now stay awake, Joe!" I warned him that if he drifted back to sleep, I was going back to sleep too. Joe kept his eyes open for the remainder of the drive back to L.A.

Joe and I both had long drives from the office to our homes. I don't recall what Joe did, but I slept in my car in the parking lot for an hour or two and then worked until later that evening before going home. It wasn't the first nor the last time I would sleep in my car, on the floor by my desk, or in the ladies' restroom. Yes, there was a couch in the ladies' room, and all the guys knew it, and many would occasionally use it. But only late at night, and only after making sure that there were no women left in the building, would the occasional tired detective go horizontal therein. After all, the women in that building were armed, and some of them—like many of the men—were of questionable sanity. The safer bet was to hit a bunk room at a nearby station, although that was less convenient.

Working around the clock was not uncommon when you picked up a fresh case. As they say, the first 48 hours are critical, and a lot of things happen during that relatively short period of time. Of course, federal law forbade us from working such hours, so on our time sheets, we had signed in at 8:00 Wednesday morning and signed out at midnight that night, though that was just about when we were heading south to San Diego. But because 16 hours were all we were allowed to work in a day, and never two days consecutively, that's what the timesheet had to reflect. There were other times we would work even longer, perhaps 36 or 48 hours straight, and the time sheets would again show only those hours we could "legally" work. The brass all knew this was the case, and the tradeoff was that nobody checked on you when you didn't come to the office. When you were sick, you stayed home, and you still put in for your regular eight-hour day. (Of course, you very likely would be working from home anyway, handling phone calls, maybe dictating reports.) It used to be called "drawer time," though by then, that term was a forbidden one. It was the unofficial timekeeping system where you kept a loose count of all of your uncompensated hours worked and took "drawer time" on those days you couldn't make it in or just needed time off. So nobody complained, at least not back in those days. I'm sure that eventually, somebody will—if they haven't already. Homicide was the best job in the county, and we were privileged to be there. But as my former lieutenant, Deac Slocumb, had said after a deputy was caught using his county car for all manner of family business, "Nothing was so good that some deputy wouldn't fuck it up for everybody."

From the onset, we believed the Carson murder was a drug deal gone bad or was somehow otherwise related to drugs. That proved to be the case, and once we figured out who the shooter was, a nationwide manhunt began. By then, Pam and I had parted ways, and Jeff Leslie and I were reunited, now partners at Homicide. I kept the case that Joe and I had started, and I would continue working on it for a long time, traveling the country to do so. More on that later.

19

FAMILIAR PARTNER

STRANGE CASES

W e started with a bang. By now, Jeff Leslie and I had been best of friends for many years and partners at several assignments. We had always worked well together, seemingly always on the same page with our thoughts and processes. We also shared a peculiar sense of humor, so it was no surprise that our first case would be a murder that played out like a twisted HBO production with a cast of characters that included a transvestite, a wannabe gangster, a trio of hoodlums, and the possibility of a sexual motive for the killing.

The victim was a divorced 47-year-old affluent male who worked for the studios constructing movie and TV sets. He was found in his front yard on a warm May morning, shot through his head at close range while doing yard work. He had left a mower in the half-mown lawn and walked over to the back of his truck, where he removed his right work glove. The victim was right-handed, so the question became had he removed the glove for the purposes of dexterity, or had he taken it off to shake somebody's hand? The position of the victim suggested he had turned from the truck and started back toward his lawnmower when the killer, evidently positioned near the open tailgate, fired a single shot at close range. The gunshot was what we call a through-and-through, meaning it entered and exited his head and kept going. After searching much of the terrain beyond the victim's position and down the line of the bullet's trajectory, we jokingly surmised that it was probably still going.

From the onset of our investigation, we were convinced that the victim knew his killer.

The victim had a roommate at the time, a coworker and friend of many years who was separated from his wife. He was the last person other than the killer to see the victim alive (or perhaps just the last person, period) and the one who found him dead. Oftentimes, the last to see a victim alive and the first to find them dead are two separate individuals, and both are always of significant interest to detectives in the preliminary stages of an investigation. The roommate, filling both of these categories, was someone we focused on early in the case.

The roommate claimed to have left a couple of hours earlier, about the time the victim had started his yard work. He claimed to have driven to Palmdale, where he had lived prior to separating from his wife, to get a haircut from his regular barber. (The barber was not sure that the roommate's visit had been on the same day as the murder.) The roommate further said he stopped by his old home to take a shower after having his hair cut. That puzzled us. He was estranged from his wife, living with the victim, yet he went by his old home in Palmdale—where his wife still lived—to take a shower late in the morning after getting his hair cut.

The roommate provided that information during an interview at Santa Clarita station shortly after we had begun our investigation. There were many parts of the interview that added to our suspicion of him, and he would be the first we would need to eliminate as a suspect. The next day we met with the roommate and his estranged wife and obtained a little more information. But all of it was bizarre. She became his alibi, and he became hers, each stating that they happened to pass each other on the freeway going in opposite directions that morning. They also seemed to be suddenly together, very much so, though separated and going through a divorce. These things added to our suspicion of the roommate and even caused us to wonder about the roommate's spouse. After that second meeting, each of them obtained counsel and asked that we not contact them again.

The victim's home was located at the end of a dirt road in a secluded canyon. The homes were spread far apart on large acreage lots. Though there was a small concrete slab in front of the garage, the victim had been killed on the dirt portion of the driveway. The only shoe impressions we found near the body were those of a patrol sergeant who seemed to have walked in circles around our victim and who sheepishly looked away when I exaggerated my glances from the shoe impressions to his feet. He admitted being by the body, though he didn't recall walking around it. He should have known better, and I made sure he realized it.

The nearest neighbors were three men who lived directly across the road from the victim. They were about the same age as our victim and were heavy drinkers, divorcees, and biker types. Two were Vietnam veterans. Only one of the three was home at the time of the murder. He didn't hear a gunshot, as he was likely in the shower, given his stated timeline. It was clear from early on that these individuals had nothing to do with the murder, but we verified the alibis of the two who were gone that morning, nonetheless. As for the one in the shower, he was relaxed, jovial, and open as he told us that he and his roommates strongly disliked the victim and thought he was an asshole. Shower Man said he certainly wasn't sad that his neighbor was dead but assured us he hadn't killed him. He cooperated with us throughout the investigation, making himself available for anything we asked of him, including a polygraph examination. (He was not given one as we never considered him a viable suspect; however, we would often ask people if they would submit to a polygraph just to see their reactions and gauge their willingness to comply.)

The victim had an adult son who was involved in drugs and gangs and who lived on the other side of the valley with his girlfriend. He certainly had a motive; he and his sister would inherit all of the victim's wealth. However, my partner and I knocked on his door late that night at our first opportunity, and he was clearly surprised at the news of his father's death—or else he was a very good actor. He and his girlfriend allowed us to search their home without a warrant, and we did. We found a handgun, but it had not been recently fired nor cleaned, and we did not believe it to be the murder weapon.

During the crime scene investigation, we found the recent tire tracks of one or more BMX-style bicycle(s), and we considered that the son could have ridden there that morning to see his father, though they were not on speaking terms. But the distance from the victim's home to his son's was considerable, and the son claimed to no longer own a bike. The son would later submit to a polygraph, the results of which were inconclusive. The victim's daughter did not live locally and was not considered a suspect.

The most bizarre part of this case was that the victim had an ex-girlfriend who was transgender and who had been over-the-top furious about their recent breakup. We learned that she had even made threats against the victim. The two had met when she was a streetwalking sex worker in Hollywood, a transvestite at the time. The victim patronized her, fell in love with her, and ultimately paid for her to have gender reassignment surgeries. She lived in an apartment not far from where the victim lived. When we interviewed her, she was honest about all aspects of their relationship, how they met, and her personal story. She even admitted to making threats against the victim after he broke up with her. However, she had one of the best alibis a person can have, one we were able to easily verify, and we did. On the day of the murder—nearly at the time of the murder—she had undergone back surgery.

We were never able to solve the case, but we worked on it diligently for many months, and we even picked the case back up a few times over the following years to see if anything had changed. We conducted surveillance of the roommate and his wife, who, interestingly enough, reconciled after the murder and moved to the beach. The more we looked at the two of them as suspects, the more convinced I was that it was one of the two—or both—who had killed the victim. Given the bizarre sexual desires of the victim and the fact that the roommate was somewhat effeminate himself, we considered that the spouse may have discovered that her husband was involved in a homosexual relationship with the victim and decided there was only one way left to save her marriage. But that was only my hunch, and unfortunately, we had no evidence against either of them.

We learned that at the funeral, the roommate had put a letter in the victim's coffin just before the burial. Through a search warrant, we looked for the pad of paper that a note may have been written on in hopes that we could recreate the letter from impressions left on the next page. It was a long shot that didn't pay off. But we wanted that letter, and now there was only one way to get it. Well, one legal way...

I prepared a search warrant for the contents of the coffin excluding the remains of the victim, accompanied by an application for a court-ordered exhumation. I obtained the chief medical examiner's blessing and included that in my affidavit. The warrant and order were issued, and my partner and I stood graveside while the victim was exhumed. We obtained the letter from inside the coffin while carefully avoiding the decomposing remains and trying our best not to inhale the rancid odor.

The contents of that letter were interesting but not what we had hoped. There was no "Sorry I had to kill you, friend," or "Sorry that crazy bitch I'm married to shot you in the back of the head." But the words "interesting" and "odd" came to mind while I studied the words that the victim's best friend had written. As my partner had said about it at the time, "It certainly isn't anything I would say in a letter to you if you were murdered."

"I'm sorry this had to happen to you." That was a line we were both hung up on. *Had* to happen? Interesting choice of words. "Sorry it happened" would have been more appropriate.

In a move seldom used by homicide detectives of major metropolitan law enforcement agencies, we solicited the help of the FBI. I've never been a big fan of the profilers, though I agree that their assessments are usually accurate. General, vague, commonly known by serious practitioners of death investigation, but accurate, nonetheless. But if ever I needed to be wowed by their talent, this was the time.

Three months later, we received the results, and to say we were sorely disappointed is my way of keeping this memoir relatively clean. I'll just say that their analysis told us nothing we didn't already know and hadn't provided to them in our case study notes.

One final thing we did—if for no other reason than to see the reaction of the roommate—was take a questionnaire that the FBI profilers had provided with their report and suggested we ask all family, friends, and coworkers of the victim to complete. The roommate and the victim were both union workers with the studios. We showed up at their shop one day and gathered a group of twenty or so and asked if they would each complete the form, that it might help us solve the murder of their union brother. All but the roommate happily agreed to do so, and they did. The roommate cited his attorney's instruction not to cooperate with us. We had anticipated that would be his reaction, and our hope was that it would raise concern or suspicion among his peers and that someone might give us a call later with helpful information. That never happened, and soon the case grew cold as new cases continued stacking up and demanding our attention.

THE NEXT CASE WE CAUGHT WAS THAT OF AN UP-AND-COMING RAP STAR, shot to death as he sat in the passenger seat of a car while the driver went to the back of a house to buy some weed. The victim, Johnny Burns, known as "Mausberg" in the hood, was affiliated with the Campanella Park Bloods. He was killed in the early morning hours of July 5, 2000, which, of course, was still the night of the Fourth of July. A lot of people were out on the streets that night and into the next morning, but not in that neighborhood. Not after that shooting.

Like most gang cases, nobody knew anything. Nobody saw anything. Nobody wanted to talk to the cops. We hit up his family, his fellow gangsters, his rap friends and associates—nothing. I believed it to be an inside hit, either by his gang or by someone in the rap industry. Lots of people got killed for reasons that remain secret in the outlaw world of gangsta rap.

It took months before information came back to us about who might have been involved. We worked long and hard with the information provided but never got a break on the case. However, we kept an eye on the two suspects, waiting for them to be back in custody (gangsters came and went from jail with predictable regularity), and several months later, our tenacity paid off; the two were both locked up on unrelated charges. We had them each sent to court, where we braced them in a holding cell that had been wired for audio recording. We took DNA samples from each of them while a "prop" poor-boy file case sat on the table. On that file folder, I had written the victim's name, his street name—in the event they didn't know his real name—the type of weapon used, along with a notation that it had been recovered, even though it had not. I also placed the word "SOLVED" in bold letters along the top, though it wasn't. This was all done—including the DNA because there was no DNA in the case itself—in an effort to elicit a conversation between the two about the murder.

The plan worked, providing us with confirmation that we were on to the right two suspects. However, the audio recording was low as the two mostly whispered once we left them alone, likely concerned that the room was, in fact, bugged. Some of the parts that could be heard included one chastising the other about the weapon, saying, "I thought you got rid of it."

But that wasn't enough to charge either of them with the victim's murder, primarily because their conversation was so unclear that any attorney would likely argue, perhaps successfully—*perhaps rightly*—that something other than that is what had been said, or that they were speaking about a different case or scenario. Both of the suspects clammed up when we attempted to interview them after that operation, no other evidence was ever discovered, and another case went cold.

Our department's homicide bureau considered a case "solved" when a suspect was charged with the crime. Some departments, such as our biggest rivals in blue, declared their cases solved the minute they had a name to put on a suspect line. This case was yet another unsolved case for us, and it would have been touted as solved by our LAPD friends. Not that it mattered, but it is worth making that known since some former cops seek fame for their great accomplishments as homicide detectives through books, movies, or shows, and in doing so, they often cite their stellar solve rates. The truth is that in a major metropolitan area where investigators carry far more cases than what "the book" suggests and where the citizenry refuses to cooperate with investigators, a solve rate of around fifty percent is probably the average. The other peeve I have along these lines is those who claim to have investigated thousands of murders, yet they were a cop in Colorado, for example. Give me a break. What that means is that maybe they supervised a homicide bureau for twenty years and are taking credit for all of the cases that all of their underlings investigated.

LESLIE AND I CONTINUED TO PURSUE LEADS ON THE CARSON MURDER THAT Joe Martinez and I had handled—the one that took us to San Diego late that night and nearly killed us on the way home—whenever we had a spare moment. We had learned from evidence we had obtained at the San Diego home of the female accomplice, and through interviews of our victim's family members and friends, that our suspect was a fugitive from New York. The family members had known the suspect, stating he had been considered a friend of the victims, which furthered my suspicion that the murder was drug related. However, we still didn't know his true identity, something he concealed from everyone he met in California.

One night, we had worked late doing some covert operations on the Santa Clarita union guy murder. We had done surveillance of the roommate's wife, and we had waited for a while after all the lights were turned off inside her home so that we could steal her trash, which had been put out for morning pickup. I was always a big fan of "trash runs," because there was a lot that could be learned from sifting through what people discarded.

In the wee hours that followed, the two of us sat on milk crates in Leslie's garage sifting through bags of trash while drinking cold beer and looking for clues. He had moved his wife's car out of the garage to give us room, though half of the garage was full of exercise apparatus, camping gear, bicycles, and sporting equipment. Fluorescent lights flickered above as we probed the debris, hoping to find a motive for the roommate and his wife to have killed their friend.

As the hours went on, our conversation turned to the Carson case, New York, and a killer on the run. That was the thing, you might be working on several murders at any given time, and while you're focused on one, you're thinking of the others. By now we were convinced that the suspect in the Carson shooting case had returned to New York, and we wondered just how he might have gotten there. We had identified the car he used to flee San Diego, and we had had airport police search local airports for it with no luck. Somehow, we came up with the idea that the suspect had driven from San Diego to Dallas-Fort Worth where he boarded a plane to New York. I honestly don't recall now how we were led to believe this to be the case, but it turned out we were right. Leslie said, while sifting through the last of the trash in his garage, "I'll call the Texas Rangers, put them on the task." He had a connection from a previous case, so it seemed like a great idea to me.

An hour later, my partner was blending margaritas and making phone calls, having decided that it was now after six in Texas, and that any self-respecting Ranger would be up and at it by then. And they were. But the Ranger he contacted referred us to the Dallas-Fort Worth police department, and provided Leslie with the name of a detective who would help us out. My partner called him next, and left a message. We continued drinking.

Another hour had passed when the Texas cop returned our call and said he was impressed by how early we started in the morning out in Los Angeles. Leslie started a second batch of margaritas in his blender, and over the high-pitched whir of the machine and the clattering of ice being pulverized, he told the airport detective, "We're still working from yesterday, pal."

The detective was going to search for the car and get back to us. Soon, the sky was showing its first signs of light and we could hear the sounds of children thundering across the second story of Leslie's home, the kids now out of bed and readying themselves for school. Apparently, we had stayed up a little too late. My partner glanced at his watch and said, "Shit, I've got court. You can crash in the guest room, and we'll hook up at the office later on."

Later that day, we learned that the DFW detective had located the suspect's vehicle in long-term parking and impounded it as evidence for us. The next day, we boarded a plane headed to Texas. We met with the detective and arranged for a team of forensic investigators to assist us in processing the car for evidence. Our hope was that there would be trace evidence left behind, such as fingerprints, DNA, blood, or anything else. Of course, we also had high hopes that the gun used in the murder would be found therein.

We didn't know it until the next day, but the detective had summoned a forensic team of FBI personnel to assist. They went to work on the car in an airplane hangar that was half filled with emergency vehicles, cop cars, bright green fire trucks, and tankers full of fire-retardant foam. It was the home of the airport's first responders. We sweated in the Texas summer heat while watching this FBI forensic team turn a simple task into an all-day affair. We didn't recover the gun or any firearms-related evidence, but several latent prints were identified and lifted. However, none of this evidence helped us identify the suspect.

Leaving Texas could be a book in itself. But the short version is that back in that time, when MD-80 planes were falling out of the sky like shot-riddled ducks, my partner and I boarded one such aircraft on the morning we were to return to L.A. When traveling "on duty," law enforcement officers are pre-boarded and usually introduced to the flight crew so that they are aware of the presence of armed law enforcement passengers. They were always very welcoming, oftentimes upgrading us to first class if it was available—without us asking. On this particular trip, my partner and I were skeptical about the two females that sat at the helm. Not to be sexist, but it was a very different experience for both of us. Occasionally you would see a woman in the cockpit, and whether she was the pilot or the copilot, I never knew. But this was the first time that either of us had boarded a plane that would be under the control of two women. We took our seats and joked about the situation.

A half hour later, as the plane labored to climb into the crystal-blue Texas sky, the passengers all grew silent together, everyone likely noticing that the plane had been sluggish in acceleration from the start. My uncle, the late, great, Lt. Col. Bascom P. Smith, a three-war combat veteran pilot, used to time the takeoffs of commercial flights and give them thirty-five seconds to be off the deck. I clocked wheels up at about forty seconds, fretting for the last five. As the nose of the jet lifted, and we began to climb into the sky, the plane growled as if working extra hard to gain altitude, and it felt sluggish as it did. Soon we were banking to the right and the climbing had mostly stopped, yet we hadn't gained much altitude. I cinched my belt tighter and studied the scant bodies of water below us, wondering if it would be better to crash into one of them or onto solid ground. The flight attendants were called to the cockpit where they huddled in the doorway for a short time. Soon thereafter, one of them feigned a smile and announced that we would be returning to DFW for "routine maintenance." Nobody was buying that line of crock.

A lady seated in front of us turned and struck up a conversation, perhaps looking for comfort or strength. She said she really could use a drink, and my partner confirmed that so could we. She said she had a bottle of wine in her carry-on but didn't think she could reach it. We encouraged her to try, but she remained seated as the plane began bouncing more than it previously had been. The jet engines still didn't sound right even though they weren't under the same load as they had been while we were trying to gain altitude. The cabin remained silent, everyone likely joining me in silent prayers and thoughts of loved ones that might be left behind. It seemed to take forever to make the big circle, but soon we were flying straight and dropping altitude at an acceptable rate, given the situation. I couldn't wait to get on the ground, but not too abruptly.

Eventually we could see the airstrip. It was easy to spot which one we'd be using as it was lined by a dozen or more emergency vehicles—police cars, firetrucks, ambulances, and several tankers filled with fire-retardant foam, red and blue lights flashing atop of each. We had spent half of the previous day with some of the very people who now waited below, prepared to do whatever they could in a worst-case scenario. Simply put, they were prepared for a crash landing, and so were we. With that thought I cinched my belt even tighter and said another prayer.

I always knew life could come to a screeching halt—we saw the aftermath of it all the time—but I never had thought that for me it would be the result of a plane crash. With a heavy heart, I pictured my children, just little girls at the time, and my wife, seeing the three of them at home, joyful in their routines, no idea of the predicament I was in. I had been in many situations wherein I could have been killed, but none that allowed considerable reflection while the scenario slowly unfolded. I had no control of this matter, no way to fix it and no say in the outcome. Honestly, these were the most frightening ten minutes of my life.

The MD-80 bounced as the landing gear struck the airstrip with a harshness I wouldn't have believed possible outside of a crash. The tires grabbed at the asphalt once more, and the jet engines roared. The fuselage shook and shuddered as we abruptly decelerated, and passengers braced themselves against the force of physics. As the plane slowed, and it finally seemed the lady pilots had us under control, my prayer giving thanks was interrupted by the voice of the skipper. It was the first time since meeting her at the helm that I heard her voice again, and she was just as calm as she had been before our departure, displaying total control in the aftermath of a harrowing event. She said, "Ladies and gentlemen, on behalf of American Airlines, we would like to welcome you back to Dallas-Fort Worth."

Passengers cheered, cried, smiled and high-fived one another as the plane then safely coasted to the gate. I still get choked up when I recall the emotion I felt as I listened to the captain's words that morning.

We thanked the flight crew on our way out, and then bounced across the passenger loading bridge and reentered the airport. Airport employees were herding our group toward an adjacent gate where another plane was prepared to take us home. Everyone went along like sheep. My partner and I looked at the new equipment that sat ominously looking back, its black nose pointed directly at us, and said, "Bullshit." It was another MD-80, and arguably two of the bravest passengers on that flight had no problem refusing to board another one. We inquired about any additional flights to Los Angeles, one that would have equipment other than the MD-80, and we learned that the next flight was six hours later. It was a bigger jet and only half full, so without hesitation, we said we'd take that flight instead, and off to the airport bar we went.

A short time after our Texas trip, I learned that the suspect's girlfriend had gone to New York herself, and through further investigation, we came up with a Brooklyn address where she might have been staying. Our thought, of course, was that this might have been where the suspect was staying also. So we packed our bags and headed to New York.

But first, I made contact with Lieutenant John Dove of the Brooklyn Cold Case squad. I explained the situation and our plans for finding our suspect in New York, and he assured me that his team would be available to assist us in whatever we needed. We would usually rent a car when we traveled, but Lieutenant Dove said not to bother—there was no place to park anyway. He said they'd pick us up at the airport and shuttle us around as needed. We were there for three or four days, and I have honestly never worked with a better group of cops in my life—and that is really saying something because I have had the privilege to work with some of the best cops in the world. But these New Yorkers were hardcore, tough, funny, and fun-loving. They made sure to give us the grand tour while there, sending us out on the harbor patrol boat for a tour of the Statue of Liberty, taking us to all five boroughs to let us see the sights. We toured Spanish Harlem, had dinner at a mobster-owned Italian restaurant in the Bronx that was chock full of mafiosos, and one night, we had dinner and drinks at O'Hara's[1], a famous Irish pub in Manhattan where police and fire uniform shoulder patches and photographs cover nearly every square inch of the walls.

After traditional *mick* dinners, we bellied up to the bar. The bartender was just what you would expect (demand?) at such a joint, an old-school Irishman with a heavy New York accent and a reverence for cops everywhere—and also a fear of dehydration, apparently. The drinks flowed freely and kept coming, cold beers stacked on cold beers, only a portion of which made the tab. I had barely noticed that our hosts were disappearing one by one over the hours. We were having too much fun to realize the time of night, and we had no idea—until closing—that the bars stayed open until 4 a.m. in New York.

The plan had been that the team would pick us up at the hotel at six. We hailed a cab, having no idea where we were, but knowing our hotel's name, we paid twenty bucks for a ride around the corner. We stumbled through the front doors and up to our room, regretting our predicament now that the fun was finished. My partner called the front desk to put in a wake-up call for five. It was now almost 4:30. He had to argue with the person on the other end of the phone, assuring him he meant 5:00 a.m., a half-hour from the time of the call. At five-fifteen, an employee was pounding on our door. Apparently, the ringing phone hadn't fazed either of us in our alcohol-induced slumbers. At six, two sharply dressed but perhaps fuzzy-minded detectives were met by a chuckling pair of New York's finest, who had parked their plain-wrapped city car on the sidewalk. Our chariot awaited.

Being kind-natured, if not sympathetic, the boys from the squad first took us somewhere for food, coffee, and copious amounts of clear liquids so that we might replenish our semi-precious bodily fluids. But then it was back to work. By seven, we had coerced our way into a row house on Flushing Avenue in Brooklyn, searching for our suspect or his girlfriend, who had relocated from San Diego. He wasn't there, but we found her enjoying that of which we had deprived ourselves: sleep. So we woke her and told her to get dressed, and she was hauled back to the squad room, where she waited while we repeated this process at three other locations throughout Brooklyn and Queens.

By the end of the day, we had our suspect identified, though we had no idea where he might be. We had spoken with a detective in Queens who had investigated a shooting that the suspect committed there a few years prior, but he had thus far eluded capture. The detective told us that the incident this suspect had been involved in was wild, remarkable, and one of the craziest he had ever investigated. The suspect had gotten into a beef with two men in a nightclub, and the fight was taken outside. The suspect gunned down one of the two on the sidewalk, and then, as the other man attempted to flee in a vehicle, the suspect jumped onto the hood of the moving car and fired numerous rounds through the windshield, striking but not killing the driver. The detective described the suspect as a very dangerous man. I told him how the same man had gunned down two men in broad daylight in Carson, and he wasn't surprised.

When we left New York, we had a positive identification of our suspect and additional evidence against him. We had met some great cops and had a grand tour of the city. Best of all, we had uneventful travel to and from, which was comforting since a week later, we would be on another flight, this time headed to South Carolina. I thought I had traveled a lot while working Fugitive, but that detail had nothing on Homicide when it came to going wheels up in the friendly skies.

After we returned from New York, I was able to get the United States Marshals Service involved in the case. The suspect was a federal fugitive now, having crossed state lines while fleeing prosecution. Our department had deputies assigned to a federal fugitive detail, and they took care of obtaining the warrant and coordinating the search for the suspect. We would pass the information on as we got it, and shortly after leaving New York, we discovered that the suspect had fled to the coast. The task force followed the leads and ultimately captured the suspect in South Carolina, and we needed to take a crack at him.

My captain suggested that we have someone there ask the suspect if he would talk to us if we flew down there, revealing his lack of investigative experience. You've got one shot at getting a suspect to talk, and you don't waste it by sending a messenger. I won the argument, and off we went. We returned with nothing—the suspect invoked his right to remain silent—so the captain gave me a big fat "I told you so" when we returned, no doubt solidifying in his own mind how much smarter he was than the rest of us.

The suspect was extradited to New York to stand trial there before we would ever get our shot at him in the courts of Los Angeles County. Either way, he would hopefully never see freedom again.

OVER THE NEXT YEAR, JEFF LESLIE AND I INVESTIGATED ANOTHER TWENTY-one death cases, eight of which were murders, seven of which had been reported as unknown causes and turned out to be something other than murder, two officer-involved shootings, a drowned child, and three suicides. We solved five of the eight murders we handled, one of which was the case of a four-year-old girl killed by her biological father.

The investigation of Lauren Key-Marer's death may have been the turning point in my career, and by turning point, I don't mean for the better. To this day, I can recall every detail of the little girl's broken body, soaked by the ocean water, where she came to rest after being thrown from a hundred-foot cliff by her father. I remember the contents of her lunch pail, barely touched as she had had no appetite, knowing, instinctively, the danger she faced and perhaps intuitively knowing the hatred her "father" had for her. She had known he would pick her up from school that day.

We had been first up for murders and were hanging around in the office during the evening of November 8, 2000, working on other cases. Toni Martinez was working the desk, and she told us about a case that had been called in as an accidental death at Inspiration Point in Pacific Palisades. She began telling us some of the details, and neither of us liked what we heard. My partner said, "That's bullshit. No one takes a four-year-old out to the end of that cliff." He had handled a suicide there not long before and was familiar with the location.

The three of us responded together, but it was quickly determined that this case would be investigated as a homicide, not an accidental death. That meant it would be mine and Leslie's to handle. It was complex, and like many of the cases mentioned in this memoir, a book could easily be written on that case alone if one were so inclined—which I am not. That little girl's death took too much out of me, and I haven't the energy to revisit it in any detail. But I would be remiss not to offer a briefing of it since this case no doubt contributed greatly to my burnout.

Lauren was conceived during a brief romantic interlude between her mother, Sarah, and a very odd man named Cameron Brown.

Brown worked at LAX as a baggage handler. When not working, he could be found surfing. His grandmother owned a beachfront property wherein he had installed a webcam that he used to monitor surf conditions constantly.

Previously, he had lived by himself in the mountains of Colorado, above the tree line, accessible only by snow machine during the winters. This while he was in his early twenties, a time in the lives of most men when they yearned to be around other people, to be in the presence of young ladies. He also drove an army surplus "deuce-and-a-half" truck (a ten-wheel, 2 ½-ton troop carrier) because it "freaked people out," and he told people his father was a CIA agent, which he wasn't.

Brown was a self-centered young man who did not desire to have children or settle down. He first demanded a DNA test at the news of Sarah being pregnant. Then, he tried to convince Sarah to have an abortion. She refused. Not long after, Brown told Sarah they should go to counseling, which she thought would be something positive for the coming child and their relationship. But that wasn't what it was; he took her to a pre-abortion counseling session.

Sarah was in the States from England and had overstayed her visa. Brown continued to urge her to abort the child and, at one point, threatened to have her deported if she didn't. Sarah worked at a travel agency. Brown called there to "anonymously" report that she was stealing from the company, being too ignorant to know there was no exchange of currency in her work. He became mean and nasty toward her during this time, and the two stopped speaking. Sarah went on to have her baby, an adorable little girl she named Lauren. Sarah never asked anything of the father, and the father wanted nothing to do with his daughter. Sarah made sure he knew he had a daughter and told him he should be part of Lauren's life. He declined.

Not long after, Sarah married a man who had custody of his young son. It was he who encouraged her to get child support from Lauren's father, and she did. Brown suddenly found himself with a substantial wage garnishment to pay support plus arrears.

By then, Brown had been kicked out of his father's home and was down on his luck when he met a woman named Patti. She had a job and a condo, and the two soon cohabitated. When Patti learned that Brown had a child, she insisted that he obtain custody of her. He wanted no part of that, but she persisted. She told him it was a way to reduce or eliminate his support payments, so he went along with her plan.

But Patti's plan meant Brown had to start spending his precious time off doing things like meeting with the child in supervised visits and attending classes on child-rearing. He could barely disguise his contempt about having to do these things, contempt toward Patti for making him do it, Sarah for putting him in the situation, and Lauren merely for her existence.

Many "incidents" preceded the day of the murder. Brown once showed up at the preschool to pick Lauren up on a visitation day on his motorcycle. Since he hadn't even brought a helmet for her, the school wouldn't allow him to take her. On the days of visitation, Lauren would report being sick to her teacher. When Brown dropped Lauren off after a visit, he would leave her in the street and drive off, never even putting the car in park. He would generally pick Lauren up, drop her off at his mother's house, and go surfing. That was how he spent his days with his daughter.

Sarah saw the change in her daughter once visitation began, and she recognized that Lauren was fearful and withdrawn, especially on the days when "Papa Cameron" was going to be picking her up. She would tell her mother she was sick and couldn't go, but Sarah forced her to anyway. As Sarah said, she was under court order, and though it broke her heart, and she instinctively knew it was a bad situation, she felt she had no option but to obey the law with regard to these visitations and shared custody.

Later, a search of Brown's internet history showed that on the morning of the murder, he had adhered to his normal routine of checking webcams showing surf conditions at various beaches across the southland. After he left their home that morning to go pick up Lauren, the internet activity changed to searches related to fathers' rights, ways to win custody of children, the processes of adoption, and so forth. Only Patti could have been on the computer during that time. It was easy to see the two opposing agendas at work: Brown wanted nothing to do with his daughter; Patti wanted nothing other than to have her in their life. Brown didn't want to spend his precious time with Lauren, but he also didn't want to keep paying child support. It was our belief that on that day, he chose to rid himself of both of those problems and also of the ongoing, often contentious dealings with Sarah.

He drove to Abalone Cove, where he paid to park at the beach. The attendant remembered the odd pairing, the frightened look on Lauren's face, and that she had a bad feeling about the situation. She considered that the child may have been kidnapped but dismissed her fears and continued collecting tolls as Brown and Lauren parked and headed south on foot.

From the parking lot to the end of Inspiration Point, where Lauren "fell" to her death, is an exhausting hike along narrow trails, across dangerous crossings, and up steep embankments. Brown would later tell us that the hike had been Lauren's idea and that he had struggled to keep up with her at times as she kept running ahead of him. But this little girl was afraid of everything and was very much the type to stay indoors and play with her dolls while other children played outside. His statement was contradicted by a witness who saw Brown carrying the little girl at one point and by yet another witness who saw him encouraging her to keep going. Both witnesses found it odd that anyone would take a young child on such a rugged course.

At the very end of Inspiration Point, the terrain gradually slopes a short distance from its highest point before ending abruptly in a cliff. Approximately 100 feet below, the Pacific Ocean crashes violently against the rocks, creating murky caverns and cold, dark pools. It was on this gradual slope, just before the cliff, where Brown said he and Lauren were enjoying the view. He claimed to have looked away for a moment, then heard a faint whimper and saw his daughter disappear over the edge as if perhaps she had thrown a rock and the momentum of it had carried her headfirst off the cliff.

After his daughter had "fallen" into the ocean below, Brown ran back to the trailhead, down to the beach below, across the rocks, and to the pool where her broken body floated. He took the time to disrobe before diving in to retrieve her, stating he knew we would be keeping him around for a while to talk to him, and he wanted to have dry clothes. He had also stopped along the way to borrow a phone from a nude sunbather, who would later tell us that the way Brown described that his daughter had "fallen," and with the lack of emotion that accompanied this proclamation, the sunbather had an image of a little girl not far away, maybe sitting on a rock with minor injuries. He couldn't have imagined what had really happened.

The 9-1-1 recording illustrated Brown's lack of concern and emotion following the horrific incident. His daughter had just plunged to her death, yet he calmly told the operator that she had fallen and needed paramedics. When she told him to hold, he must've not realized that the line was still being recorded. He said to the nude man before him, "Sorry about that, dude. You're probably going to have to put some clothes on because the cops will be coming." (This is my recollection of his actual words, though they may have varied slightly.) When I first heard the recorded call, I couldn't believe it. I remember saying that I had ordered pizza with more emotion. My partner aptly pointed out that at no time during the five-minute call did Cameron tell the operator to hurry up or express any urgency. Anyone who has ever worked 9-1-1 lines will tell you that people get really upset when an operator continues asking questions, and all they want is for help to be there right then. That wasn't the case with this call.

Over the months to follow, I would wake up in the middle of the night thinking about Brown tossing his child off that cliff in the same way he might load and unload baggage at the airport. On several occasions, I got up, checked on my daughters—the two of them on either side of the age Lauren would forever remain—and then went in to work, unable to sleep and with too much to do to waste the day. Several times, I arrived at the office at three or four in the morning to see my partner sitting at his desk, he too having been unable to sleep. We had a nearly impossible case, a perfect murder, one might say. I've always said the perfect murder is to push someone off a boat in the middle of the ocean. No eyewitnesses, no way to prove it was murder. Unless—UNLESS—a couple of tenacious investigators could put together a circumstantial case—a couple of bulldogs on the bite.

For the next three years, that's exactly what we did. We interviewed scores of people who knew and had interacted with either Brown or Lauren during her short four years. We had experts review the evidence, a professor of mechanical engineering among them who, after extensive study and testing, concluded that Lauren had been propelled off the cliff rather than having fallen unassisted.

By the time we were able to file this case and arrest Brown for murder, Jeff and I had split up as partners but remained on the same team. I had been asked to train a new investigator at the bureau, Bob Kenney. When the case would eventually go to trial, I would be retired from law enforcement. Leslie did an outstanding job of carrying the ball in my absence, withstanding two hung-jury trials before finally convicting Brown of murder in 2015, fifteen years after the horrific murder.

This was a case in which many doubted we would ever be able to charge a suspect, much less obtain a conviction; the evidence was mostly circumstantial, and it would be very difficult to prove Brown had murdered his child. Many speculated that, at best, we might hope to get manslaughter charges against him—reckless endangerment—something a first-time offender might not do any time for at all. But Brown was convicted of special circumstances murder and sentenced to life in prison. Lauren never saw her fifth birthday.

As my children grew up, I often thought of Lauren, especially during the early years when they were still young. I would watch them play in the yard and laugh and giggle, and I would think back to a video I had watched in which Lauren had done the same, and each time, I was left with sorrow and rage and undeserved guilt. I think of her still, the images sometimes those of nice portraits I've seen, and at other times, the images are more tragic, vivid memories that were seared into my mind that cool November evening at the bottom of Inspiration Point.

I've been back to the cliff where a nice memorial of Lauren stands near the trailhead, the ominous point a distance beyond it, the unrelenting waves below. I stood and pondered the tragic event of that day the way I've done thousands of times before. I walked out to the edge and stared across the ocean as the sun began to set, my wet eyes shielded from the glare. This case took a serious toll on me. *This job* took its toll. [2]

I WAS FORTUNATE TO BE INVOLVED IN THE INVESTIGATION OF THE CONTRACT murders of motorsports legend Mickey Thompson and his wife, Trudy. They were gunned down by two hooded professional killers on the morning of March 16, 1988, as they prepared to leave their upscale home in a gated community in the city of Bradbury, within the LASD Temple station jurisdiction. Thompson's former business partner, Michael Goodwin, had been a suspect in the killing, though the actual shooters were described as two black males—Goodwin is white. Thompson and Goodwin had had a nasty falling out, and Goodwin had made threats. But the case went cold and remained unsolved for many years after the murder.

My very good friend, Mark Lillienfeld, had reopened the cold case and worked on it in his spare time for several years before the pieces began coming together. By then, wiretaps, surveillances, and other investigative activities had been implemented in an effort to stimulate conversations between Goodwin and his ex-wife. Lillienfeld needed a couple of investigators to go to Virginia to oversee parts of the investigation that were taking place there, and he chose me and my partner, Jeff Leslie, to go. The suspect's ex-wife now lived there, and the theory was that she had known about the murders and might talk about the case if stimulated.

In order to legally be involved in a wiretap case in Virginia, we had to be sworn peace officers of that state, according to the state's statutes. As such, we were sworn in as "Special State Police Officers" and given limited police powers throughout the duration of our investigation there.

Not only were we sworn in, we were also issued Virginia State Police certificates, identification cards, and badges.

Our work mostly involved gathering intelligence and overseeing the wiretap operation. We were assigned two state troopers to shadow us, a man and a woman. They were a serious pair of troopers, if not a bit uptight. The practices of cops vary from jurisdiction to jurisdiction, sometimes from assignment to assignment within the same jurisdiction. The first time we all stopped for lunch (at a Hooters), Leslie and I ordered a pitcher of beer for us, and the troopers reacted as if we had asked for bindles of cocaine and extra straws. Apparently, they weren't accustomed to homicide luncheons.

At the conclusion of our time in Virginia, the badges and IDs were whisked away from us in spite of our passionate pleas to keep them. This was in 2001, before cell phones came equipped with cameras, so we couldn't quickly snap some pictures for memory's sake. I think Virginia had had all it could take of L.A. cops.

Goodwin was eventually tried and convicted of contracting the murder of his former business partner, thanks to the great work by Lillienfeld, a true bulldog and one of the best cops with whom I've ever had the privilege to work. The two shooters were believed to be brought in from another country and returned shortly after the murders. They were never identified. [3]

---

1. Here you can find a wonderful array of photographs of the interior and exterior of O'Hara's in Manhattan, New York. https://www.google.com/maps/uv?hl=en&pb= !1s0x89c25a10ac02e5b9%3A0xfad36691304b0f8b!3m1!7e115!4shttps%3A%2F%2Flh5. googleusercontent.com%2Fp%2FAF1QipOlmKwTGZ3bnw-L89RYsa1dROiaooRml6u EhT5l%3Dw426-h320-k-no!5so%27hara%27s%20in%20new%20york%20-% 20Google%20Search!15sCAQ&imagekey=!1e10!2sAF1QipOlmKwTGZ3bnw-L89RYsa1 dROiaooRml6uEhT5l&sa=X&ved=2ahUKEwil3_2P-YHpAhWyJzQIHW7EC_wQoiowE3oECB4QBg

2. This is a fairly accurate news article on Lauren's case with quotes from the investigators and the prosecutor. https://truecrimedaily.com/2017/11/22/over-the-edge-dad-convicted-of-throwing-tot-over-cliff-after-15-years-3-trials/

3. Wikipedia provides some details of Mickey Thompson's life and murder. https://en.wikipedia.org/wiki/Mickey_Thompson

20

TRAINING OFFICER AT HOMICIDE

MAY 2001

I n the spring of 2001, my lieutenant asked if I would train a newly assigned investigator. We were getting some bodies at the bureau, and our team could take two to bring us up to full staff. But that meant that some partners would need to split up. I was reluctant at first but agreed to be a training officer when I learned an old friend and roommate, Bobby Harris, was coming to the bureau. I asked my lieutenant if he would try to get him to our team and let me train him. Bobby was an excellent cop who would be a breeze to train, plus a lot of fun to work with. But that didn't work out as I had hoped. Bobby Harris went to another team in the bureau, and I was assigned to train Bob Kenney, whom I had known since our days working patrol at Firestone.

There were no incentives to be a training officer at Homicide beyond the pride of having been selected to do so and in watching the ones you've trained succeed. In patrol assignments, training officers are paid a five percent bonus. At Homicide, you double your workload, as the trainee won't be able to work independently without your oversight for at least a few months, and you are paid what every other investigator is paid.

Nobody goes to Homicide without being an experienced detective, but death investigation is honestly that much more difficult, technical, and demanding than any other detective assignment. To be an effective homicide detective requires substantial training and plenty of experience—lots of death scenes.

During Bob Kenney's first four months, we handled an industrial accident death, an accidental drowning, a suicide, and six murders, and we assisted with the investigation of a cop's murder. Deputy Jake Kuredjian was shot and killed in Santa Clarita's jurisdiction while assisting federal law enforcement officers on a warrant service, and as in other murdered cop cases, it was an all-hands-on-deck scenario.

The pace never seemed to slow at Homicide Bureau, and once again, we were killing ourselves trying to figure out who killed somebody else.

Two weeks prior to the towers collapsing in New York City, 67-year-old Nada Lazarevic disappeared from her home in Palmdale. A first-generation American, she lived a modest lifestyle and carefully managed her meager income, money made from working as a seamstress. She worked from home and had built a substantial clientele over the years. Her home and car were both paid for in cash with the money she had saved.

There were two daughters. Kenney and I referred to them as the good daughter and the bad daughter.

Good Daughter lived in Simi Valley, a considerable distance from her mother's home in Palmdale. She was married with children, and she and her husband each worked hard to realize the American dream. In many ways, she was much like her mother, whom she spoke to daily and loved dearly.

Bad Daughter, Vanessa Walker, lived a mile or so from her mother with her second husband, Ken Walker, and their two daughters. They lived in debt, spent extravagantly, and were always asking their mother for financial help.

Spoiler Alert: Before getting too far into the facts of the case, it might be worthwhile to know that many years before her mother mysteriously disappeared, Bad Daughter had shot her first husband while he slept in their Northern California home. (Now even Stevie Wonder can see where this is going.)

But Bad Daughter had paid her debt to society, serving *nearly eighteen months* in a low-level women's prison for plugging her slumbering hubby with a bullet from her pistol. She had first claimed it was a case of suicide, and the police foolishly assumed it to be during the initial stages of the investigation. Several days later, an autopsy revealed that the husband had been shot in the back of his head, not by his own doing. The case was ruled a homicide, and police hurried to interview Bad Daughter again and confront her with this new revelation. She eventually admitted to shooting her husband as he slept, saying that she did so because he abused her and she was in fear for her life. (I'm just going to leave that there for a beat.)

Good Daughter was unable to reach her mother by phone one day and immediately became concerned. She called her sister and asked if she had seen or talked to their mother. Bad Daughter said she hadn't and told Good Daughter not to worry. A few hours passed. Good Daughter had tried several more times to reach her mother. Again, she called Bad Daughter and expressed her concerns, only to have them dismissed again. Good Daughter asked Bad Daughter to go check on their mother, but Bad Daughter argued that it wasn't necessary. Eventually, she succumbed to Good Daughter's persistence, or at least said that she would. A short time later, Bad Daughter called Good Daughter and said their mother wasn't home, but again assured her she shouldn't worry. Good Daughter insisted that Bad Daughter make a report to the police, but Bad Daughter refused to do so.

Good Daughter drove the hour or so to her mother's home and found it eerily silent and vacant. Her car was gone, yet her personal belongings and heart medication had been left behind. Good Daughter made a report in spite of Bad Daughter insisting they should wait. It had now been several days since anyone had seen Nada Lazarevic alive.

Missing Persons, a detail within the Homicide Bureau, was assigned the case. Within days, they requested that the case be assigned to a homicide team, concluding there was a strong chance that a murder had occurred.

When we interviewed the two daughters, it was apparent which of the two was concerned about the welfare of her mother and which seemed to have a dark secret concealed. Bad Daughter was dismissive, deceitful, and mostly uncooperative, as was her husband. Good Daughter told us that her mother had recently been upset about something that had to do with Bad Daughter and her husband borrowing money, though she didn't have a lot of detail. We later would learn that the couple had opened up lines of credit under the mother's identity and had racked up over $50,000 in credit card debt, for which the victim would now be responsible. The day the victim was last seen, she had told Good Daughter she was going to confront Bad Daughter and her husband about money.

On September 11, 2001, a surveillance team set up on Ken Walker early that morning at our direction. They followed him to work at about the same time I sat in my living room with tears in my eyes, glued to the live footage of our country under attack. Our department went on county-wide tactical alert, which meant that every sworn member—detectives included—was subject to being activated for tactical response. I phoned our bureau and was told that we at Homicide were not assembling; however, we were to be prepared to respond if needed. There was nothing my partner or I could do to help our fellow first responders on the other side of the country, so we went to work. The surveillance of Walker was terminated as the team was pulled off by their supervisors and ordered to assemble at headquarters. However, Bobby and I went forward with our plans to spend the day canvassing the neighborhood for witnesses.

We went door to door speaking with the neighbors of Nada Lazarevic, and most often found ourselves standing in living rooms asking about the night she went missing while televisions played in the background, continuous loops showing the airplanes striking the towers and Americans leaping to their deaths. It was surreal, possibly the strangest day of my career. Continuing with our investigation, under the circumstances, seemed almost insensitive, but what else could we do? Because of the pace at which new cases arrived, you were always working against the clock, and there was only so much time available for any given case. So we continued on as if the world hadn't changed, and we learned that Bad Daughter and her husband had been at Nada's home on the last night she was seen alive. The husband was observed driving Nada's car the day after, followed by Bad Daughter in her vehicle. Ken began to pull into Nada's home but seemed to change his mind when he noticed the neighbor watching. We believed they had planned to put Nada's car back in the garage to add to the mystery of her disappearance. Instead, they abandoned it a short distance from their own home.

The following day, we interviewed Ken Walker. He didn't exactly confess, but he came close, making statements that would later be used against him in a court of law, as he had been duly warned might happen. After he failed a polygraph examination, we interviewed him again and then arrested him. We went to their home and told Bad Daughter that we had arrested her husband for the murder of her mother and that we knew she was also involved. She adamantly denied any knowledge or involvement. Once I put my handcuffs on her, she changed her tune, now willing to sing any song to keep from going to jail. She led us to her mother's vehicle, which was parked in a vacant lot in an industrial area.

That night and the following day, we executed search warrants at the home and businesses of Ken and Vanessa Walker. The victim's personal keyring with keys to her home and vehicle was recovered from Ken's locked toolbox at the car dealership where he worked as a mechanic.

We didn't know it at the time, but Nada Lazarevic's body had been recovered several days earlier in a remote area of Kern County, a hundred miles from her home. It was a body dump case. Though we had sent teletypes a week prior, the authorities in Kern County had not made a connection, and their case remained unidentified, a Jane Doe.

We charged both Ken and Vanessa Walker with murder without having recovered the body of Nada Lazarevic. A "no body" murder case is difficult to prove, but we felt we could prove this one, and the district attorney concurred. We successfully took the case through a preliminary hearing without having recovered the body of Nada Lazarevic, and both defendants were held to answer.

Sometime after the preliminary hearing and before trial, we received a response to one of the many teletypes we continued to send to the various agencies of Southern California. Kern County had a Jane Doe that was recovered on September 8, 2001, and they thought the remains might be those of our missing person. We drove to Kern County with the dental records of Lazarevic, and the medical examiner there was able to positively identify the found remains as Nada Lazarevic. Her body had decomposed and been ravaged by animals, preventing the coroner from determining an actual cause of death. However, the case was ruled a homicide based on the totality of circumstances.

Bad Daughter was once again off to the pokey with her new un-murdered, murdering husband in tow.

Vanessa Walker is eligible for parole in 2026; her husband was denied parole in 2015, 2018, and 2020. He will be eligible again in February 2023.

ON JULY 9, 2002, AS THE SOUTHERN CALIFORNIA SUN DROVE THE MERCURY to three digits by 10:00 a.m., Bob Kenney and I were sent to a recycling center in the City of Carson. The remains of a newborn had been found by an employee whose job it was to sift through trash as it made its way along conveyor belts. I shed my suit jacket, rolled up my shirt sleeves, and loosened my tie as I gazed across the parking lot to the mountains of debris that awaited us. It was another day at Homicide, and it would be a miserable one—certainly one for the books.

The employee who found the remains said he was sorting trash when he smelled the pungent odor of decomposing flesh. He assumed it to be a dog or cat, but then he saw a baby's arm. He called for the lines to be shut down, pulled the bag containing the baby from the conveyor, and notified a supervisor. But before the belts stopped, the trash near the remains had moved beyond his workstation and dropped into an enor-mous pile below. Finding evidence that might help us would be nearly impossible.

A coroner's investigator joined my partner and me. We donned latex gloves and went to work, sifting trash into the evening hours, hoping to find something that would lead us to its origin, to a place where a new mother held a dark secret. With literally tons of trash to sort through and search, there was no way to pinpoint a geographical area from where the trash had come. We were finding addresses from every region of the vast county and beyond.

We pulled log sheets and saw there were dozens of companies with trucks that had delivered trash during the previous twenty-four hours. The geographical boundaries were nearly non-existent, stretching to the outskirts of a hundred-mile radius, and it became clear that we would not be able to determine where the baby had come from by sifting through the mountains of garbage. We took the story to the media and asked the public for information—if anyone knew anything, we needed them to call. We included details of the Safely Surrendered Baby law, which states there are no questions asked of any parent or grandparent who leaves an unwanted baby at a fire station or hospital within 72 hours of birth. It was a plea of sorts, perhaps a public service announcement, a message to the frightened and confused. But we never received a single phone call in response to the substantial media coverage.

The next day, my fortieth birthday, I attended the postmortem examination of the infant's remains. It was determined that he had died within hours of birth and had taken at least one breath. Which meant he wasn't stillborn; this was a case of murder. Mode of death: homicide. Manner of death: suffocation.

As the autopsy concluded, I stood inches from the cold, stainless steel table, staring at the delicate body of a newborn baby boy, considering what might have been. It occurred to me how few are cursed with the knowledge of these horrific incidents of violence against children and burdened with the memories. I thought of the man who, day after day, silently sifted through the waste of others—likely for minimum wage or not much more—and I wondered how the discovery of Baby Doe affected him. I was accustomed to death, and it did a number on me. I also thought about my fortieth birthday, a milestone that some people make a big deal of and celebrate grandiosely. The day meant nothing to me, and the thought of any celebration repulsed me. I'd purposely put in a long day so there would be nothing planned by any of my loved ones; the last thing I wanted to do was meet the family for dinner and have people ask about my day.

I knew I'd have a drink later, but it wouldn't be celebratory.

WHEN A HOMICIDE DETECTIVE IS CALLED OUT FOR A NEW CASE AND TOLD that the suspect is in custody, he/she is likely to do a happy dance—even if it *is* three o'clock in the morning. This type of callout is referred to in the business as a *walkthrough*, the idea being that there is less follow-up to be done and you're guaranteed to have another check mark in the "Solved" column. The process is more streamlined than that of a complex murder—a whodunnit—as your work on one of these is reduced to the bare-bone practices: document the crime scene, interview witnesses (and the suspect if he/she will talk), collect the evidence and process it through the crime lab, and show up for the autopsy. Every good homicide investigator attends the autopsies of their cases, regardless of the fact that there is nothing worse to observe in a civil society. After that, it's just a matter of dictating a report, gathering the reports of others, and presenting it all to the District Attorney for filing.

One night, I was the recipient of just this type of slow-roller ground ball play, and as such, I gleefully responded to the Vermont District of Los Angeles County. My partner and I stood not far from a deceased Hispanic gang member as a deputy on scene provided a summary: there had been a drive-by shooting, there was a witness who saw it, and Lennox station deputies had located, positively identified, arrested, and booked the offender.

This was terrific news.

However, I would be remiss to not question this gift horse: "How is it you were able to locate the suspect so quickly?"

"Well, we were speaking with our witness," the deputy said, and pointed toward a Hispanic woman who stood nearby clutching her wrap against the cool night air, "when the suspect drove past us. She pointed him out and said that was him. He was stopped and detained for a field show-up, and she positively identified him."

The witness had said she heard gunshots and saw the suspect's vehicle driving past the location. The vehicle stood out; it was a black Cadillac Escalade with custom chrome rims and a loud, thumping stereo. The driver, the sole occupant of this vehicle, was arrested as a result of the identification.

The crime scene was an elevated residence lawn surrounded by a four-foot retaining wall. The home sat on the corner of a major street.

There were shell casings near our victim, grouped together nicely on the grass. This evidence alone disputed the theory of a drive-by shooting, and supported the idea that a close-range, walk-up shooting had occurred. It seemed the witness may have been mistaken. It happens. It's why nobody sees the hangman over statements alone; there must be corroborating evidence. We needed to interview this alleged suspect sooner rather than later, as I feared a mistake had been made.

Kenney and I drove to Lennox station and found the accused detained in an interview room, awaiting our arrival. This man who had already been booked on murder charges was not anything like what I expected to find. He was clean-cut, athletic, polite, handsome—to be truthful about it—and also terrified of the situation in which he found himself. The young man played football for a major university in the northwest. He had grown up in Compton, California, had never been arrested, and he claimed no gang affiliation. From his physical appearance and the absence of gang tattoos, I had no doubt he was telling us the truth about that.

His having grown up in Compton, yet being free of gang affiliation and judicial intervention, told me this was an exceptional young man. I'm not sure I could have grown up in Compton and stayed out of jail.

The arrestee pleaded his innocence, and then asked if he needed a lawyer. I told it to him straight. "You get a lawyer, he's going to tell you not to talk to me. That means you stay in jail until you've finished paying for his new boat. This is one of those times in your life when you're going to want to trust the cops."

"But I didn't do *anything!*"

I had heard those words a thousand times by that point in my career. But this time, I believed they were true. I read him his rights and said, "Now, tell me what happened, and don't bullshit me."

He said he was in town for the weekend, visiting family. A friend wanted to go to a party on the west side (of Los Angeles). On the way, they stopped at an apartment complex up the street from where the shooting occurred so his buddy could buy some weed. There was no parking available on the street, so College Boy double-parked and waited in the car, listening to his loud music while his friend went to score the dope. After a couple of minutes, a police car drove past, so our "suspect" went around the block rather than staying put where he was illegally parked. When he returned to where he had first parked, his friend still hadn't come out from the apartments. A few more minutes passed, so he drove around the block again. When he stopped in front of the apartments this time, a cop car sped past him with its lights and siren activated. He again drove around the block, and on this lap—his final one—there were several cop cars gathered at the corner, their lights flashing. He passed by slowly, gawking to see what had happened, and when he continued on, the cops came after him and pulled him over.

It was clearly a case of mistaken identity. The woman had heard gunshots and her attention was drawn toward the flashy vehicle with the loud music, which had driven past at exactly the wrong moment, probably the first time our "suspect" had circled the block. The driver never even heard the gunshots and was oblivious to the action on the corner until it was filled with cops. Even someone who has never been arrested knows not to stay around and take victory laps after shooting someone.

College Boy didn't want to provide us with his friend's name; he was concerned about the dope component of his alibi. I explained to him that we didn't care if he had a kilo of cocaine up his ass, we were there investigating a murder, and we wouldn't be looking. He took some convincing, but he ultimately decided to trust us and provided us with all the details. Later that morning, he was glad he had.

My partner and I spent the next two hours tracking down the friend, and another hour convincing him to tell the truth about what had happened. He had no idea his friend had been arrested; he only knew he didn't come back to get him. He finally gave us a statement that matched the one told by the man who had been arrested, providing the same details that they had been headed to a party and stopped to buy some weed.

We never did solve that murder case, but justice was served that next morning at the Lennox station jail when I filled out the form to release an innocent man. When the reports were completed, Kenney and I presented the case to a prosecutor and asked for a formal rejection. We didn't have to do that. Releasing him would have been sufficient, and it is often the protocol in such situations. However, we took the extra steps to be certain that his education, his career, and his life would not be derailed by a terrible mistake.

In the end it was far from being a "walkthrough," but it is honestly one of my fondest memories of being a homicide detective. In a job that deals with death and the destruction it leaves behind, there are few opportunities to feel great about the outcome of a case, especially an unsolved one.

PERHAPS THE MOST PITIFUL OF CASES I HANDLED WAS THE SUICIDE OF A starving artist in West Hollywood who was being evicted from his rent-controlled apartment. He had had no income for a great many years, rarely, if ever, selling any of his so-called art. For his grand finale, he hung a blank canvas on the wall, placed the side of his head against it, put the barrel of a snub-nose revolver on the other side of his head, and pulled the trigger. The .38 caliber round-nosed bullet traversed his head cleanly, continued through the wall, across the hallway and into a neighbor's apartment, narrowly missing the elderly woman who lived there.

Before implementing his exit strategy, he had scrawled a note across the top of this blank canvas, a final message to the world: "My last great piece of work."

The would-be artist must have believed that the canvas would be painted by a terrible mess of brain matter and spattered blood in vivid colors and bold patterns by a simple pull of the trigger. But he was wrong. He used the wrong type of bullet and he stood too close to the canvas. All that was left, marking his *last great piece of work*, was a small hole in the center of an otherwise blank canvas. The irony of it did not escape me.

HELL SEEPED INTO MY SKIN AND FLOWED THROUGH MY VEINS ONE NIGHT IN Lancaster as I held the hand of a killer.

"You're not a bad girl, Valerie," I told her, staring into her hollow eyes.

There was no remorse, no emotion, nothing beyond her obvious plotting, trying to find a way out.

"This thing was out of your control," I continued.

Kenney sat on the other side of the table from us, listening carefully to every word she said. Both of us knew this would be our last chance to break her, to get her confession to murder.

"Yeah?" she said, her voice lilting with the possibility.

"But, you know, Valerie, I've been doing this for a long time. I've investigated a lot of murders, talked to plenty of killers. I know when someone's being deceitful."

"What's that?"

"Lying about your involvement, your knowledge. You know more than you're telling me. You need to start telling the truth."

"I'm trying—"

"You have to do better than try, Valerie. I want to hear your side of the story. You'd be wise to give it to me before someone else cuts a deal."

"I don't know anything."

When the tape recorder clicked off, I held my hand up to stop her. I inserted the third, ninety-minute audiotape, knowing if it didn't come soon, it wouldn't come at all; confessions of murder never came easy.

"We'll forget everything you've said until now," I told her, "and I'm going to let you in on a little secret."

"What's that?"

"One of the boys has given us a statement. He gave the whole thing up. I don't need your statement, but I think you have something to say. I don't think you're the monster he made you out to be."

Her brows crowded her eyes. "Who... not Ronnie?"

Ronald "Ray-Ray" Kupsch was her son, sixteen at the time of the murder. A tweaker, a skinhead, a cockeyed evil son of a bitch, literally. "I can't say," I lied.

"Whoever... he's lying. I didn't have nothin' to do with what happened."

"I think you did."

"No."

"Valerie?"

Hiding behind stringy blonde hair covering her face, she seemed to be focused on her shoes. "What?"

"You're making it worse with the lies."

Without looking up, she shook her head. "I'm not lying."

"You're not telling me the truth. I can prove you made the call and sent your boyfriend to pick up your boy, Ray-Ray."

It took a while, but she began, "I had no idea... I didn't think they'd kill him." She sighed heavily, the stench of cigarette breath assailing my senses.

She was the one who had set it up; we knew this from the confession of a co-conspirator, and not her evil son, Ray-Ray. She needed the money for drugs and wanted her pain-in-the-ass, strait-laced boyfriend out of her face. She planned the robbery, told her kid to get the ATM card from the victim's wallet—she knew the code—and then called the victim, her boyfriend, just before midnight when he was due to get off work, asking him to go pick up Ray-Ray and give him a ride. She directed him to a remote trailer court out on Desert View Drive.

William Dolphus Whiteside was a 61-year-old Native American, separated from his wife and living in a modest mobile home in Lancaster. He had met 35-year-old Valerie Martin at the hospital where both of them worked. They dated, and soon after, she moved into his trailer with him. Soon after, her 16-year-old son was released from juvenile hall and joined his mother. Whiteside didn't like having Ray-Ray there, and he liked it less when Ray-Ray's skinhead friends began coming around also. Soon enough, Valerie was back to using meth with her son and his friends, and Whiteside had had it. He wanted all of them out.

That night, Whiteside drove to the desert where Valerie had asked him to go, and there he found Ray-Ray waiting with two other thugs. The boys entered Whiteside's car and immediately jumped him. They beat him with small wooden bats—weapons they referred to as "nigger beaters"—and then tossed him into the trunk of his car. They drove him farther into the desert, stopping along the way to beat him again after hearing him move about in the trunk; they were surprised he hadn't already died. They cracked his skull, took his wallet—Ray-Ray remembered that his mom had told him to get the ATM card—and then proceeded to the remote desert backroad where they waited for Valerie. She brought a can of gas, and they burned him alive in the trunk of his car.

You didn't know they would kill him? What the hell would you say to him the next morning over breakfast? Sorry my son beat and robbed you last night. You ought to see a doctor for that head. "I'm sure you didn't know they'd kill him, Valerie," I told her, "you're too good a person to be a part of that."

She lifted her slouched shoulders, pushed her chest out, and sucked in her stomach. "I am."

"You have a lot going for you," I assured her.

She tugged at the collar of her shirt and ran a finger down the center of her chest. Her eyes softened as she raised her brows. "I do."

"You didn't need this shit, these youngsters getting out of control that night."

"That's what it was."

"But you set up the robbery, Valerie, and we can prove it."

It was all we needed. Prove her knowledge and involvement in planning the robbery, and she goes down for murder. The conspiracy makes her culpable regardless of whether or not she was there.

She looked down and away, forced the sounds of crying, then looked back. Her eyes were dry. "What's going to happen to me? You know, like if I knew they were going to rob him, but that's all?"

"I'm not going to lie to you." I was lying my ass off. "You're going to do some time." *Like twenty years while you're awaiting death penalty appeals.*

"I didn't want him to get hurt."

"Of course, you didn't," I told her. "You really got wrapped up in a bad deal. It was beyond your control." *You're an evil, conniving bitch, and I only hope you're stupid enough to keep talking.* I stroked her forearm. It gave me the creeps, as it always would to use the practice of physical touching during interviews of killers. But a gentle touch can sometimes significantly affect the psyche of the subject and break down barriers between you and them. "You didn't mean for this to happen."

"No, I didn't. What about Ray-Ray? What's going to happen to him?"

"Your boy's no damn good, Valerie... you know that. It's not your fault how he turned out. You wouldn't be in this mess if it weren't for him. Write him off; he's going down hard for this."

"Yeah?"

I put my hand over hers. It was large, like a man's, damp with perspiration. "He deserves what he gets, Valerie. William didn't deserve to die like this. He was a good man, worked hard to make it, never hurt a soul."

I detected the first hint of true emotion. She knew it was true; William Dolphus Whiteside *was* a good man, and he didn't deserve to be beaten and burned to death in the trunk of his car. She knew it, possibly even regretted what they had done to him. Maybe she only regretted being caught, or perhaps she regretted not planning it better. The few hundred dollars they pulled from several ATMs after the murder was likely not worth it, in retrospect.

I placed a second hand on hers and said, "I know you took the gas out to the boys."

Her expression meant to express shock. "I did what?"

"You took the gas. Ray-Ray called you, and the cell phone records show it. You drove out to the desert and brought the gas with you."

"No—"

"We have surveillance video from the gas station," I said, hoping to God she had, in fact, purchased the gas that night. Hoping the bluff wouldn't backfire. Once they catch a bluff, the momentum turns.

"Video?" she said, her bloodshot eyes darting side to side, recalling the night. I wondered if she was seeing the gas station in her mind.

I pushed it. "You're on video, buying the gas."

"Ray-Ray said they needed gas."

"Like they ran out?"

"Yeah, like that."

"So, you bought some gas."

"Yeah."

"You put it in the gas can I found in your car?"

"Yeah."

"Took it out to them?"

"Yeah."

"They told you where to go?"

"Yeah, I guess."

"You were there when the car was torched."

"No... I didn't—"

"You were there, Valerie; we can prove it. Don't make this worse by lying about something as insignificant as driving out there with the gas." *Insignificant. Burning your boyfriend to death in the trunk of his car.*

Her gaze roamed as she processed the information. "I remember going out there..."

"Yeah?"

"But I don't remember the fire."

"You were there when they torched the car."

"I didn't see—"

"You saw the whole thing, Valerie."

"I left before—"

"No."

"What?"

"You drove the boys home, remember? You need to think before you lie."

She paused. "Okay."

"You were there."

"But I didn't watch."

"How could you not?"

Small beads of sweat formed over her upper lip. "This is so messed up... I get confused. You're making me confused."

She was close to giving it up. I could feel it. It was time to push her over the edge. "Did you hear him scream?"

Her head jerked up. Her hazel eyes drilled me, studying me the way I'd studied her, trying to read my thoughts through my eyes, looking for something that said I was bluffing. At that moment, I realized she hadn't known that her boyfriend was still alive when the car was set afire. She must have assumed he was dead, that the fire was just a way to destroy evidence. Her breathing was now labored, and I could see her pulse beating in her throat.

"Oh God," she murmured.

"Yeah, they burned him to death."

The tears came, showing me I had found the small piece of her heart that hadn't been destroyed by drugs, greed, and a lifetime of bad turns and hard knocks. It's what I needed to finish the job.

"He felt it, every bit of it. A slow, torturous death he never deserved," I continued. "Your kid, him and his buddies, they beat him with sticks and a bat, stuffed him in the trunk after cracking his skull. Then they torched the car while he was fighting for his life. While you watched. William was probably thinking of you and your son as he slowly died that night."

Tears now streamed down her cheeks. "Oh my God!"

"You took the gas out there so they could finish him off."

"No. Oh God, please, no! I didn't know..."

"The least you could do is tell me the truth. You owe him that. If you believe in anything at all—God, Buddha, karma—you'll tell me the truth now. Tell me who doused the car with gas and who torched it."

"I never meant for that."

"I know, you're not a bad person." *You evil bitch.*

Her shoulders rocked back and forth, her eyes staring past me. She was likely recalling the night, the way it went down, the horror, the flames, the death... the point of no return. She bit at her lower lip, tearing the skin, and a trickle of blood oozed from a small crack. "Chris poured the gas, then Ray-Ray lit the fire before he was ready. Chris was still pouring the gas, and the flames got him, burned his arm and leg. He yelled—called Ray-Ray a dumbass or something. Ray-Ray just laughed. He was high. They were all high."

"You saw it?"

"Yeah," she said, her words now barely audible.

I slowly pulled my hands back and straightened in my chair, satisfied with her statement. It was mostly self-serving but more than enough to nail her. "Thank you, Valerie. You did the right thing, being honest here."

"I've told you the truth."

"I know."

"That will count for something?"

"Yeah, it will count for a lot. I'll make sure the D.A. knows you cooperated." *While we file murder charges with the special circumstances of lying in wait, robbery, kidnap, arson, financial gain, and torture, making it a death penalty case.*

"Do you feel better after getting it off your chest?" I asked, the knowledge needed for future interrogations.

She swept the hair from her face with the back of a hand and sniffed away her emotion. "Yeah, I think so."

"You did the right thing, proving you're not a bad person."

"I'm not."

"No."

"Am I charged now?"

"You'll be arrested. It'll be up to the D.A. whether you're charged."

"What happens next?"

"You'll be booked."

She pursed her lips and folded her arms over her chest. "Can I have a cigarette?"

"Sure," I told her. "Come on, we'll step out on the patio before I walk you over to the jail."

She stood and smiled, seeming to accept her journey to Hell.

For me, it was time to turn back; I'd been as close to Hell as I cared to be during this dance with a demon.[1]

Bob Kenney and I stayed together long after his one-year training period, as we worked well together and enjoyed being partners. At one point, I was asked to take a new investigator, but declined. Bob and I were together for two and a half years, and we were partners on the day my doctor told me I was finished. During our partnership, we were assigned more than fifty cases: thirty-four murders, seven deputy- or officer-involved shootings, and a variety of other death investigations. We assisted on three murdered deputy cases: Deputy Jake Kuredjian, Deputy David March, and Deputy Steve Sorenson.

We investigated an industrial accident wherein a construction worker was run over by a rubber-wheeled scraper on a Friday afternoon, one hour before he would have been done for the week and home with his family for the weekend. He had stepped into the path of the grader once it passed to "shoot" the grade (checking the leveling or sloping of the earth being moved/altered). The driver came upon an obstacle, stopped, and quickly reversed direction in order to have room to go around it. He would have had no way of knowing that a man had stepped behind his tractor and had crouched in the tracks of the machine to shoot the grade.

We handled a suicide in Palmdale wherein a man hanged himself in the garage in such a way that his wife would find him staring out at her when she returned from work that night, the beam of her lights washing over his rapidly cooling carcass. There is no limit to the cruelty of mankind.

There were two cases Kenney and I were called out to investigate as murders that turned out not to be so. One was that of a woman found in the brush near an RV campground. Though it rightly caused concern to the handling patrol deputies, it only took a few minutes of analysis to note that it was likely a natural death. Her shoe was recovered up the trail from where she was found, and a handbag was found between it and her body. There were no obvious signs of trauma and no evidence along the dirt trail that any other person had accompanied her. I assumed she had died of a heart attack, and at the onset, she had panicked and run downhill, perhaps toward potential help (other campers). An autopsy would later confirm my suspicions; she died from a cocaine-induced heart attack.

A similar situation occurred in the home of a man who lived alone and was found dead in his bathroom, the porcelain toilet lid broken, the mirror cracked, and superficial injuries to the decedent's arms, hands, and face. Within moments, I called it a natural, to the dismay of both my partner and lieutenant. I explained that neither the injuries nor the damage to the bathroom rose to the level of violence that it takes to murder someone without a weapon. Also, there was no evidence of anything occurring outside the small confines of that bathroom: though there was blood therein, there were no signs of blood tracking out, no smears on door handles or light switches, and no bloody shoe prints anywhere to be found. He, too, it turned out, had died of a heart attack. Sometimes, even natural death can be violent.

We handled a murder-suicide of two gay lovers in Compton, another drowned child, an "unknown cause" infant death (SIDS), and an accidental/recreational death in Santa Clarita wherein a young adult male was killed as the result of a mountain biking accident. Had anyone known where he was or what had happened to him, he could have been saved—there was evidence that he lived for a considerable length of time before being found dead the next day.

Compton PD was taken over by the sheriff's department in 2000. As a result, our bureau inherited all of their unsolved or open homicide cases. Kenney and I were given—among several other unsolved Compton cases —a triple murder with no witnesses and little evidence. Not long after, we assisted teammates Tim Cain and John Laurie on another triple murder in Compton. It was amazing to me how many people could be killed at once in that city and how often it happened.

As a homicide detective in Los Angeles, there were times when we were called to investigate the deaths of celebrities or public figures. On February 3, 2003, actress Lana Clarkson was murdered in the Alhambra mansion of famous music producer Phil Spector. Our team was up for murders when it occurred, and Paul Fournier and Rich Tomlin were assigned as the primary investigators. Kenney and I assisted, as did Lillienfeld and several others from our team. I was tasked with writing the crime scene search warrant (a Mincey warrant) and affidavit. Once a warrant was issued, we went to work processing the crime scene and searching the nearly nine-thousand square feet of mansion, otherwise known as the Pyrenees Castle, while news crews lined the streets outside and circled in helicopters above. Spector was ultimately convicted of second-degree murder and sentenced to eighteen years in prison.[2]

When Deputy Steve Sorenson was shot and killed in the high desert region known as the Antelope Valley, I was at my home in the north end of the county on a day off. Since I wasn't far from where it happened, relatively speaking, I was called and asked to respond and take control of the scene until the assigned investigators could arrive.

My wife had gone shopping, and I was home with the girls, six and eight at the time. While still on the phone with the desk getting information about the location where I was being sent, I hastily changed into a suit while gathering the kids, and I headed east toward Palmdale with my children in the back seat of my Crown Victoria. They held on for the ride of their lives as I raced across the highway with a red light flashing on the dash. Eight miles away, I dropped them off with their grandparents and then doubled my speed for the rest of the drive.

I arrived at about the same time Eddie Brown from Homicide did. He, too, lived in the north county, and he, too, had been called and asked to respond. When cops are killed, our bureau puts forth a tremendous effort, and anyone and everyone who is able to assist does, especially at the onset when someone needs to take control of a chaotic scene. Few are better fit to do so at a law enforcement officer's murder scene than seasoned homicide detectives.

Eddie and I began doing just that, taking control of the scene, designating duties, calming those who were propelled by anger and emotion, and rightly so. I had been in their shoes. I had experienced the rage and emotion of having a colleague murdered—several times, actually—and I had, by then, been involved in the investigations of several murdered cop cases.

Deputy Sorenson was killed at a remote desert trailer location. Afterward, the killer moved the body, trying to distance it—and the deputy's vehicle—from his home. Not knowing any better way to move the dead weight of a large man, the killer had tied Sorenson to the back of the patrol vehicle and dragged him farther out into the desert. This act caused even more rage with the local cops—his partners and friends—if that was possible. They saw it as an act of intentional disrespect. I believed that the killer, deranged as he was, simply understood the dilemma that he now had after shooting a deputy in front of his own trailer.

The fact that the killer had dragged the body away from the scene created a large and complex area to be documented as the crime scene. Sorenson's body was found with his pistol and handheld radio missing, and a search of the area would be imperative to see whether either could be found or if the suspect, now on the lam, was armed with these items.

While we were still trying to organize the efforts of everyone assisting at the scene, a helicopter was set down in an area between the location of the murder and the area where Deputy Sorenson's body and vehicle had been recovered. As a passenger in a suit and tie popped out of the bird and started toward me, I, too, started toward him. I recognized him as the undersheriff, the second in command of our department. It was not uncommon for executives to arrive at the scene of a murdered deputy, and in fact, it was appropriate that they did. However...

He reached out to shake my hand as we came together. Holding my hat on my head with one hand, keeping it from being blown back to the city by the wash of the helicopter blades, I shook his hand with the other and said, "Sir, with all due respect, you've set down in the middle of our crime scene, and we need you to get that helicopter the hell out of here." He, likewise, addressed me as "sir," apologized, and immediately saw to it that the bird lifted off.

Joe Purcell, a veteran homicide detective with the experience to handle such a fiasco, was given the case. When he and his partner arrived, Brown and I briefed them about what we knew by then and our actions to that point. Joe asked that we stay and assist, and we did.

A task force was formed, and during the following days and nights, deputies from all over the county were utilized to assist in the search for the fugitive and to handle calls and keep order in the remainder of Palmdale station's jurisdiction. Because crime doesn't allow cops to call a timeout when a colleague is murdered.

SWAT teams worked around the clock, searching the vast desert for any trace of the suspect. At night, helicopters equipped with thermal imaging cameras scoured the land, searching for clues. But the killer was a desert rat who could survive in environments and situations where the average man without training could not. As an indication of this, outside his trailer, there was a five-gallon bucket full of live rattlesnakes—table fare for a man living on little means.

Each day after that first day when I had responded to the scene, I dressed in jeans and boots as I set out to continue working on the case. We tracked down leads, interviewed people, and checked locations where the suspect might seek refuge throughout the high desert region. Most of the time, I was driving on old dirt roads going from one desolate area to another, all the while knowing that a killer, armed with some type of assault weapon (which he had used to kill Deputy Sorenson), the deputy's 9mm pistol, and a handheld radio that could be used to monitor traffic, could be anywhere. As such, I had both a scoped, bolt-action hunting rifle and an AR-15 in my trunk, neither of which I was authorized to carry at Homicide.

In the late morning of August 8, 2003, I was out in the remote high desert on my way to the home of a person who might have had information about the killer when a radio call went out announcing that the suspect might have been seen at a particular home. I was less than a half mile from that location, and I responded, arriving before anyone else. I positioned myself approximately 400 yards from the residence with a clear view of the house and the detached garage, which the suspect was said to have been seen entering. I parked perpendicular to the location, grabbed my rifle from the trunk of my car, and took cover behind the engine compartment. I knew that at this distance, the suspect would be unlikely to shoot with any accuracy. On the other hand, I was completely confident that I could kill a man at 400 yards with my scoped rifle. The previous fall, I had shot a deer at 350 yards, killing it with one shot.

Soon, two radio cars arrived, pulling in close to the house. I radioed for them to back out of the kill zone, that they were far too close given the firepower of the suspect. The goal was to contain the location and take the suspect into custody but on our terms. They backed out, and soon, the place was surrounded by a dozen or more patrol cars. A helicopter circled above, and we waited.

Though nothing happened over the next several hours at the location where we believed the suspect would be found, a tremendous amount of activity was occurring behind the scenes. The suspect had been contacted by phone, and negotiators tried convincing him to surrender peacefully. SWAT teams were assembling and heading in our direction. The few residents scattered throughout the desert region were evacuated, and roads were closed.

The trunk of my car was always full of equipment, most of it stored in milk crates for organizational purposes. I had extra water, extra clothing, boots, shoes, rain gear, hats, sunscreen, a county blanket (all patrol cars are equipped with blankets which have a multitude of uses, and I always kept one in my detective cars as well), extra guns, ammunition, and even food. I set a milk crate on its end, put the folded blanket on the hood of the car, lathered myself in sunscreen, donned a floppy field hat, and settled in with a sniper's mentality. I knew I would take him out if I saw him and he was armed. There was no playing with a cop killer. And I envisioned it unfolding perhaps hundreds of times in my mind as I watched through the scope of my rifle, the barrel of which I kept pointed at the garage wherein the suspect was believed to be holed up.

As members of the SWAT teams began arriving several hours later, they relieved patrol deputies from perimeter positions. The airship above coordinated this movement, addressing radio cars by their rooftop numbers to tell them they had been relieved and needed to depart the location. I had already decided that I wasn't leaving, and nobody was going to tell me otherwise. By this time, I had been sitting there baking in the desert sun for half the day, and I wasn't going to *not* be a part of the ending however it might go down. Also, I was from Homicide, and this was *our* case. The airship finally announced, "Who do we have in the gray Crown Vic?" I responded with my call letters, following up with clarification that I was from Homicide and I was fine where I sat. "Ten-four," was the response.

LAPD had sent their SWAT team to assist, and they brought with them their infamous tactical vehicle, an armored tank equipped with a .30 caliber machine gun and a battering ram capable of injecting gas. Sheriff's officials had advised the suspect that he had until sundown to surrender. The justification for the ultimatum was that for a week, the suspect had successfully avoided detection while moving through the desert at night, using the cover of Joshua trees and burrowing beneath sagebrush to avoid detection from the thermal imaging equipment that was being used to find him. He was clever and crafty—a man who could survive in extreme conditions. Survive and kill again. And he was a cop killer, something that, by this time, he had admitted to one of our detectives over the phone.

Shortly before darkness swept across the desert, the battering ram moved forward, crashed the turret's long barrel through the garage door, and turned it side to side, tearing the door apart to allow a view inside. I watched through the scope of my rifle, waiting for a clear target. Shots rang out, a few muted pops that sounded like they came from inside the structure. That set off a chain of events: tear gas canisters were shot into the garage, and deputies and LAPD officers all around the perimeter opened up on the garage, firing pistols, rifles, and automatic weapons.

I didn't know if any of them had acquired a target. I hadn't. My previous visions of the suspect appearing outside of the structure with his weapon pointed my way was now replaced with a vision of him running from the fiery garage, indiscriminately spraying bullets from his assault rifle while absorbing bullets fired in return. I squeezed the trigger, working hard to control my breathing during this extraordinary event, one which I knew at that time would be a part of history, one of several big standoff/shootouts that went down in the history books of L.A. law enforcement. I didn't blink for fear of missing the fleeting instance I thought might be offered, a glimpse of the suspect inside the burning structure, his attempt to flee through the side of the garage that favored my position—anything. Any opportunity to engage the suspect. For I was armed with the equivalent of a sniper rifle, and with a sniper rifle, you didn't lay down cover fire; you waited for the shot. The one perfect shot. Most, if not all, of the dozens of shooters that night never saw their target. They shot blindly into the structure toward where the gunfire had come from. They did so wisely, overwhelming the suspect with gunfire to keep him from advancing, to keep him from being able to acquire a target, and to put him down before he killed another cop. Had I chosen to use my AR-15, I would have done the same. I would have sent lead downrange just to be a part of putting down the killer. But I had a scoped rifle and a sniper's mentality, so I waited, unblinking, narrowly focused on the target, anticipating a kill shot. One shot, one kill. It never came.

Thousands of rounds were fired that night. The gunfire tapered off after a while, and eventually, it stopped. All that could be heard then was the crackling of fire as flames shot into the darkening sky and a calmness fell over the desert. It was over.

I waited another half hour before packing up and heading to the command post, where all *normal* homicide detectives mingled with department executives, administrators, and other emergency personnel. Of course, I almost immediately ran into my captain, who had apparently been advised that I had been out at the scene of the standoff and subsequent shooting and that I had been the first on scene and had remained through the final gunshot. He said, "What in the hell were you doing out there!"

By then, I knew what mattered to my captain, so I went directly to the point. "I didn't fire any shots, Skipper." He studied me for a long moment and said, "Well, thank God for that." He asked why I had stayed out there, and then it was my turn to pause and consider my reply. We had our differences, but he was a good captain, and he did take care of his investigators. I said, "Because I had a rifle and a clear shot at the suspect if he emerged from the garage. Besides, I felt it would have been more dangerous for me to try and move from my position." He nodded, and that was it, no questions about the unauthorized deployment of a long gun. I never heard another word about it.

Early the next morning, I returned to the location as several teams of homicide investigators began processing the scene in the budding daylight, my good friend Scott Fines among them. The charred remains of the suspect sat on a concrete slab where a corner of the garage had been but where only ashes now stood. He had huddled there in his final moments, his rifle and Deputy Sorenson's pistol at his side.

Had I fired my rifle that night, I would likely have received some form of discipline for using an unauthorized weapon. That was a chance I had been willing to take, knowledge that weighed on me during the very long, hot day. Perhaps knowing that had contributed to my restraint amidst the chaos.

Two years earlier, Jake Kuredjian was shot and killed in Santa Clarita. Kenney and I had been in Santa Clarita working on another case, along with Jeff Leslie and his partner, Brian Steinwand. The four of us responded to the command post and were there while shots were still being fired at the nearby location. The suspect was ultimately shot and killed by our SWAT team and, incidentally, also burned to the ground along with his home, the result of teargas being inserted into the structure.

THERE WAS A NOTICEABLE CHANGE IN MY ENERGY AND DISPOSITION DURING the months following Deputy Sorenson's murder. My wife had noticed, and on several occasions, she asked if I was depressed. Maybe deep down inside, I knew I was, but I sure wasn't ready to admit it. Not to her, not to anyone. I was tired, burned out, stressed, in pain—anything but depressed.

The neck pain had gradually returned and worsened to the point where it could be unbearable at times, the usual numbness and tingling becoming sharp, shooting, and, at times, debilitating. I feared that the second disc had ruptured and was, like the first disc had, now compressing my spinal cord, as once again, I was experiencing nerve pain down my arm. At the time of the first surgery, a decision had been made only to remove one disc. It was a decision made in part by my surgeon but also by the county's insurance carrier. In hindsight, they should have taken them both.

I had a supply of pain pills that went unused after my first surgery, and I eventually resorted to using them. I didn't like to, and I did so as sparingly as possible, but during the most stressful times at work, my neck would freeze, my spine would quiver, and blood would pulse violently through my head. On one such occasion, I was arguing with the captain. Another time, I was arguing with a sergeant from the crime lab, a man with a chip on his shoulder who wouldn't deviate from his policy to accommodate an unusual request related to polygraph testing. Looking back, the real problems were the administrative bullshit, the red tape, and the stubbornness of little Caesars with their empires who were blind to the greater cause of what we were literally killing ourselves to accomplish. The enemy within caused far more damage than any of those on the outside. I spent thousands of hours over the course of my career interacting with evil men and women, killers and thieves, hustlers and whores, and the only time other than during deadly encounters that my blood pressure would spike to the point where my heart pounded and pulsed, seemingly on the verge of failure, was when dealing with administrators and their bullshit, defense attorneys and their lawyerly tones and attitudes, and the overall function of the justice system. Those things regularly pushed me to my breaking point, especially toward the end.

At the preliminary hearing of the Whiteside case, there were four defendants: the three skinheads and Valerie, the mother of one of them. As a reminder, these people had beaten, robbed, kidnapped, tortured, and burned alive a Native American, a man they called a nigger, a man they killed for a couple of hundred bucks and to remove him as an obstacle to their using meth and living the high life. There was an attorney for each of them, and these people coddled the unrepentant killers throughout the six-week fiasco called the preliminary hearing, gently touching their shoulders and smiling widely while whispering in their ears. There were three witnesses, all tweakers and skinheads themselves, all of whom we had arrested and whom the judge had ordered held in custody throughout the hearing because otherwise, we would have never seen them in court. They, too, were each appointed a lawyer by the court. There were two lawyers on the prosecution side as a case of this magnitude required it. Of course, the judge was a lawyer, too. All of these lawyers filling the courtroom chatted and joked as if out for coffee or back at their frat houses. It seemed to elude them all that we were there because the four assholes at the table had tortured and burned a man to death. Throughout the six weeks of long, grueling days, it was only Kenney and I, and the victim's ex-wife and her mother, who sat solemnly at all times. Which caused me to want to stand up and scream for everyone to shut the fuck up and act like this was something to take seriously. But I didn't, and the pressure built.

Then I took the stand. At one point, one of the snarky attorneys questioned my integrity, and I lost it. He had pointed his finger at me and raised his voice, and I rose from the witness chair, returning the gesture, and I admonished him to never point his finger at me again. The judge slammed his gavel down, yelled at me, and then admonished me that he would hold me in contempt if there were any further outbursts. Well, I certainly was contemptuous; there was no doubt about it. Shortly after, while in the restroom on a break, the same attorney sidled up next to me at the urinals and made some irrelevant comment in an attempt to be friendly. I pictured myself grabbing him by his thick head of black, slicked hair and cracking his head against the tile wall. To him, it was a game. To all of them, it was nothing but a game. It seemed it was only me and those like me who took these processes to heart, and it was killing me. Was it me? Was I wound too tight for the job? Or was everyone else an asshole for being lighthearted about the horrific murder of a decent man?

By now, my blood pressure was through the roof, and my doctor wanted to start me on medications. I resisted, not wanting to do that at 41 years of age. In the fall of that year, I went to Idaho to hunt elk with my friend and former colleague, John Terry. Before going, I consulted the doctor due to frequent chest pain. I had known another deputy who had died of a heart attack while hunting, and I feared it would happen to me since, by then, I seemed to be wound so tightly at all times I honestly felt I was going to explode. Given my physical ailments, I was second-guessing the idea of being secluded in the mountains, and I was fully ready to cancel the trip. However, my doctor said that my high blood pressure was directly related to stress and encouraged me to go on the trip. It would be good for me, he said.

We were on a mountain without cell service and had very little human contact outside of our small group of close friends for seven days. One of the men in our party had come to hunting camp sick, and by the time we came off the mountain, each of us had caught whatever he had. Before starting the long drive home, I went to a walk-in clinic so that I could get started on antibiotics, having felt miserable for the last three days. They took my blood pressure there and noted it was 110/70. I couldn't believe it was literally perfect, given that it had been 150/95 just weeks before. I asked the nurse to take it again. The results were the same. During the twelve-hour drive home, I heavily contemplated what I was doing to myself, and I knew then that the end was near. I could feel it. With mixed emotions, I acknowledged that I was more than burned out, tired, and stressed; I was literally killing myself because of *how* I did the job.

I recalled a conversation with a mentor who was known by all in our department, a distinguished deputy sheriff and remarkable homicide detective. We had become close while working on an unsolved case together, and one day, he told me about his breakdown, something that many knew had happened, but few were privy to the details. There had been nothing unusual about his day, just another day at the bureau. He was at the office in downtown Los Angeles when he was sent out to handle a murder, something so routine he didn't provide the details. Driving along under a blue sky with the sun shining brightly, he was headed for the crime scene in South Los Angeles when he suddenly burst into tears. He had no idea why he was sobbing, and he was unable to stop. He pulled over to the side of the road and wept uncontrollably, alone in the darkness within him. All the stresses, hardships, and pressures he had endured over time finally caused him to crack an egg, and it changed the course of his career.

Earlier, I talked about Mike Bumcrot. He was the complete opposite of me and the mentor I just mentioned who cracked. Bummer—and there were others: Mike Robinson, Joe Purcell, Mark Lillienfeld, Davey Castillo, and John Laurie, to name a few—was the type of investigator I respected greatly and admired for his ability to remain calm and collected in a chaotic environment. He and those others knew how to let things go like water off a duck's back, and I envied them for it and wished I were more like them. I possessed the skills to be an effective homicide detective, and I was. But eventually, I came to admit—if only to myself—that I hadn't the temperament for the job. It was literally killing me.

Jeff Leslie told me about a conversation he and Rich Tomlin had had a while after I retired, where Jeff had made a comment to the effect of "We have no idea what this job is doing to us." Tomlin smiled and said, "Oh yes, we do."

There are many other cops in this world who find themselves ready to crack, but nobody else ever knows it. They live in a darkness that nobody sees, and they die with broken hearts. Some go off and eat a gun. Others drink themselves to death. Fortunately, some get out in time before they get to that place or come to grips with where they are and bravely seek help. No cop likes to admit to a weakness, and that is what PTSD and depression are often mislabeled as being, if only by the ones afflicted. This is why I tell people that breaking my neck was a blessing from God. It probably saved my life by allowing me out before it was too late, because I might not have ever conceded to myself or anyone else that I was in a very dark place by the end. And honestly, who knows where *that* road might have led.

A few months after the hunting trip came the head hanging in a tree case and the incident of my neck locking up as I glanced over my right shoulder while speeding down the Long Beach Freeway. The head turned out to be what remained of a suicide. The deceased had gone to a remote area where he hanged himself, and his remains had gone undetected for several months. Eventually, the corpse had decomposed, and it had been pulled apart by scavengers and spread around the mountainous terrain. The head had remained, along with part of the neck, cinched tightly in the rope. So it hadn't been the beginning of a Hannibal Lecter story, but still, it was a human head, and it was hanging in a tree ominously. And it was the final encounter with death I would have, professionally.

That same day, Bob Kenney saw me pop another pain pill and said, "You've got to get that neck taken care of, Bubba. You can't keep going like this."

---

1. The dialogue used to recount the interview of Valerie Martin is based solely on the author's memory of that event which occurred twenty years prior to this writing. Though it is contextually accurate, the dialogue is not taken from transcripts of the interview and is not to be considered an exact representation of that interview.
2. Details of the Lana Clarkson murder: https://en.wikipedia.org/wiki/Murder_of_Lana_Clarkson

PART V

AN ABRUPT ENDING

OF A WHIRLWIND CAREER

21

THE SHRINK

On the way home from the doctor's office on what turned out to be my final day of work as a Los Angeles County Sheriff's deputy, I called my wife and told her I was on my way home. It was relatively early in the day, and she knew something unusual had happened. I told her that I had gone to the doctor because my neck had locked up while driving and that he had taken me off work. She had questions, but I was in no shape to answer them while driving in traffic after having just recently composed myself.

We talked when I got home, and I told her what had happened, all the doctor had said, and how I had broken down at hearing his words. Then I told her that because of it, the doctor asked if I thought I was depressed. She was gracious enough only to nod knowingly and not remind me that she had said several times over the previous year that she believed I was. I told her he had prescribed a medication for depression and had given me a sample, and as I said it, another wave of emotion crashed over me. I don't know if others who battle depression feel as if they are broken, but I sure did. And for me, that equated to failure. I hadn't been able to finish the game. I wasn't as tough as the other players. I was embarrassed about my predicament and told her so through teary eyes and a runny nose.

She said, in part, "Don't you think you've done enough? You have nothing left to prove."

My good friend Frank LaFlamme, one of the most philosophical people I know, would later break it down for me with a statement I've hung onto, words that allowed me to hold my head high again eventually. He said, "You put in more than twenty years with one of the greatest departments in the nation, and you worked nothing but tough assignments throughout your career. You did twenty years in the fast lane, pal, and you have nothing to be ashamed of." He went on to say that the work I had done over the past twenty-plus years was equivalent to working a hundred years as a cop in many places. It sure felt like I had.

I couldn't stand taking the medication the doctor had prescribed for the depression, so I stopped. During those few days I did take it, everything seemed brilliant, brighter, crisper, and louder, and I wondered if taking meth provided a similar experience. From what I'd been told, it seemed like the two experiences weren't that far apart, and I was no fan of it. I told my doctor that the meds weren't for me and asked what else he suggested. His first thought was that we try a different prescription, but I protested. I didn't want to take any antidepressants. I knew I could conquer this depression without them; after all, the source of my stress had been removed since he had taken me off work with permanency in mind. He relented about the medication but with one caveat: he wanted me to see a counselor. I readily agreed to do so because I honestly wanted the help and looked forward to the experience.

The "counselor" turned out to be a shrink. I realized this when a questionnaire was sent to my home that was to be completed and returned before my scheduled appointment. There were only about six questions, as I recall, and there was room to answer in about five or six sentences beneath each question. I read a couple of the questions before responding to any of them, and I laughed at the absurdity of them: *Do you feel like you are under stress? Do you think your job causes you stress? What about your work creates stress?* And so on. I chuckled, but not from amusement. Then I scribbled across the page, "SEE ATTACHMENT."

I began typing my response on a computer, my fingers blazing across the keyboard as I spilled my soul to this new doctor I had yet to meet. As often is the case, once I start writing—when I get on a roll—the words flow effortlessly, magically. Soon, I had thirteen typewritten pages that would very clearly answer everything the good doctor wanted to know with regard to what about my job caused stress.

When I met with him, I was oddly at peace with all of it: I was depressed; I was done with law enforcement; I was now part of the rubber gun brigade, having joined the ranks of other cops who had left the job before their time, unable to continue coping with the death, the violence, the red tape, the broken system called justice, the administrative bullshit, and *the public*. I had been away from work for more than a month by then and had come to terms with the fact that I wasn't returning. I had even obtained an attorney for the workers' comp case and instructed him to file for a medical disability retirement on my behalf. One of the advantages to being part of the rubber gun squad is you don't have to put up with any more shit—others do that for you. So I settled into a plush leather chair across the imposing wood desk of a man with all sorts of initials before and after his name, and I waited while he flipped through the pages of my response that succinctly explained what had turned me into a fucking banana.

Finally, he lowered the papers but kept them in both hands as he met my gaze. His first words to me—since he had welcomed me and shown me to my seat—were, "You should write for a living."

I had never considered writing outside of what the job necessitated, but now that I am officially an author, I wish I had. If I had known that I would someday write about and from my experiences, I would have kept a daily journal of all the fun, crazy, and bizarre things I witnessed over the years. It's easy to recall the best and worst moments and days, but the many daily treasures that seemed routine at the time are difficult to recall—many of which would certainly entertain the world if written.

Even as the good doctor said those words, it didn't resonate with me that I should write, so I said nothing in response.

It was like high school football practice when Coach Ford put me at tight end as we practiced against the starting defense. He sent me on a short pattern across the middle and threw a high pass, which I leapt up and caught. I held onto the ball, though I was immediately nailed by two of our top players at once, which sent me twirling through the air, the world upside down for a moment. I landed flat on my back but still held the football firmly in my hands. Coach Ford ran up to me, poking his finger at my face guard, spittle landing in my eyes, saying, "Goddamnit, Smitty, you've got hands! Why the hell haven't you told me you've got hands!" But instead of admitting that yes, I could catch the ball and I'd catch it every time if given the chance, I didn't say a thing. I silently returned to the huddle, convinced I could never be anything but a second or third-string player because I lacked speed and experience compared to many of my teammates. Those guys who hit me had played organized football all their lives, as had most others on the team. On my side of the tracks, we played on the street or at the elementary school, and we hit and tackled, but we had never worn gear nor had any instruction, and I was certainly out of my league playing at William. S. Hart High.

I didn't stick with football in high school because I didn't realize at that time in my life that a lack of experience didn't equal a lack of ability. I would later learn this in all aspects of life: police work, writing, and cowboying, to name a few. Those are the things in life that I've been most passionate about, and I haven't allowed anything to stand in the way of my successes.

"Seriously," Doc said, raising the papers to emphasize his point, "you have an incredible way with words. I've read this several times since I received it, and I've honestly never had any other patient articulate their feelings and pain the way you have here."

I smiled. "Yeah, so what do you think, Doc? I'm nuts, right?"

He smiled back. "We're going to do some testing, but my guess, given your work history and this response, is that you probably have PTSD. You know what that is, right?"

I nodded.

He said, "We'll work on how you cope and move on."

Several medical appointments followed, and it would be weeks before I met with him again. In the meantime, I was given the infamous MMPI (Minnesota Multiphasic Personality Inventory), the foolproof measure of one's sanity. The doctor would later tell me that I had a valid rating, which is not always the case. The test is designed to detect manipulation of the results, so it comprises 567 questions requiring a true or false answer. The test results showed that I hadn't been deceptive and exhibited signs of depression and PTSD.

There were other tests that seemed to be designed to test motor skills, but apparently (I asked) were intended to gauge one's ability to work through frustrating situations. I was given the old inkblot test, which I found both silly and amusing, but perhaps I should have been less thoughtful while answering. I assumed that the more violence, death, and destruction I saw in those vague patterns, the bigger a banana I would have been deemed to be. So, instead, I allowed myself to see more pleasant images, many of which were sexual in nature. This caused a notation in the final report that I might have a strong, perhaps even unhealthy sexual appetite, which made me think these shrinks were taking the banana thing too damn far.

But in the end, the good doctor—whom I had come to trust through our meetings—informed me that I most certainly suffered from chronic Post-Traumatic Stress Disorder. He explained that the difference between chronic and acute was best summarized thusly: acute PTSD is often found in victims of a single violent encounter, whereas chronic PTSD is more often detected in those who have experienced multiple deployments in battle. The latter type is often found in cops who have spent their time in fast-paced, violent jurisdictions. He said, "Your experiences as a cop have been affecting you for a long time, and you just didn't know it."

Next came the *what-to-do-about-it* part. Ongoing counseling would be very beneficial, he said. When he mentioned group counseling, I looked him in the eyes and said, "Doc, you can't be serious about that." He smiled and said, "Yeah, I don't know what I was thinking." I made my case for what I believed would keep me out of counseling and off the prescription meds. I reminded him that I was no longer in the stressful work environment and wouldn't be returning. I'd be moving out of state very soon, which would help me immeasurably. There weren't many places in L.A. County where I hadn't stood over a dead person, and for a while, by then, geographic locations would trigger memories of various cases. I remember taking my family to a water park in San Dimas and thinking of a dead woman in the bushes as we traveled along the 210 Freeway. At the park, I thought about the three cases of drowned children I had handled while kids laughed and splashed and enjoyed the times of their lives. All these things and many more were ever-present in my mind and probably always would be. I knew I had to get away. I wanted to run away from home but take my family with me, and ultimately, that is what I did.

He studied me for a moment and told me I was probably right, but again, he said I should consider writing a book or a journal, which is one of the most therapeutic things one can do. But as had been the case with Coach Ford, I knew better than the expert. I was no writer.

When we got down to where the ass meets the saddle, as my former bullfighting friend Daryl "Deedub" Knight likes to say, the primary concern of my shrink was whether or not I had experienced suicidal ideation. No, I hadn't, I assured him. I have a wonderful wife, two lovely daughters, and a great family. I had (have) no intention of taking my own life, though sometimes my actions might cause one to wonder. (More on that later.) In the end, we shook hands, and he wished me the best of luck. He also said he had no doubt I would be okay because I was the type of person who would never give up. He had that right. He had a few other things right, too, but it would take me a long time to realize it.

22

SNEAKING OUT IN THE DARK

A great number of cops have retirement parties when they leave. I didn't want one. Again, I was ashamed of how I left, and I found no cause for celebration. I left in the dark of night, cleaned out my desk on a weekend, and said goodbye only to my closest friends. My lieutenant at the time, Dan Rosenberg, called and asked about a party. I told him I didn't want to have one. He said he understood that some guys didn't want to make a big deal of retiring, and suggested we could have a small get-together, maybe a team luncheon. I said no, I wasn't interested. Then he asked if I could come by the office sometime, explaining he had some things for me. I had no idea what that meant.

I don't recall now what my strategy had been, but I clearly remember figuring out a time that I could go by the office when Dan would be there, but few others would, and that is what I did. Dan presented me with the department medal for distinguished service, a certificate of retirement thanking me for twenty-one years, two months of "loyal public service," letters of congratulations and appreciation for my service from Sheriff Leroy Baca, District Attorney Steve Cooley, United States Senator Barbara Boxer, California Governor Arnold Schwarzenegger, and President of the United States, George W. Bush. I received a Homicide Bureau gold card, something given to investigators who retire with more than five years of service as a homicide investigator, and a personal thanks from my lieutenant, who lamented that it would have been much nicer to present these things to me as part of a celebration of my career, but nonetheless, I had earned them. And he wished me the best of luck with my future.

I departed the office that day feeling a sense of pride but also a helping of guilt. Over the weeks, months, and even years that followed, I would hear from former colleagues, all of whom congratulated me on my retirement, and many of them said they wished I would have had a retirement party. Geody Okamoto accused me of pulling a Forrest Gump, saying that one day, I just stopped running and said, "I'm tired. I'm going home."

23

THE ART OF WRITING

ANOTHER COP-TURNED-AUTHOR

In the following months, I moved my family to a farming community in Idaho, away from the city. I found a new surgeon in not-too-distant Boise and soon learned that a second neck surgery was in fact, necessary. The bulging disc that had been left alone had ruptured, and it was compressing my spinal cord just as the other one had, though less severely. I again had to wait nearly a year before the county insurance carrier would approve surgery, but at least I was no longer carrying a stressful workload.

And that's when I began writing.

Having the shrink's words in my head, I decided to try my hand at fiction. It was the obvious choice since the last thing I wanted to do was revisit those things that agitated me. As I write this now, it has been sixteen years since I left the job, and still, I find my body temperature rising, my blood pulsating hard through my veins, and feelings of anger as I write parts of this memoir. Some of those feelings might have been obvious during the latter parts of the previous section when I described, in particular, the courtroom drama regarding the William Whiteside murder case. Had I tried to write this memoir in the early years of my retirement, it would have been detrimental to my health and recovery, and it would likely have read more like a Stephen King horror novel.

They say you have to write a book to learn how to write a book, and I believe it is true. I wrote a book, and not long after, I attended a local writers conference where I met with an agent who had reviewed the first three chapters of my prose. It was a humbling experience, to say the least, and the takeaway was that I discovered I knew nothing about creative writing. Yes, in truth, I had written professionally for years. I had written thousands of police reports, hundreds of which were contested mightily by opposing counsel. I had authored hundreds of affidavits, and untold volumes of homicide investigation reports, all of which have withstood the scrutiny of supervisors, attorneys, various municipal, superior, and appellate courts, and even the California Supreme Court. But none of that prepared me to write creatively, to write in a manner that would entertain, perhaps even captivate readers. And that was now my goal.

So, I discarded the first book and applied myself to learning the art of writing. I immersed myself in books, blogs, and seminars that offered instruction on the topic, and I enrolled in online college courses to refresh my grammar and English skills. I read everything I could get my hands on. But most of all, I wrote.

With the newly acquired knowledge of writing prose, and still, with nothing but time on my hands, I began writing a detective novel in which the characters, cases, and some of the action are loosely based on the adventures of working Homicide Bureau, and I named it *A Good Bunch of Men*. I had fun writing it, and my longtime partner and friend, Jeff Leslie, read it chapter by chapter as I did. I would send him pieces of it as it was written, and he thoroughly enjoyed it. Then I sent the book to my good friend, Patti Barrick Brennan, who offered to look it over for me and, as she says, move a few commas around. That's an understatement. Patti not only edited that first book for me, but she has edited everything I've written since. Through the process of it all I've learned much more about writing, and I've honed my skills. But back to the first book, *A Good Bunch of Men*, Patti raved about it, saying it was just great and that I should publish it. I thought she was only being nice, as I still lacked confidence in my writing, and it would be many years before it would be published.

24

A NEW BEGINNING

SECOND, THIRD, AND FOURTH CAREERS

L ife started up again and the days of sitting in my chair writing gave way to the daily grind of my second career while I started a third.

Though I received a pension, I knew then that it wasn't enough to live comfortably on for the rest of my life while raising two daughters. I took a job as an investigator with the Oregon Department of Corrections, but that was a disaster. (In fairness, my shrink warned me that it would be, but I ignored his admonishment because I had to get back to work.) My first day on the job the big boss from Salem, across the state from Ontario where I was assigned, called to welcome me and tell me that one of the reasons they had hired me was so that I could teach my boss there in Ontario how to be an investigator. "He's a nice guy but he has no investigative background." I flatly told Mr. Salem that I was not about to do that, though I would gladly answer any of his questions or assist him or anyone else if they came to me and asked for my help. I saw what a disaster that could be.

Apparently, Salem had also told my boss in Ontario the same thing, that they had hired me, in part, so that he would benefit from my investigative experience. This man became my greatest nemesis in record-breaking time. He would reject my reports and request corrections that weren't necessary, just to show me who was boss. This former farmer and prison guard who had been promoted far beyond his skill set to the position of supervisor in the investigations unit pressed his big, fat thumb on me, and I didn't do well with that. I never have.

Within the first few months, I began planning a prison break; I had to get out of that place. The shrink was right, it never works out when experienced, proficient workers take jobs for which they are overqualified. But in order to escape I needed a strategy, an idea and a plan of how I could make a living elsewhere, since I truly had no marketable skills outside of being a cop or an investigator. Obviously, I could never be a cop again, and so far, this being an investigator for the prison—a far less challenging job than any assignment I had held as a deputy sheriff—hadn't worked out. It was also at this time that I realized and admitted to myself that I had been spoiled. I had loved my first career. There were only a handful of days that were bad—and those days were horrible—but overall, it was a terrific career and I was suddenly more grateful for it than I might have ever previously been. The assignments I had held and the work we did mattered greatly, and now here I was investigating misconduct complaints such as the case of an inmate smuggling an extra apple out of the chow hall. *Now* I wanted to kill myself. Not truly, but I would often tell my wife that I spent many hours in my new office looking up at the rafters and thinking about tossing a rope over them.

. Then one day a phone call changed my life.

Jerry Thompson, a former Lynwood deputy whom I had known since our early days working at the jail, called me out of the blue. He had heard that I retired and was living in Idaho, as was he. When he asked what I was doing, I told him I was working at the prison, and I hated it. "Why not be a PI?" he asked. I couldn't imagine being a private investigator, having known a few of them over the years. Most of them were former cops who, in most cops' opinions, had sold their souls and become sleazy advocates for defense attorneys. It was not an industry I wanted to be a part of. But Jerry pointed out the positives: I would work for myself (I would later describe this as having to work for only one asshole) and make my own hours. Jerry had done some PI work himself, and he gave me a few ideas about how to start a business.

As I contemplated the idea further, I thought of another good friend who I knew had started a PI company, a former detective from the sheriff's department named Gary Lynn. I called Gary and had a long conversation with him, and then over the first year or two of my starting a PI business, I called him often with questions about where to go for certain information, or how to market to certain industries. Gary was more instrumental in my success than he probably knows.

Soon I was working two jobs: prison detective by day (my actual title there was "Inspector," which I also found absurd), and super sleuth private eye by night. Eventually the PI business grew enough that I could quit my job at the prison, and I had decided that the next time my boss pissed me off, I would be gone. That happened often, so it didn't take long for that day to come, and you can bet I voiced my displeasure with that supervisor before I left.

The PI business soon thrived, and it wasn't long before I needed to hire additional investigators to work for me. The business allowed my family to live comfortably, and with the girls doing their parts working and earning many scholarships, my wife and I were able to put them through college without them having to take on student loans. I was also able to pay for parts of two weddings and keep mama in new shoes all the while.

And to avoid embarrassment about what I did for a living—and with a nod to Harry Truman—I told people I played piano in a whorehouse.

ONCE I WAS HEALED UP FROM MY SECOND NECK SURGERY, I DISCOVERED A love of horses, which led me (eventually) to a love of horsemanship and cowboying. Fortunately, now living in the heart of what local cowboys and buckaroos call "the ION" (southwest Idaho, southeast Oregon, and northern Nevada), I was surrounded by knowledge and opportunity. I could write a book about my experiences riding and roping, gathering and branding calves, sorting and driving cattle—all of which I had the opportunity to do once I became proficient in the saddle. I've earned paychecks "day working," a common term used by cowboys who are paid by the day for the work they do on various ranches without being an employee of the outfit. I once spent the better part of a week working on

DANNY R. SMITH

a large ranch that spans the vast deserts of southern Idaho and Eastern Oregon, many miles from a paved road. We slept in tents and worked from dawn to dusk, gathering hundreds of cows the first several days, and then branding the calves the last couple of days. The work was hard, not only on the cowboys, but on our horses too. As fun as it was, I was happy when it came to an end and I was back to the office for a few days.

One of my greatest horse adventures was the spring I traveled to Craig, Colorado and participated in the Great American Horse Drive, an annual event in which forty or so cowboys gather to move the Sombrero Ranches' herd of 600 saddle horses from winter grounds back to the main ranch, a sixty-mile trip that is made over two days. Horses are led, unlike cattle which are driven, and when they are first turned out for the trip, they are fresh and ready to go. So the first couple miles of that trip are wild and western as the herd leaves its winter grounds with a start, and each of the riders along for the adventure becomes part of the herd, galloping down a long dusty road until the horses begin to settle.

It is not an event for the inexperienced and unprepared rider, and you can almost count on a wreck or two from what I saw and what I was told by the wranglers who worked there. The only wreck I personally witnessed was the result of a horse trying to jump a creek and the rider hadn't maintained his balance. Not all who start out on the ride finish it, because it really is a tough two days. Those who do are rewarded with a Sombrero Ranches "Gate to Gate" Great American Horse Drive buckle, signifying that you made the entire ride from start to finish. Even though I would go on to win three trophy buckles in team roping events, the Sombrero Ranches buckle has a very special place in my heart, and the memories of that week are priceless.

One of the highlights of the horse drive is when, at about halfway home, the herd is routed through the middle of Maybell, Colorado, a quaint town with the bulk of its businesses located along the main drag, Highway 40. For local residents, the event is celebrated. Spectators line the street shoulder to shoulder to take in the remarkable sight, sounds, and perhaps even smell of some 600 horses coming through town. The onlookers seemed to marvel at the show, and I felt proud to be part of it.

I mentioned earlier that although I never had any intention of taking my own life, that it might have appeared otherwise at times. Part of learning to cowboy at an "older" age means you had better be tough. Kids bounce, men don't. When you're learning to ride—at any age— you're going to come off your horse at some point if you do anything other than trail ride on old horses. When you ride young horses and you push the tempo of learning beyond your comfort zone, you're going to crash more often. One might argue that it wasn't smart for a man with three fused vertebrae to put himself at that much risk, and they might be right. One day I had come home bloody and dirty with a torn shirt and a crunched straw hat. When my wife asked what happened, I told her how I had actually had two wrecks that day, one in which my horse had stumbled, fallen, and rolled over me. She said, "Are you *trying* to kill yourself?"

No, I wasn't, I assured her. But if I died doing these things, she should know that I died living life my way and to its fullest. Isn't that what it's really all about? I never want to sit on a porch and look back over my journey with regrets about the things I hadn't done. I have lived an exciting life—before, during, and after my career in law enforcement— and I've made enough memories to last several lifetimes, though I only have one to live. At least the kids will have good stories to tell their children and grandchildren when I'm gone, and honestly, that is my primary motivation for writing this memoir.

I could easily prattle on about cowboying and horses, but I won't. Though I do owe it to my very lovely wife to include another great quote from her, if for no other reason than to show the world what a wonderful woman I married. I came home one day from branding cattle, and I was frustrated. Although I had had fun and felt like I roped well and that everything went smoothly, one of my cowboy mentors had gotten on my case afterward, telling me the things I needed to do better. Normally, criticism from that cowboy would have been well-received, but this time it had felt mean-spirited and unwarranted. So I bitched to my wife about it while unsaddling my horses and sipping a beer. She said, "Who cares what he thinks? You've done far more important things in your life than roping cattle."

And that put the entirety of my life into perfect perspective.

In the fall of 2015, Jeff Leslie was diagnosed with a rare blood cancer that was considered terminal, and he was given six months to live. He outlived the six months and fought a long, hard battle, and now, as I write this memoir in the summer of 2020, he is cancer-free and thriving.

But while he was sick, I made several trips to L.A. to spend time with him, mostly while he was in the hospital. On one of my visits early in his battle, he asked what I had done with "our book," which is how we referred to the manuscript of *A Good Bunch of Men* whenever it was mentioned.

"Nothing," I replied, surprised by the question. I hadn't even thought of the book for years. Though writing truly had been therapeutic for me—as my shrink had assured me it would be—and although I thoroughly loved doing it, the PI business and cowboying left no spare time, and my writing had come to a halt. I said, "Why do you ask?"

"I was just thinking," he said, "that I'd like for my family to be able to read it."

Those words changed the course of my life once again. He had made the request because the two main characters in that book and its series are "loosely" based on him and me, though the stories are (mostly) fictionalized. Given his diagnosis, I did not take the request lightly.

So I brushed off the keyboard and went back through the book, effectively doing what I would later learn is called the rewrite. I asked Patti to go through it and edit it for me once more, and she did at least that. I knew there was a method by which I could publish it myself, but I had no idea how that was done. But I also didn't know how much time we had, and I wanted to accomplish this before...

In the next two months, I educated myself about self-publishing and made a cover using Amazon's design software. The truth was, I figured I would sell four or five copies and give a couple dozen away to his family, mine, and friends of us both. But the book somehow took off, first through parts of the department, then through larger parts of the law enforcement community, and then far beyond. I was hooked by the feedback and the excitement of those who read it, and that is what fueled me to continue writing and in fact, to go forward with the series.

I hired a marketing coach once I realized this could be the real deal, and soon after, I hired a professional cover artist. *A Good Bunch of Men* became an Amazon #1 best-seller, *Echo Killers*, the third book in the series, was an Amazon #1 release and also a second-place winner of the 2019 Public Safety Writer's Association writing contest, and *Death After Dishonor*, the fifth in the series, won Best Crime Fiction in the 2020 Indie Excellence Awards. Just as this manuscript was about to be sent to the publisher, I learned that *Unwritten Rules*, book 6 in the series, won second place in the 2021 Public Safety Writer's Association. Far more readers have warmly received the entire series than I could have ever imagined, and writing has become my fourth career and yet another passion.

EVERY DAY OF MY LIFE, I COUNT MY BLESSINGS. AS YOU'VE READ IN THESE pages, many close calls could have ended the party far too soon. I had a great career and worked some of the most prestigious assignments alongside some of the best men and women to ever wear the badge. Somehow, I also got lucky and married the exact woman I was meant to spend the rest of my life with, the most patient, selfless woman any man could hope to marry. Trust me, it takes a very special woman to be married to a cop, and she is that and ever so much more. Truthfully, she's a saint for putting up with me for all these years.

Together, Lesli and I have raised two wonderful daughters, who in turn have married terrific men whom we couldn't love more nor be prouder to have welcomed into our family. We have our health, and, amazingly, I have my (relative) sanity in spite of the things I've seen and done.

If the death business teaches anything, it is that we never know how much time we have on earth and that every day above ground is a good day. I am truly thankful for each sunrise the good Lord allows me to see, and I'm beyond grateful for the many blessings God has bestowed upon me and my loved ones. Clearly, He has been very generous with me—if not amused by some of my antics.

And while new passions constantly drive me, and I aspire to accomplish many more things before I'm gone, I am finally at peace with who I am, what I've done, and that I have nothing left to prove.

Academy photo of the author with his nephew, Cameron, who has followed in his uncle's footsteps - 1984

Century Crime Impact Team - marijuana bust

Smith and Leslie with Lt. Dove and another detective assigned to the Brooklyn Cold Case Squad

Compton crime scene - Smith and Leslie

Smith and Leslie exhuming a body for evidence

The author in a New York precinct

Smith and Leslie cruising the harbor in New York

Smith and Leslie in Virginia with state troopers

Monterey Park crime scene

Command post near the scene where Dep. Jake Kuredjian was killed in the line of duty

The author (left) and his good friend Riley Stringer roping at the Payette County Rodeo, 2016

The author riding his best horse, Benny, while training the colt he named Stoney Boy

The Great American Horse Drive, 2011

Recent photo of the author and his warden, AKA: "trophy wife"

BOOK REVIEWS

Independent authors count on word-of-mouth and paid advertising to find new readers and sell more books.

Reviews can help shoppers decide about taking a chance on authors who are new to them.

I would be grateful if you took a moment to write a review wherever you purchased the book.

Thank you!

Danny R. Smith

ALSO BY DANNY R. SMITH

THE DICKIE FLOYD DETECTIVE SERIES

- A GOOD BUNCH OF MEN
- DOOR TO A DARK ROOM
- ECHO KILLERS
- THE COLOR DEAD
- DEATH AFTER DISHONOR
- UNWRITTEN RULES
- THE PROGRAM
- THE FIRST FELONY
- HARD-BOILED: BOXSET - FIRST THREE DICKIE FLOYD NOVELS

THE RICH FARRIS DETECTIVE SERIES

- THE OUTLAW

DICKIE FLOYD SHORT STORIES

- In the City of Crosses
- Exhuming Her Honor

AVAILABLE AUDIOBOOKS

- A Good Bunch of Men
- Door to a Dark Room
- Nothing Left to Prove

NON-FICTION — MEMOIR

- Nothing Left to Prove: A Law Enforcement Memoir

SUBSCRIBE TO MY NEWSLETTER

I love staying connected with my readers through social media and email. You can also sign up for my newsletter at murdermemo.com and receive bonus material, such as the Dickie Floyd short story, EXHUMING HER HONOR.

As a newsletter subscriber, you will receive special offers, updates, book releases, and blog posts. I promise to never sell or spam your email.

Danny R. Smith

Dickie Floyd Novels

ACKNOWLEDGMENTS

I can never sufficiently thank my good friend Patricia Barrick Brennan for all of her help. She edits, she proofreads, she provides endless feedback to all of my projects, and she centers me when I find myself out of sorts and on the verge of a literary meltdown. Thank you, Patti, I could not do this without you.

A special thanks to my team of terrific beta readers: Scott Anderson, Jacqueline Beard, Michele Carey, Teresa Collins, Lyn Findlay, Bud Johnson, Phil Jonas, Michele Kapugi, Ann Litts, Moon Mullen, Kay Reeves, Andrea Self, Dennis Slocumb, and Heather Wamboldt. You are definitely All Stars in my book (pun intended).

ABOUT THE AUTHOR

Danny R. Smith spent 21 years with the Los Angeles County Sheriff's Department, the last seven as a homicide detective. He now lives in Idaho where he works as a private investigator and consultant. He is blessed with a beautiful family and surrounded by an assortment of furry critters whom he counts among his friends.

Danny is the author of the *Dickie Floyd Detective Novel* series and the *Rich Farris Detective* series. He writes about true crime and other topics in his blog, The Murder Memo.

He has appeared as an expert on numerous podcasts and shows including True Crime Daily and the STARZ channel's WRONG MAN series, and is the host of *Unsolved Murders with Danny Smith* on the Dr. Carlos Crime Network podcast.

Danny is a member of the Idaho Writers Guild and the Public Safety Writers Association.

f X 󰋙

Made in the USA
Las Vegas, NV
10 March 2024

86980023R10177